Advanced Marathoning

Pete Pfitzinger
Scott Douglas

Human Kinetics

Library of Congress Cataloging-in-Publication Data

Pfitzinger, Pete, 1957-
  Advanced marathoning/Pete Pfitzinger, Scott Douglas.
    p. cm.
  Includes bibliographical references and index.
  ISBN 0-7360-3431-5
    1. Marathon running--Training. I. Douglas, Scott. II. Title.

  GV1065.17.T73 P45 2001
  796.42'52--dc21   00-47236

ISBN: 0-7360-3431-5

Acquisitions Editor: Martin Barnard; **Managing Editor:** Cynthia McEntire; **Assistant Editor:** John Wentworth; **Copyeditor:** Barbara Walsh; **Proofreader:** Erin T. Cler; **Indexer:** Daniel A. Connolly; **Graphic Designer:** Fred Starbird; **Graphic Artist:** Dody Bullerman; **Photo Manager:** Clark Brooks; **Cover Designer:** Jack W. Davis; **Photographer (cover):** ©Victah Sailer; **Art Manager:** Craig Newsom; **Illustrator:** Tom Roberts; **Printer:** Bang Printing

Human Kinetics books are available at special discounts for bulk purchase. Special editions or book excerpts can also be created to specification. For details, contact the Special Sales Manager at Human Kinetics.

Printed in the United States of America

10   9   8   7   6   5   4   3   2   1

Human Kinetics
Web site: www.humankinetics.com

United States: Human Kinetics
P.O. Box 5076
Champaign, IL 61825-5076
800-747-4457
e-mail: humank@hkusa.com

Canada: Human Kinetics
475 Devonshire Road Unit 100
Windsor, ON N8Y 2L5
800-465-7301 (in Canada only)
e-mail: hkcan@mnsi.net

Europe: Human Kinetics, P.O. Box IW14
Leeds LS16 6TR, United Kingdom
+44 (0) 113 278 1708
e-mail: humank@hkeurope.com

Australia: Human Kinetics
57A Price Avenue
Lower Mitcham, South Australia 5062
08 8277 1555
e-mail: liahka@senet.com.au

New Zealand: Human Kinetics
P.O. Box 105-231, Auckland Central
09-523-3462
e-mail: hkp@ihug.co.nz

To all runners willing to work hard and intelligently
—Scott Douglas and Pete Pfitzinger
To the memory of my parents, Harry and Gloria
—Pete Pfitzinger

Contents

Foreword

I was in the lead pack of the 1984 Olympic Marathon Trials when Pete Pfitzinger surged ahead around the halfway mark. At the time, I knew Pete as a solid marathoner, but I sure didn't think he'd keep his lead for another 13 miles. After all, among those in the pack with me were Alberto Salazar, Greg Meyer, and Tony Sandoval; we had all run a few minutes faster than Pete for the marathon. Besides, I had beaten Pete in a 10-mile race just a month earlier. I wondered how long Pete's time in the sun would last.

As you probably know, it lasted pretty darn long, as Pete won that day, becoming the first American to beat Alberto in the marathon. At the Olympics a few months later, he was again the top American, placing 11th. By the time Pete placed 14th in the 1988 Olympic Marathon—again as the top American—his reputation was sealed: Pete was the peaker par excellance, a marathoner who always seemed to reach his potential when it mattered. What he lacked in innate talent compared to those he competed against, he made up for with hard work, focus on his long-term goals, and intelligently applying scientific principles to his training and racing.

In the last several years, the running world has come to know a different side of Pete—the exercise physiologist who tells you not only how but why to train most effectively for your key races. What differentiates Pete from the many others who do this, of course, is that he tested and used the methods he prescribes while competing at the highest level. As seen in Pete's column in *Running Times,* the result is a rational approach to running that never loses sight of the fact that, for runners, any scientific theory has to meet one major criteria: will it make me faster?

I can safely say that if you absorb and follow the advice in this book, the answer will most definitely be yes, you will get faster. I sure wish I'd read *Advanced Marathoning* and had the knowledge conveyed within it before my first marathon. I dropped out of that one, as I did seven others, usually because of dehydration and lack of proper recovery before race day.

What's great about *Advanced Marathoning* is that it discloses the key points to successful marathoning for all those who wish to improve their times—and almost everyone, after finishing their first marathon, is in that category. Even better, it imparts this information to you with some of the clearest, cleanest writing you'll ever read about running. Pete's co-author, Scott Douglas, is well known for writing with finesse. Readers of Pete's and Scott's first book, *Road Racing for Serious Runners,* know that, working together, they have an unsurpassed ability to explain sometimes complex running concepts in an engaging way that always focuses on what you want to know—how can I use this information to run faster?

Having written two books with Scott, I also know that he's ever mindful of your need to fit in your running with the rest of your responsibilities. That commitment to helping motivated runners succeed in the real world really comes through in *Advanced Marathoning.*

I think of Pete and Scott as friends and fellow road warriors. Pete and I used to train together occasionally, and Scott paced me through the 100th Boston Marathon in 1996. Those are strong bonds. But even if those bonds didn't exist, I would recommend *Advanced Marathoning* without reservation. I have never read a book more useful to the tens of thousands of marathoners who want to know how to meet their ambitious goals.

Best wishes for smooth roads and satisfying marathons.

Bill Rodgers

Preface

Would you like to run fast in your next marathon? If so, then this book is for you.

Advanced Marathoning is unique. In our first book, *Road Racing for Serious Runners*, we showed how to train for the most popular distances by applying the latest findings of exercise science. The positive response to this approach showed us that many runners are hungry for scientifically based, ambitious training schedules that they can follow while still living in the real world.

Advanced Marathoning follows a similar philosophy—use exercise science to determine the types of training most needed for success in a distance, and base training schedules on those needs—but applies it solely to the marathon. No other book devotes its entirety to showing you how to run a fast marathon using this strategy.

Read *Advanced Marathoning*, and among other benefits you'll

- learn the physiological requirements of successful marathoning;
- discover which types of training are most relevant to marathon success and which are a waste of your time;
- see how to do your long runs and other important workouts to best prepare your body and mind for a strong pace on race day;
- learn what types of nonrunning training have the biggest impact on your marathon times;
- understand how to eat and drink for top performance, both in training and during your race;
- get advice from leading runners on how to find the time and energy for marathon training while working;
- learn the best approach for running two marathons within a few months of each other; and
- receive extensive, day-by-day training schedules leading to your goal marathon and targeted to your level of weekly mileage.

As you can see, *Advanced Marathoning* isn't just for elite runners hoping to shave a few seconds off their time. This book is for all runners who are ready to do more than merely complete their next marathon. This can mean setting a personal best, qualifying for the Boston Marathon, competing in your age group, or any number of performance-oriented goals.

From our place in the sport—one of us is a former Olympic marathoner and a current exercise physiologist and coach, and the other is a running journalist who has always fit hard training around a job—we know that many marathoners are willing to do the work necessary to run their fastest. If that's you, welcome aboard. *Advanced Marathoning* will show you the hows and whys of accomplishing your marathoning goals.

Acknowledgments

Our thanks go to . . .

- Our wives, Christine Pfitzinger and Stacey Cramp, for undying support.
- Annika and Katrina Pfitzinger, for being quiet while Daddy was writing.
- Martin Barnard and Cynthia McEntire at Human Kinetics, for bringing this book to fruition.
- Bill Rodgers, for writing the foreword.
- Jack Daniels, PhD, for many phone calls and e-mails over the years.
- Bill Rodgers, Bill Squires, David Martin, PhD, Lorraine Moller, Bill Dellinger, Kevin Ryan, and Arthur Lydiard for their valuable insights into marathon training.
- The world-class marathoners profiled in these pages, for sharing how they've succeeded.
- Mark Crimmins, for designing the calculator that helped us construct our pace charts.
- Jim Whitnah, for eagle-eyed proofreading of the pace charts.

PART

I

Training
Components

Guidelines for Advanced Marathoning

What is advanced marathoning? What, for that matter, is *Advanced Marathoning*?

The marathon has reached levels of popularity that were unheard of at the height of the first so-called running boom of the late 1970s and early 1980s. The number of finishers in North American marathons, for example, continues to grow by about 10 percent a year. Obviously, with nearly half a million marathon finishers annually just in the United States, the key to being able to run 26.2 miles isn't a secret: train long to go long.

But what about when you want to race a marathon? Then things aren't so simple. Besides gaining enough baseline endurance to complete the distance, now your concerns turn to matters such as how fast to do your long runs, what types of interval sessions to do, how to manipulate your diet for maximum performance, how to schedule hard workouts to allow both progress and recovery, and so on. The best answers to these questions aren't so obvious, and they require a solid base of knowledge. You'll acquire that knowledge in this book. When you've run a marathon and want to move beyond the basics—or if you're an accomplished runner at shorter distances planning a marathon debut—then it's time to graduate to *Advanced Marathoning*.

Advanced Marathoning

What do we mean by advanced marathoning? Simply this: that many runners aren't content with saying, "I finished." They want to run the

3

marathon as they do shorter races, namely, as fast as possible. That doesn't mean that they're going to drop everything in their lives and do nothing but train, but it does mean that they're committed to doing their best, taking into consideration such factors as their age and real-world commitments. The runners for whom we wrote this book have goals such as setting a personal best, qualifying for Boston, or running faster than they did 10 years ago.

> **Advanced marathoning is preparing to run the marathon as fast as possible.**

Competing in the marathon, as opposed to completing the distance without regard for time, requires thorough, intelligent preparation. Being dedicated to improving your marathon performance requires knowing such things as how fast to do your long runs given your goal race pace, how far and how fast your hard sessions should be, what to eat so that you're able to run as fast at mile 25 as at the start, and so on. Advanced marathoning has to be based on more than common sense and running folklore. *Advanced Marathoning*, therefore, is based on exercise science.

The training schedules in the second section of this book are based on a simple but often-ignored concept: research in exercise physiology has revealed that the fastest marathoners have a few key attributes in common. These include an ability to store a large amount of glycogen (the stored form of carbohydrates) in their muscles, an ability to sustain submaximal speeds for prolonged periods, an ability to send large amounts of oxygen to muscles and for muscles to use that oxygen, and an ability to run faster than others using a given amount of oxygen. We know which of these attributes are most important for successful marathoning, and we know what types of training best improve these attributes. Marathon training, then, should be a matter of balancing these types of training with adequate recovery so that your body's ability to sustain a good pace for 26.2 miles improves as your goal race approaches.

We could, of course, simply present the training schedules found in the latter part of this book and say, "Just do what we tell you. Trust us." But we think that the more that you understand why you're running a given workout, the more motivated you'll be to stick with your training and the better prepared you'll be to assess your progress toward your marathon goal. For that reason, before the training schedules are several chapters that explain the principles of successful marathoning. These chapters explain what is critical for marathon success, and why. Digesting the information in them will help you be a better marathoner. Let's look at the contents of the first part of this book.

Grete Waitz

Fastest Marathon: 2:24:54
Marathon Career Highlights: First place, 1983 World Championships. Second place, 1984 Olympic marathon. Four world records. Won New York City Marathon nine times.

© Sailer Ltd. 1988

After a world-class career at short track distances, Grete Waitz entered the 1978 New York City Marathon because of the promise of a free trip for her and her husband. In 2:32:30, she broke the world record and revolutionized women's marathoning.

When Waitz started running seriously at the age of 16, the longest international championship event for women was 1,500 meters. Although 3,000-meter races became more common in invitationals during the 1970s, even that event wasn't added to the Olympic program until 1984. Because, Waitz says, "I did not have a lot of natural speed, I had to work very hard to be competitive over those distances." She ran 85 to 100 miles a week to train for the short races—"which was very unusual in those days," she says—and twice set a world record at 3,000 meters.

After achieving much at events not suited to her, "I considered retiring in 1978," she says. "I was working full-time as a high school teacher and had lost some of the motivation to run twice a day besides working for a living." Enter the lure of free travel. "Jack, my husband, talked me into running New York in 1978," she recalls. "He convinced me I was a better runner than the women who ran the marathon at that time. Since I had never been to the United States and New York, I was tempted—not to run, but to see the city that never sleeps.

"So I said okay, if the organizer would pay the expenses for the two of us to come to New York. They did, and I won and ran a world best in my first road race ever. That was the start of a new career."

(continued)

Grete Waitz *(continued)*

Her new career was helped substantially by her old one. "Having that speed background, I was very comfortable going through 10K in a marathon in 35:00," she says. In addition, even when she was concentrating on middle-distance events, "Much of my training was hard tempo runs so that I could maintain even lap times on the track." She was already used to running high mileage and bumped her weekly totals up to 90 to 110 miles.

In addition to providing the high-quality background that helped her redefine the role of speed in women's marathoning, Waitz also thinks that her track career helped her to remain competitive for so long in the marathon. (For example, when she won her ninth New York title in 1988, she ran 2:28:07, nearly 4½ minutes faster than she had in her first victory 10 years before.)

"I don't think I would have achieved more in the marathon if I had started earlier," she says. "I ran my first marathon when I was 25, which I think is a good age for that distance. I had a good solid foundation running-wise and was physically prepared to move up to longer distances. I believe if I had started with longer distances earlier I would have been burned out and injured a lot before the age of 30."

Your Guide to Understanding the Marathon

Chapter 2 is by far the longest chapter in this book. We don't expect that everyone will sit down and read it at once; in fact, you could start on the training schedule of your choice right now and not have to worry that you haven't looked at chapter 2. Eventually, though, you'll want to read this chapter carefully and understand its key concepts because it explains the exercise science we used in constructing the training schedules.

Chapter 2 gives an in-depth examination of the physiological attributes needed for success in the marathon. These include an ability to store a large amount of glycogen in your muscles and liver, a well-developed ability to use fat as fuel, a high lactate threshold, a well-developed maximal oxygen uptake, and good running economy. (Don't worry if any of these concepts are unclear to you—you'll fully understand them and their relation to marathoning after chapter 2.) We look at the traits your body must have to run a good marathon, and then we detail how to train to provide the largest stimulus for these traits to improve.

Understanding the concepts in chapter 2 is critical. Contrary to what some people think, training for a fast marathon doesn't mean running as many miles as possible as quickly as possible. Regardless of how inspired you are to run your best marathon, you most likely have to prepare for it while not neglecting those annoying little details such as your job. Your training, then, should provide the biggest return for the time you put into it. After you read chapter 2, you'll know why the targeted training the schedules call for is optimal for marathoning success.

Chapter 3 explains the crucial role that proper nutrition and hydration play in successful marathoning. What marathoners should eat and drink is the subject of much ill-informed discussion—perhaps almost as much as training is. After reading chapter 3, you'll know what marathon training and racing require in terms of fuel and how your diet contributes to meeting your marathon goal. You'll also understand how just a small amount of dehydration can significantly reduce your performance and the strategies you can use to avoid it in training and on race day.

As we said previously, intelligent marathon preparation means more than accumulating repeated days of hard

Your body adapts to the rigors of marathoning through intelligent training.

mileage. You'll make more progress toward your goal by doing one of the key workouts described in chapter 2, allowing your body to absorb the benefits of that workout, and then doing another targeted session. In other words, you should allow your body to recover after an especially long or hard run. Chapter 4 shows how to maximize your recovery, including how far and how fast to run, plus the types of nonrunning aerobic training that have the most relevance for marathoners.

If you follow one of the training schedules in this book, your training will contain all of the running elements you'll need for a fast marathon. But there are things you can do in your nonrunning hours that can help your overall improvement as a marathoner. In chapter 5, we detail the types of flexibility, resistance, and other sorts of supplemental training that will make you the best marathoner.

All of the training schedules incorporate the principle of gradually improving your marathon-specific fitness as your goal approaches. In chapter 6, we show how to track your progress so that you'll know whether you're getting the most benefit from your hard work. We'll also show you how to know what to do when those nearly inevitable setbacks occur during the long weeks of your marathon buildup. Dealing with injury and illness is, alas, often a fact of marathoning life. Reading chapter 6 will help you to avoid being derailed by such interruptions. We'll also show you how you can evaluate and improve your running form.

The final background chapter details what to do on race day. Chapter 7 discusses race strategy, with mile-by-mile pacing advice, and presents information on other crucial matters, such as what to eat on race day and how to drink on the run to minimize dehydration.

The Training Schedules

Chapters 8 to 10 apply the principles detailed in chapters 2 to 7 to day-by-day training schedules leading to one goal marathon.

The chapters are divided on the basis of weekly mileage. Chapter 8 contains the schedules that call for the lowest weekly mileage; these peak at 55 miles per week. Chapter 9 contains schedules that call for 50 to 70 miles per week. Chapter 10 is for the high-mileage crowd, those who regularly run more than 70 miles per week. The one you follow is up to you. Making that decision should be based on your running history, your tendency

© Tom Messenger

Your marathon goal will determine which training schedule is right for you.

toward injury above a certain level of mileage, what else will be going on in your life in the months before your goal race, and so on. Regardless of which schedule you follow, it will contain the workouts that will lead to the biggest gains in marathon-specific fitness for that level of mileage.

Chapters 8 to 10 present you with another decision to make. Each chapter contains a 12-week, 18-week, and 24-week schedule. Although we recommend that most readers follow the 18-week schedule, we realize that some readers don't mind maintaining such a specific running focus for nearly half a year; hence, the 24-week program. In the same way, we realize that some readers will want to prepare for a marathon that's only a few months away. The 12-week schedules are for these readers, and while they're more compact than is optimal, they nonetheless contain the workouts needed to make significant progress in such a short time.

These chapters are meant to be self-contained. For that reason, we provide an abbreviated description in each chapter of all the types of workouts called for in the schedules. We also provide race strategy advice specific to marathoners training at a given chapter's level of weekly mileage.

The schedules are designed to be easy to read vertically and horizontally. Horizontally, they show you how your mileage and training emphases change as your marathon approaches. This helps you to understand your key training goals for a given period. Looking at the schedules vertically enhances that understanding because you can quickly grasp the key workouts in a given week. The schedules specify the purpose of each day's workout. That way not only will you know what you're trying to achieve on a certain day of the week but you can look down through the week to see your most important training goals for that week.

You'll note that the schedules specify what to do every day of the many weeks leading up to your marathon. We realize, of course, that it's the rare reader whose life will so perfectly coincide with such a detailed schedule. Again, looking at the schedules vertically and horizontally will prove helpful because you'll know what types of training are most important for wherever you are on the schedule so you'll know which workouts to emphasize if you need to juggle a few days around.

Chapter 11 is a bit different from the other training-schedule chapters, and it's for marathoners who themselves are a bit different. Chapter 11 is for multiple-marathon runners who want to run two or more marathons within 12 weeks or less. Following such a schedule usually isn't the way to run your fastest marathon, but it's not our place to say categorically that you should never attempt such a feat. Chapter 11 acknowledges that some runners want to tackle this challenge, and it provides schedules that will maximize your chances of success in the second (or third or fourth) marathon of your recent past. Using the principles behind the other schedules, chapter 11 provides schedules for your best possible marathon 4, 6, 8, 10, and 12 weeks after another marathon.

Now that you know what's in this book and how to use it, let's get going on understanding the basics of successful marathoning.

chapter

2

Elements
of Training

The marathon demands respect. The physiological and psychological demands of the marathon are extreme; therefore, you must plan your preparation intelligently and thoroughly.

Unfortunately, "intelligent" and "thorough" aren't the two words that most readily come to mind when thinking about some marathon-training programs. Search the Web under "marathon training" and you'll find thousands of well-meaning but only intermittently helpful sites. The training advice on many of these sites is based more on personal anecdotes and handed-down folk wisdom than exercise science. You'd be hard-pressed to cull through these sites and summarize why they're prescribing the type of preparation they present.

> **Training for a marathon should be relatively simple.**

That's too bad, because while running a marathon isn't easy, training for it should be relatively simple. Running a marathon requires specific physiological attributes. The task at hand is to run 26.2 miles as fast as possible. The requirements for this feat in terms of fuel use, oxygen consumption, biomechanical requirements, and even psychological attributes are highly predictable. In this chapter, we look at the physiological demands of the marathon and how to train most effectively to meet those demands.

First we look at the physiological demands, such as having a high lactate threshold and the ability to store large amounts of glycogen in your muscles and liver. Then we look at the types of training that are most effective for improving marathon performance and explain why. Next we investigate how to structure your training so that it progresses logically to your desired end point. Finally, we look at the importance of using shorter races as tune-ups to the marathon.

This chapter is long, and some of the concepts may seem complex. Nonetheless, it's important that you read it thoroughly. After reading this chapter, you'll see the logic underpinning effective marathon training and will better understand which types of training to emphasize and why.

Marathon Physiology

Successful marathoners have many factors in common. Most of these factors are determined by both genetics and training. Genetics determines the range within which you can improve; training determines where your current abilities fall within that range. In this section, we'll consider the physiological variables necessary for marathon success.

Successful marathoners have these physiological attributes:

- High proportion of slow-twitch muscle fibers. This trait is genetically determined and influences the other physiological characteristics listed here.
- High lactate threshold. This is the ability to produce energy at a fast rate aerobically without accumulating high levels of lactate in your muscles and blood.
- High glycogen storage and fat utilization. These traits enable you to store enough glycogen in your muscles and liver to run hard for 26.2 miles and use fat for fuel.
- Excellent running economy. This is the ability to use oxygen economically when running at marathon pace.
- High maximal oxygen uptake ($\dot{V}O_2$max). This is the ability to transport large amounts of oxygen to your muscles and the ability of your muscles to extract and use oxygen.
- Quick recovery. This is the ability to recover from training quickly.

Remember, no one factor makes a successful marathoner. Frank Shorter, for example, had 80 percent slow-twitch fibers and a $\dot{V}O_2$max of 71.4 ml/kg/ min (milliliters of oxygen per kilogram of bodyweight per minute). In contrast, Alberto Salazar had 93 percent slow-twitch fibers and a $\dot{V}O_2$max of 78 ml/kg/min. Still, each was arguably the best in the world at his peak. It's the combination of these physiological factors, in conjunction with biomechanical variables and psychological makeup, that determines marathoning success. Let's look more closely at each of the main physiological factors.

High Proportion of Slow-Twitch Muscle Fibers

Your thousands of muscle fibers can be divided into three categories—slow-twitch, fast-twitch A, and fast-twitch B. The higher the percentage of slow-twitch fibers in your muscles, the greater your likelihood of marathon success. Slow-twitch muscle fibers are naturally adapted to endurance exercise. They resist fatigue and have a high aerobic capacity, a high capillary density, and other characteristics that make them ideal for marathon running.

Priscilla Welch

Fastest Marathon: 2:26:51
Marathon Career Highlights: Women's masters world record in the marathon of 2:26:51. Won the 1987 New York City Marathon at age 42. Sixth place, 1984 Olympic Marathon.

© Sailer Ltd. 1987

Priscilla Welch shows that excellence in marathoning is possible regardless of age and background, if you're willing to do the work.

Welch started running in 1979 at age 34 for health and fitness. She had completed a stint in the British military while on a NATO assignment in Norway and had met her future husband, Dave. She stayed in Norway; was unemployed; and, she says, "was miserable not working." She had also been a smoker and more-than-occasional drinker while in the military. Out of concern for her health, Dave introduced Priscilla, who had been sedentary her whole life, to jogging.

She ran her first marathon—"not properly trained," she says—that year in 3:36.
"I didn't realize at all that I could be good," she says. After she placed second in a 10K cross-country race, however, that began to change. "I think Dave realized that maybe I had something, and he just promoted it," she says. Dave, a 2:46 marathoner at his peak, read training theory voraciously and began to apply scientific principles to Priscilla's training.

She improved rapidly. In her first marathon that she prepared properly for, she ran 2:59 at London in 1981. By 1983, she was down to running 2:32 for a third-place finish at New York City. A couple more fast times secured her a spot on the British team for the first women's Olympic marathon in 1984. A 2:28 at age 39 in the heat of Los Angeles earned her sixth place and a British national record. Welch had her best year in 1987. At the age of 42, she ran 2:26:51 at London in April and then, in her 25th marathon, took the overall title at New York City.

The Welches decided early on to concentrate on success in the marathon. The majority of shorter races that Priscilla ran were either tune-ups during marathon preparation or entered as tempo runs. "We tried to give at least one day's rest before

(continued)

Priscilla Welch *(continued)*

these races," says Dave, "and some of the results were fairly reasonable under the circumstances—49:35 for 15K and several 32:00 10Ks."

Still, the shorter races were viewed as feedback on the marathon training, not as ends in themselves. "We didn't set goals for these shorter races," says Dave. "I think it can be disastrous to set goals for development races during hard training for marathons. For instance, 3 weeks before London '87, Priscilla ran a 33:47 10K in the Boston Milk Run after an intense week of training. Three weeks of taper followed. In the marathon, a very rested and peaked Priscilla ran through the first 10K in 33:04 and sailed through the half marathon in 1:10:46 (a PR) to her 2:26:51 finish. A goal of sub-33:00 in Boston could have had disastrous results. Fortunately, we were pleased with the effort and knew not to panic, as it was a small part of a much bigger plan."

The Welches knew they had to approach Priscilla's training a bit differently because of her relatively late start in life. "When we started training for the marathon seriously," says Dave, "we realized that to reach the top at late 30s/early 40s, the training had to be at least as tough as for the youngsters but with more refinements—diet, sleep, et cetera. We also realized we needed a very careful, scientifically based buildup, to develop at the right pace and avoid injuries. Rest and recovery become more important as you advance in age.

"However," he adds, "we get sick of reading in U.S. publications about the importance of rest and never about how hard you have to train to become successful!"

The proportion of slow-twitch fibers in your muscles is determined genetically and is believed not to change with training. World-class marathoners often have more than 75 percent slow-twitch muscle fibers, whereas the general population has about 50 percent slow-twitch fibers. Although your fast-twitch muscle fibers can't be converted to slow-twitch fibers, with general endurance training they can gain more of the characteristics of slow-twitch fibers, especially the fast-twitch A fibers. These adaptations are beneficial because your fast-twitch fibers become better at producing energy aerobically.

A muscle biopsy is the only method of determining your proportion of slow-twitch muscle fibers. In a biopsy, a small amount of tissue is cut out of your muscle and analyzed. Though it is interesting (and painful), for most runners this procedure is pointless—once you know your fiber-type distribution, there's nothing you can do about it. In contrast, you can improve other physiological characteristics with training.

High Lactate Threshold

A high lactate threshold is the most important physiological variable for endurance athletes. Lactate threshold most directly determines your performance limit in any event lasting more than 30 minutes. You select your marathon race pace based on preventing the accumulation of lactate (a by-product of carbohydrate metabolism) in your muscles and blood. A close

© Kim Karpeles/Kim Karpeles.com

Elite marathoners generally have substantially more slow-twitch muscle fibers than the general population.

relationship exists between your lactate threshold and marathon performance because lactate threshold reflects both the ability of your heart to transport oxygen to your muscles and the rate at which your muscles can produce energy aerobically. Successful marathoners typically race at a speed very close to their lactate threshold pace.

The average runner's lactate threshold occurs at about 75 to 80 percent of his or her $\dot{V}O_2$max. Successful marathoners generally have lactate thresholds of 84 to 88 percent of $\dot{V}O_2$max; elite marathoners tend to have lactate thresholds of about 88 to 91 percent of $\dot{V}O_2$max. This means that elite marathoners can use a larger proportion of their maximal aerobic capacity before lactate starts to accumulate in their muscles and blood.

Lactate is produced by your muscles and is used by your muscles, heart, liver, and kidneys. The lactate concentration in your blood represents a balance between lactate production and consumption. Even at rest, you produce a small amount of lactate. If your blood lactate were measured right now, you would have a lactate concentration of about 1 millimole. As you increase your effort from resting to walking to easy running, your rates of lactate production and lactate consumption increase, and your blood lactate concentration stays relatively constant. When you run harder than your lactate threshold, however, your lactate concentration rises because the rate of lactate clearance can no longer keep up with lactate production.

When you accumulate a high level of lactate, the hydrogen ions associated with lactate production turn off the enzymes used to produce energy and may interfere with the uptake of calcium, thereby reducing the muscles' ability to contract. In other words, you can't produce energy as quickly when your lactate level is high, so you're forced to slow down. This explains why you run the marathon at an intensity just below your lactate threshold. If you were to exceed your lactate threshold, you would accumulate lactate quickly and wouldn't be able to hold the pace for long.

> *Running at just below lactate threshold keeps lactate concentration constant.*

With the correct training, adaptations occur inside your muscle fibers that allow you to run at a higher intensity without building up lactate. The most important of these adaptations are increased number and size of mitochondria, increased aerobic enzyme activity, and increased capillarization in your muscle fibers. These adaptations all improve your ability to produce energy using oxygen.

Increased Number and Size of Mitochondria

Mitochondria are the only part of your muscle fibers in which energy can be produced aerobically. Think of them as the aerobic energy factories in your muscle fibers. By fully utilizing your ability to produce energy without accumulating high levels of lactate, lactate threshold training increases the size of your mitochondria (i.e., makes bigger factories) and the number of mitochondria (i.e., makes more factories) in your muscles fibers. With more mitochondria, you can produce more energy aerobically and maintain a faster pace. This is a very relevant adaptation for marathoners because more than 99 percent of the energy needed to run a marathon is produced aerobically.

Increased Aerobic Enzyme Activity

Enzymes in your mitochondria speed up aerobic energy production (i.e., increase the rate of production in your aerobic energy factories). Lactate threshold training increases aerobic enzyme activity; this adaptation improves the efficiency of your mitochondria. The more aerobic enzyme activity in your mitochondria, the faster you produce energy aerobically.

Increased Capillarization of Muscle Fibers

Oxygen is necessary to produce energy aerobically. Your heart pumps oxygen-rich blood to your muscles through a remarkable system of blood vessels. Capillaries are the smallest blood vessels, and typically several border each muscle fiber. With the correct training, you increase the number of capillaries per muscle fiber. With more capillaries per muscle fiber, oxygen is more efficiently delivered where it's needed. Capillaries also deliver fuel to the muscle fibers and remove waste products such as carbon dioxide. A more efficient delivery and removal system provides a constant supply of oxygen and fuel, and waste products don't accumulate in your muscles as quickly. By providing oxygen to the individual muscle fibers, increased capillary density allows the rate of aerobic energy production to increase.

High Glycogen Storage and Fat Utilization

Glycogen is the form of carbohydrate stored in the body, and carbohydrate is the primary fuel used when racing a marathon. The two ways to ensure that glycogen stores last throughout the marathon are to train your body to store a large amount of glycogen and to train your body to conserve glycogen at marathon pace.

A large supply of glycogen in your muscles and liver at the start of the marathon enables you to work at a high rate throughout the race without becoming carbohydrate depleted. During the marathon, you use a combination of carbohydrate and fat for fuel. When you run low on glycogen, you rely more on fat, which forces you to slow down because fat uses oxygen less efficiently. With the correct training, your muscles and liver adapt to store more glycogen. Design your training so that toward the end of certain workouts, you run very low on glycogen; this provides a stimulus for your body to adapt by storing more glycogen in the future.

Design training so that you run low on glycogen at the end of certain workouts.

Because your body can store only a limited supply of glycogen, it's an advantage to be able to use as much fat as possible at marathon race pace. Successful marathoners have developed their ability to use fat; this trait spares their glycogen stores and helps to ensure that they make it to the finish line without becoming glycogen depleted. When you train your muscles to rely more on fat at marathon race pace, your glycogen stores last longer. In the marathon, that means that the Wall moves closer and closer to the finish line and eventually disappears. (The concept of the Wall is really a reflection of improper marathon preparation and pacing.) Later in this chapter, we'll look at how to train to improve glycogen storage and fat utilization. In chapter 3, we'll examine how your diet affects these vital processes.

Excellent Running Economy

Your running economy determines how fast you can run using a given amount of oxygen. If you can run faster than another athlete while using the same amount of oxygen, then you're more economical. This concept is similar to the efficiency of an automobile engine—if a car can travel farther using a given amount of gasoline, then it's more economical than another car.

Running economy can also be looked at as how much oxygen is required to run at a given speed. If you use less oxygen while running at the same speed as another runner, then you're more economical. If you know how much oxygen a runner can use at lactate threshold pace, as well as that athlete's running economy, you can generally predict marathon performance fairly accurately. In fact, a study by Farrell and colleagues found that differences in pace at lactate threshold predicted 94 percent of the variation among distance runners in racing speed (Farrell et al. 1979).

Running economy varies widely among runners. While testing elite runners in the laboratory, Pete has found differences of more than 20 percent in running economy among athletes. Obviously, a large advantage exists in being able to use oxygen as economically as possible during the marathon—your aerobic system supplies nearly all of the energy for the marathon, and oxygen is the main limiting factor in the rate of energy production by the aerobic system.

For example, say two athletes with identical lactate threshold values of 54 ml/kg/min are racing at a pace of 5:55 per mile. Although it seems that they should be working equally hard, this often isn't the case. If Stacey has an oxygen requirement of 51 ml/kg/min at that pace and Christine requires 57 ml/kg/min, then Stacey will be comfortably below lactate threshold and should be able to maintain 5:55 pace. Christine will steadily accumulate lactic acid and will have to slow down. Stacey has a faster pace at lactate threshold because she uses oxygen more economically.

The primary determinants of running economy appear to be the ratio of slow-twitch to fast-twitch fibers in your muscles, the combined effect of your biomechanics, and your training history. The proportion of slow-twitch muscle fibers is important because they use oxygen more efficiently. One reason that successful marathoners tend to be more economical than slower marathoners is because they generally have more slow-twitch muscle fibers.

Running economy is also related to the interaction of many biomechanical variables, but no single aspect of biomechanics has been shown to have a large impact on economy. We don't know, therefore, how to change biomechanics to improve economy. One of the problems is that it's impossible to change one biomechanical variable without affecting others.

High Maximal Oxygen Uptake ($\dot{V}O_2$max)

Successful marathoners have high $\dot{V}O_2$max values. This means that they're able to transport large amounts of oxygen to their muscles, and their muscles are able to extract and use a large amount of oxygen.

The average sedentary 35-year-old man has a $\dot{V}O_2$max of about 45 ml/kg/min, while the average 35-year-old male runner has a $\dot{V}O_2$max of about 55 ml/kg/min. A locally competitive 35-year-old male marathoner tends to have a $\dot{V}O_2$max in the range of 60 to 65 ml/kg/min, whereas an elite male marathoner would tend to be in the range of 70 to 75 ml/kg/min. Although successful marathoners tend to have high $\dot{V}O_2$max values, they aren't as high as the $\dot{V}O_2$max values found in elite 5,000-meter runners, whose maxes can reach as high as 85 ml/kg/min. Women's $\dot{V}O_2$max values tend to be about 10 percent lower than those for men because women have higher essential body fat stores and lower hemoglobin levels than men.

The primary factors in increasing $\dot{V}O_2$max appear to be related to improvements in the ability to transport oxygen to your muscles. This ability is related to four factors: your maximal heart rate, the maximal amount of blood your heart can pump with each beat, the hemoglobin content of your blood, and the proportion of your blood that is transported to your working muscles.

Your maximal heart rate is determined genetically. In other words, it doesn't increase with training. In fact, recent evidence indicates that maximal heart rate decreases as a runner's $\dot{V}O_2$max increases. Successful marathoners don't have particularly high maximal heart rates, so it isn't a factor in determining success.

> **Maximal heart rate is genetically determined.**

The maximal amount of blood your heart can pump with each beat is called your stroke volume. If the left ventricle of your heart is large, then it can hold a large amount of blood. If your left ventricle is strong, then it can contract fully so that not much blood is left at the end of each contraction. Filling the left ventricle with a large amount of blood and pumping a large proportion of that blood with each contraction result in a large stroke volume. Stroke volume increases with the correct types of training. In fact, increased stroke volume is the main training adaptation that increases $\dot{V}O_2$max.

The hemoglobin content of your blood is important because the higher your hemoglobin content, the more oxygen can be carried per unit of blood and the more energy can be produced aerobically. Some successful marathoners train at high altitude to increase the oxygen-carrying capacity of their blood. Other than by training at altitude (or through several illegal methods), the hemoglobin concentration of your blood won't increase with training.

We've talked about the amount of oxygen per unit of blood and the amount of blood that your heart can pump. The other factor that determines the amount of blood reaching your muscles is the proportion of your blood transported to your working muscles. At rest, just more than 1 liter of blood goes to your muscles per minute. During the marathon, approximately 16 liters of blood are transported to your muscles per minute. When you're running all out, it's more than 20 liters per minute. Much of this increase is due to increased heart rate and stroke volume, but redistribution of blood to your muscles also contributes. At rest, approximately 20 percent of your blood is sent to your working muscles; during the marathon, it rises to roughly 70 percent. With training, your body becomes better at shutting down temporarily unnecessary functions, such as digestion, so that more blood can be sent to your working muscles.

Quick Recovery

Successful marathoners are able to recover quickly from training. This allows them to handle a larger training volume and a higher frequency of hard training sessions than those who recover more slowly. The ability to recover quickly is related to genetics, the structure of your training plan, your age, lifestyle factors such as diet and sleep, and your training history. (The 30th 20-miler of your life will probably take less out of you than your first one.)

Runners vary in how many workouts they can tolerate in a given time. Recovery runs are an important element of your training, but they must be handled carefully. If you do your recovery runs too hard, you run the risk of overtraining and reducing the quality of your hard training sessions. This is a common mistake among distance runners, particularly marathoners—many runners don't differentiate between regular training runs and recovery runs. The purpose of your regular training runs is to provide an additional training stimulus to improve your fitness; the purpose of your recovery runs is to help you to recover from your last hard workout so that you're ready for your next hard workout.

Recovery runs improve blood flow through the muscles; this process improves the repair of damaged muscle cells, removes waste products, and brings nutrients to your muscles. These benefits are lost, however, if you do recovery runs so fast that you tire yourself out for your subsequent hard training sessions. In addition, by doing your recovery runs slowly, you use less of your glycogen stores, so more glycogen is available for your hard training sessions. Optimizing your diet to enhance recovery is discussed in chapter 3. Recovery runs and other strategies to improve your recovery are discussed in depth in chapter 4.

/// Head Games

"Mind is everything; muscle, pieces of rubber. All that I am, I am because of my mind." So said Paavo Nurmi, the Finn who won nine Olympic gold medals at distances from 1,500 meters to 10,000 meters. Although he wasn't a marathoner, Nurmi knew the need for psychological strength in distance running.

Most of this chapter deals with the physiological attributes that most directly determine your marathoning success. Traits such as your lactate threshold and $\dot{V}O_2$max can measured; if we were to gather 10 readers of this book and run them through a series of laboratory tests, we could reasonably predict their order of finish in a marathon.

What we couldn't so easily measure and predict, though, would be which of those runners would come closest to reaching their physiological potential. That's where the mind comes in. Just as there are wide variations among runners in attributes such as percentage of slow-twitch muscle fibers, so too are there great ranges in the less quantifiable matter of what we'll call, for lack of a better word, "toughness." We all know midpack runners who have a reputation for thrashing themselves in races; at the same time, most followers of the sport could name a few elite runners who often seem to come up short when the going gets tough.

Despite being unmeasurable in a scientific sense, mental toughness can be improved. In fact, it's one of the few determinants of marathon performance that you can continue to better after even 20 or more years of running. Maturity, years of training, and some positive reinforcements along the way can enhance such necessary weapons in the marathoner's arsenal as perseverance and willingness to suffer in the short term for long-term gain.

Nurmi also said, "Success in sport, as in almost anything, comes from devotion. The athlete must make a devotion of his specialty." Having a challenging but reasonable marathon goal provides you with the necessary object of devotion. Intelligent, thorough preparation for that goal—such as that provided in the training schedules in the second section of this book—provides the confidence needed to attack that goal. Do the right training, and both your body and your mind will benefit.

How to Train to Improve the Key Physiological Attributes

Now that we've discussed the physiological requirements for successful marathoning, let's look at the components of training that improve the key physiological variables and how to do each type of session most effectively in your marathon preparation. Of the six physiological variables we've discussed, all but muscle fiber type improve with the appropriate training. In this section, we'll look at how to train to improve your lactate threshold, ability to store glycogen and utilize fat, running economy at marathon pace, and $\dot{V}O_2$max. We'll also consider a specialized training session that integrates the various aspects of your training. In chapters 3 and 4, we'll look at strategies to enhance your recovery from this targeted training.

Improving Your Lactate Threshold

The most effective way to improve lactate threshold is to run at your current lactate threshold pace or a few seconds per mile faster, either as one continuous run (tempo run) or as a long interval session at your lactate threshold pace (cruise intervals or LT intervals).

These workouts make you run hard enough so that lactate is just starting to accumulate in your blood. When you train at a lower intensity, a weaker stimulus is provided to improve your lactate threshold pace. When you train faster than current lactate threshold pace, you accumulate lactate rapidly, so you won't be training your muscles to work hard without accumulating lactate. During these workouts, the more time that you spend at your lactate threshold pace, the greater the stimulus for improvement.

Lactate threshold training should be run at close to the pace that you could currently race for 1 hour. For serious marathoners, this is generally 15K to half marathon race pace. Slower runners should run closer to 15K race pace on tempo runs; faster runners should run closer to half marathon race pace. This should be the intensity at which lactate is just starting to accumulate in your muscles and blood. You can do some of your tempo runs in low-key races of 4 miles to 10K, but be careful not to get carried away and race all out. Remember that the optimal pace to improve lactate threshold is your current LT pace, and not much faster.

A typical training session to improve lactate threshold consists of a 15- to 20-minute warm-up, followed by a 20- to 40-minute tempo run and a 15-minute cool-down. The lactate threshold workouts in this book mainly fall within these parameters, although most of the schedules include one longer tempo run in the 7-mile range. LT intervals are typically two to five repetitions of 5 minutes to 2 miles at lactate threshold pace with 2 or 3 minutes between repetitions.

For runners competing in shorter races, tempo runs and LT intervals are both excellent ways to prepare. For marathoners, however, tempo runs are preferable to LT intervals. After all, the marathon is one long continuous run, and tempo runs simulate marathon conditions more closely. There's both a physiological and a psychological component to the advantage of tempo runs. The extra mental toughness required to get through a tempo run when you may not be feeling great will come in handy during the marathon.

///// *What's Your Lactate Threshold?*

The most accurate way to find out your lactate threshold is to be tested at the track or in a sport physiology lab. During a lactate threshold test in a lab, you run for several minutes at progressively faster speeds until your lactate concentration increases markedly. The tester measures the lactate concentration in your blood after several minutes at each speed by pricking your finger and analyzing a couple of drops of blood. A typical lactate threshold test consists of six increasingly hard runs of 5 minutes each, with 1 minute between runs to sample your blood. By graphing blood lactate concentration at various running speeds, testers can tell the pace and heart rate that coincide with lactate threshold. You can then use this information to maximize the effectiveness of your training.

The lower-tech method to estimate lactate threshold is to use your race times. For experienced runners, lactate threshold pace is very similar to race pace for 15K to the half marathon. Successful marathoners generally race the marathon 2 to 3 percent slower than lactate threshold pace.

In terms of heart rate, lactate threshold typically occurs at 80 to 90 percent of maximal heart rate, or 76 to 88 percent of heart rate reserve in well-trained runners. (Heart rate reserve is your maximal heart rate minus your resting heart rate.)

Improving Glycogen Storage and Fat Utilization

Your ability to store glycogen and use fat for fuel tends to improve with the same types of training. Pure endurance training stimulates these adaptations and increases the capillarization of your muscles. For marathoners, the primary type of training to stimulate these adaptations is runs of 90 minutes or longer. Your total training volume, however, also contributes. That's one reason to include two-a-day workouts and relatively high weekly mileage in your training program.

Long runs are the bread and butter for marathoners. For all marathoners, including the elite, the marathon distance is a formidable challenge. To prepare to race 26.2 miles at a strong pace, train your body and mind to handle the distance by doing long runs at a reasonable pace.

The long run also provides psychological benefits. By running long, you simulate what your legs and body will go through in the marathon. When your hamstrings tighten 23 miles into the race, for example, it helps to have experienced a similar feeling in training— you'll know you can shorten your stride a few inches, concentrate on maintaining your leg turnover, and keep going. More generally, you'll have experienced overcoming the sometimes overwhelming desire to do anything but continue to run. During your long runs, you encounter many of the experiences, good and bad, that await you in the marathon.

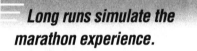

Long runs simulate the marathon experience.

No scientific evidence will tell you the best distance for your long runs as you train. However, a clear trade-off exists between running far enough to stimulate physiological adaptations and remaining uninjured. If you regularly do runs longer than 24 miles, you'll become strong but slow because you won't be able to run your other hard workouts at as high a level of quality. You'll also increase your risk of injury because when your muscles are very fatigued, they lose their ability to absorb impact forces, greatly increasing your risk of muscle strain or tendinitis.

Experience suggests that steadily building your long runs to 21 or 22 miles will maximize your chances of reaching the marathon in top shape while remaining healthy. Experienced marathoners who are not highly injury prone should include one run of 24 miles in their preparation.

When Are Long Runs Too Long?

My experience as a runner and coach indicates that long runs greater than 22 miles take much more out of the body than do runs in the range of 20 to 22 miles. I occasionally included runs of 27 to 30 miles in my marathon preparations and believe that I ran slower in my marathons because of those efforts.

(continued)

The only time I really got carried away with long runs was in preparing for the 1985 World Cup Marathon in Hiroshima. The previous year, I had won the Olympic marathon trials in 2:11:43; 3 months later, I placed 11th at the Olympics. I figured that training even harder would bring even greater success. During a 4-week period, I did two very hilly 27-milers and a 30-miler in New Zealand, and I ran them hard, trying to drop my training partners, Kevin Ryan and Chris Pilone.

The World Cup Marathon was on a lightning-fast course. I was very strong but had little speed, and I finished 18th. Although my time of 2:12:28 was satisfactory, the conditions were excellent and I blew my best opportunity to run 2:10.

Pete Pfitzinger

Your long runs should be run 10 to 20 percent slower than your goal marathon race pace. If you use a heart monitor, your long run pace should be in the range of 73 to 83 percent of maximal heart rate, or 65 to 78 percent of your heart rate reserve. This will ensure that you're running with a similar posture and are using similar muscle patterns as when you run at marathon pace. If you do long runs much slower than this, you risk being unprepared for the marathon. Slow long runs reinforce poor running style and do a poor job of simulating the demands of the marathon. If you run long runs too fast, of course, you risk leaving your marathon performance out on your training loops because you'll be too tired for your other important training sessions. Using the suggested intensity range of 10 to 20 percent slower than marathon goal pace, table 2.1 lists suggested long run paces for a wide range of marathoners.

The first few miles of your long runs can be done slowly, but by 5 miles into your long run, your pace should be no more than 20 percent slower than marathon race pace. Gradually increase your pace until you're running approximately 10 percent slower than marathon race pace during the last 5 miles of your long runs. In terms of heart rate, run the first few miles at the

Table 2.1 Sample Long Run Paces

Marathon goal pace	Early part (20% slower than goal pace)	Latter part (10% slower than goal pace)
5:00 mi	6:00 mi	5:30 mi
5:30 mi	6:36 mi	6:03 mi
6:00 mi	7:12 mi	6:36 mi
6:30 mi	7:48 mi	7:09 mi
7:00 mi	8:24 mi	7:42 mi
7:30 mi	9:00 mi	8:15 mi
8:00 mi	9:36 mi	8:48 mi

low end of the recommended intensity range and gradually increase your effort until you reach the high end of the range during the last 5 miles. This makes for an excellent workout and provides a strong stimulus for physiological adaptations. These workouts are difficult enough that you should schedule a recovery day the day before and 1 or 2 days after your long runs.

If you do long runs in this intensity range, a 22-mile run will take approximately the same amount of time as your marathon. By running for the length of time you hope to run the marathon, you also provide psychological reinforcement that you can run at a steady pace for that amount of time.

//// What's Your Maximal Heart Rate and Heart Rate Reserve?

Throughout this book, we'll prescribe specific intensities for various types of workouts to help you prepare most effectively for the marathon. Heart rate monitors are a useful tool you can use to check the intensity of your training. Training intensity can also be described in terms of speed, but unless you train daily on a track or measured stretch of road, you don't really know how fast you're training most of the time. Monitoring the intensity of your training in terms of heart rate, however, is simple.

MAXIMAL HEART RATE

The intensity of your runs can be stated relative to your maximal heart rate or as a percentage of your heart rate reserve. Your maximal heart rate is, quite simply, the fastest that your heart will beat during maximal-effort running. There are several formulas for estimating maximal heart rate, but they're all quite inaccurate. All you really know from the formulas is that there's a 95 percent chance that your maximal heart rate is within 20 beats per minute of the predicted value. For example, using the formula of 220 minus your age equals your maximal heart rate, a 42-year-old would have a predicted maximal heart rate of 178. That simply means that there's a 95 percent likelihood that this individual's true maximal heart rate is between 158 and 198 beats per minute. Using an estimated maximal heart rate can lead you to train too hard or not hard enough, so it's better to do a performance test to determine your actual maximal heart rate.

You can find your maximal heart rate quite accurately during a very hard interval session. An effective workout is to warm up thoroughly and then run three high-intensity 600-meter repeats up a moderate hill, jogging back down right away after each one. If you run these 600s all out, your heart rate should be within two to three beats of maximum by the end of the third repeat.

HEART RATE RESERVE

Heart rate reserve is an even more accurate way of prescribing training intensities because it takes into account both your maximal heart rate and your resting heart rate. Your heart rate reserve is simply your maximal heart rate minus your resting heart rate, and it reflects how much your heart rate can increase to provide more oxygen to your

(continued)

muscles. By resting heart rate we mean your heart rate when you first wake up in the morning. As an example of calculating heart rate reserve, Scott's current maximal heart rate is 188 and his resting heart rate is 38. His heart rate reserve, therefore, is 188 minus 38, which equals 150 beats per minute.

To calculate the proper heart rates for a workout using heart rate reserve, multiply your heart rate reserve by the appropriate percentage, and then add your resting heart rate. For example, if Scott wanted to do a lactate threshold workout at 76 to 88 percent of his heart rate reserve, he would stay in the range of 152 ([heart rate reserve of 150 × .76] + resting heart rate of 38) to 170 ([150 × .88] + 38) beats per minute. This compares closely to using 80 to 90 percent of his maximal heart rate, which would put him in the range of 150 to 169 beats per minute.

The prescribed training intensities used in this chapter and chapter 4 are summarized in table 2.2.

Table 2.2   Heart Rate Intensities for Standard Workouts

	Maximal heart rate (%)	Heart rate reserve (%)
$\dot{V}O_2$max	94–98	93–98
Lactate threshold	80–90	76–88
Long runs	73–83	65–78
Recovery	<75	<70

ALLOWING FOR HEART RATE DRIFT

During a lactate threshold session or long run, your heart rate will tend to increase several beats per minute even if you hold an even pace. On a warm day, your heart rate increases even more because of dehydration and as your body sends more blood to your skin to aid in cooling. This phenomenon is discussed in greater detail in chapter 3. The implication for your lactate threshold sessions and long runs is that you should start these sessions at the low end of the specified intensity zone and allow your heart rate to increase to the high end of the zone during the workout.

On a low-humidity day with temperatures in the 70s, increase your zones by two to four beats per minute to gain the same benefits as on a cooler day. On a high-humidity day in the 70s or a low-humidity day in the 80s, increase your zones by five to eight beats per minute. On a high-humidity day in the 80s, just take it easy (Lambert 1998).

The total volume of your training also improves your ability to store glycogen and use fat, and reinforces some of the other positive training adaptations, such as increased capillarization. There is some benefit, therefore, in doing relatively high mileage. The best marathoners in the world train from 100 to 170 miles per week.

More is only better to a point, however. You have a unique individual current mileage limit that is dictated by your biomechanics, past training, injury history, shoes, running surface, diet, and various other life stresses. (For starters, most of those people running 150 miles a week don't commute to a 50-hour-per-week job.) The challenge in pursuing marathoning excellence is to find the mileage range that you can handle without breaking down.

Also, although racing performance improves with increased mileage, the incremental improvement decreases the more mileage you do. In *Daniels' Running Formula* (1998), renowned coach and physiologist Jack Daniels, PhD, explains the principle of diminishing return: "Adding more and more mileage to your weekly training does not produce equal percentages of improvement in competitive fitness" (page 26). Increasing from 70 to 90 miles per week, therefore, will not improve performance as much as increasing from 50 to 70 miles per week, but it may produce a benefit nonetheless.

Although you have an individual current mileage limit, this limit changes over time. The mileage that contributed to your shinsplints 5 years ago will not necessarily cause problems for you again. You need to be a good detective and figure out the causes of your past injuries. Many runners say, "I tried high mileage once years ago, and I just got tired and hurt," and they permanently return to what they consider to be their safe mileage range. They don't consider that in the ensuing years their bodies may well have gained the ability—and their minds the wisdom—to handle higher mileage and to reap the concomitant benefits.

//// *Increasing Mileage While Minimizing the Risk of Breakdown*

As with most aspects of running, there are no guarantees, but the following guidelines will help you increase your mileage without getting injured or overtrained:

◆ Bite off small chunks. Over a few years, you can double or triple your mileage, but increasing mileage too much at once is almost certain to lead to injury or overtiredness. Unfortunately, there's no scientific evidence indicating how much is safe to increase at one time. A commonly used, but unvalidated, rule of thumb is to increase mileage by a maximum of 10 percent per week. Jack Daniels recommends increasing mileage by no more than 1 mile for each training session that you run per week. For example, if you run six times per week, you would increase your mileage by up to 6 miles per week.

◆ Increase in steps. Don't increase your mileage week after week. That approach is very likely to lead to injury. Instead, increase your mileage 1 week, then stay at that level for 2 to 3 weeks before increasing again.

◆ Avoid speed work while upping your mileage. Don't increase your mileage during a phase of training that includes hard speed work. Fast intervals put your body under

(continued)

a great deal of stress. Increasing your mileage adds more stress. Save the majority of your mileage increases for base training, when you can avoid intervals.

◆ Reduce your training intensity. When increasing your mileage, it helps to slightly reduce the overall intensity of your training. By backing off the intensity, you can increase your volume without increasing the strain of training. You can then return the intensity to its previous level before upping your mileage again.

◆ Not all miles are created equal. When building your mileage, it's particularly important to train on soft surfaces to reduce the accumulated jarring on your body and to wear running shoes that suit your needs and are in good repair.

◆ Give yourself a break. Don't let mileage become a goal in itself. Aimlessly running high mileage can lead to chronic overtiredness and burnout. Your training should be focused on a target race such as a marathon. When you have run your target race, give your body a break before building your mileage for your next goal.

PETE'S PROGRESSION

My highest sustained mileage was before the 1984 Olympic trials marathon. With Alberto Salazar, Greg Meyer, Tony Sandoval, and Bill Rodgers in the race, making the Olympic team necessitated no compromises. My previous training had peaked at 125 miles per week. At the time, I thought that was all my body could handle.

The trials were held in May. For 8 weeks during January and February, I averaged 143 miles per week, with a high week of 152 and a low week of 137. Most of this was run at a fairly brisk pace (5:40-6:10 per mile), but I was in base training and didn't need to do much speed work.

After I cut my mileage to 100 to 120 miles per week for the last 2 months before the trials, my legs felt fresh and strong all the time. Having adapted to the higher volume, I was able to do high-quality intervals and tempo runs while still running well over 100 miles per week. While that mileage looks daunting to me now, there's little question that January's and February's high-mileage training contributed to the improvement that allowed me to win the 1984 trials.

Besides the physiological benefits, high-mileage training provided me with psychological benefits for the marathon. When I was coming up through the ranks, 2:10 marathoner Gary Bjorklund revealed to me that he was running 160 miles per week. When I asked him if that much mileage was necessary, he said, "It's not necessary before every marathon, but you need to do it at least once to know you can."

SCOTT'S SCHEDULE

High-mileage training—and its many benefits—needn't be solely the domain of the elite. During the 1990s, I averaged 72 miles per week, with a peak of 125 miles in a week; in 1993, I averaged 95 miles per week for the year. All of this occurred while I usually worked 45 hours a week or more at a regular job and put in additional time as a freelance writer.

For many people, our priorities are reflected in how we spend our time. I enjoy running, and I would rather try to be modestly good at it than to simply accept being mediocre, as I would definitely be without hard training. So to the question "Where do you find the time?," the answer is simply, "I make it." I've chosen to have running be one of the few things that I concentrate on, and I allot my time accordingly. (Which means you won't see me at a lot of after-work happy hours.)

For the most part, running a decent amount while living a "normal" life means giving a day's one or two runs as much importance in planning my schedule as I do work and other obligations. Besides setting aside time for running, this also means getting to bed at a decent hour most nights; allowing time for a few good stretching and weightlifting sessions each week; and not cramming my weekends with activities, so that I can use these days to recharge physically and mentally.

If you're devoted to getting in the miles, you can almost always find ways to squeeze more time out of your schedule. For example, my current job is the third one in which I've run to or from work at least once a week.

Of course, you might have other high priorities in your life besides running. In the months before a marathon, however, it's worth setting some of them aside to concentrate on your training. High mileage and the real world aren't inherently incompatible.

Improving Your Running Economy

An important determinant of marathon performance is running economy at marathon race pace. Although some evidence shows that economy improves with training, no one fully understands the secrets of improving running economy. Various studies have found running economy to improve with weightlifting, biofeedback, relaxation training, hill training, exhaustive distance running, and long intervals. Jack Daniels (1998) recommends running fast intervals to reduce wasted motion and to train the body to recruit the most effective combination of muscle fibers. A variety of biomechanical factors, such as a narrow pelvis, small feet, and "faster rotation of shoulders in the transverse plane," have been suggested as contributors to running economy.

According to Don Morgan, PhD, who has conducted a large number of studies on running economy, the most important factor for improving economy may be the number of years (and accumulated miles) that you have been running rather than the specific types of workouts that you do. The mechanism for improvement may be that with training your fast-twitch muscle fibers gain more of the characteristics of the more economical slow-twitch fibers. Morgan speculates, however, that different types of training may improve economy depending on the specific strengths and weaknesses of the individual athlete. This individuality in response may explain why no clear consensus exists on how to improve running economy.

Putting all of the evidence together suggests that your running economy should gradually improve over the years and that there may be ways to help hurry the process along. For marathoners, probably the two most worthwhile ways to try to improve running economy are increasing mileage over time so that your fast-twitch fibers gain the positive characteristics of slow-twitch fibers and running short repetitions (80-120 meters) fast but relaxed.

Running short repetitions quickly but with relaxed form—strideouts—may train your muscles to eliminate unnecessary movements and maintain control at fast speeds. These adaptations may translate to improved economy at marathon pace. Along with improved running form, you'll gain power in your legs and trunk that may also contribute to improved running economy. Because these intervals are short and are performed with sufficient rest between them, lactate levels remain low to moderate throughout the workout. As a result, they won't interfere with your more marathon-specific workouts.

A typical session is 12 repetitions of 100 meters in which you accelerate up to full speed over the first 70 meters and then float for the last 30 meters. It's critical to remain relaxed during these accelerations. Avoid clenching your fists, lifting your shoulders, tightening your neck muscles, and so on. Concentrate on running with good form, and focus on one aspect of good form, such as relaxed arms or complete hip extension, during each acceleration.

These sessions aren't designed to improve your cardiovascular system, so there's no reason to use a short rest between accelerations. A typical rest is to jog and walk 100 to 200 meters between repetitions. The most important considerations are to maintain good running form and to concentrate on accelerating powerfully during each repetition.

Improving Your $\dot{V}O_2$max

The most effective running intensity to improve $\dot{V}O_2$max is 95 to 100 percent of current $\dot{V}O_2$max. Well-trained runners can run at $\dot{V}O_2$max pace for about 8 minutes. Ninety-five to 100 percent of $\dot{V}O_2$max coincides with current 3,000-meter to 5,000-meter race pace. This coincides with an intensity of approximately 94 to 98 percent of maximal heart rate or 93 to 98 percent of heart rate reserve. Running intervals at this pace or intensity is part of the optimal strategy to improve $\dot{V}O_2$max. (Be sure to use an accurate assessment of your current 5K pace, namely, a race run under optimal conditions, not a hilly course on a hot day.)

The stimulus to improve $\dot{V}O_2$max is provided by the amount of time you accumulate during a workout in the optimal intensity range of 95 to 100 percent of $\dot{V}O_2$max. This fact has implications for how best to structure your $\dot{V}O_2$max sessions. Consider two workouts that each include 6,000 meters of intervals—one of 15 × 400 meters and the other of 5 × 1,200 meters. When you run 400-meter repetitions, you're in the optimal zone for perhaps 45 seconds per interval. If you do 15 repetitions, you accumulate just more than 11 minutes at the optimal intensity. When you run longer intervals, you are in the optimal intensity zone much longer. During each 1,200-meter interval, you would be in the optimal intensity zone for 3 to 4 minutes and would accumulate 15 to 20 minutes in that zone during the workout. This would provide a stronger stimulus to improve your $\dot{V}O_2$max.

The optimal duration for $\dot{V}O_2$max intervals for marathoners is approximately 2 to 6 minutes. Intervals in this range are long enough so you accumulate a substantial amount of time at $\dot{V}O_2$max pace during each interval but short enough so you can maintain 95 to 100 percent of $\dot{V}O_2$max. Intervals for marathoners should generally be between 800 and 1,600 meters. The training schedules in this book include some workouts of 600-meter repeats during weeks when your top priority lies elsewhere, such as when the week also calls for a tune-up race.

The training schedules don't include 2,000-meter repeats. Although repeats of this length can provide a powerful boost to $\dot{V}O_2$max, for all but the elite they take more than 6 minutes to complete. That's fine if you're focusing on a 5K or 10K, where $\dot{V}O_2$max is the primary determinant of success. As a marathoner, though, you want to be fresh for the week's more important endurance workouts, so you don't want your $\dot{V}O_2$max workouts to require several recovery days before and after.

The total volume of the intervals in a marathoner's $\dot{V}O_2$max session should be 5,000 to 10,000 meters, with most workouts in the range of 6,400 to 8,000 meters. Any combination of repetitions of 800 to 1,600 meters will provide an excellent workout. Longer intervals (e.g., 1,200s or 1,600s) make for a tougher workout, physically and psychologically, and shouldn't be avoided.

The optimal amount of rest between intervals is debatable. One school of thought is to minimize rest so that your metabolic rate stays high during the entire workout. This strategy makes for very difficult workouts (which can be good), but you risk shortening your workouts. Another school of thought is to allow your heart rate to decrease to 70 percent of your maximal heart rate or 60 percent of your heart rate reserve during your recovery between intervals.

For the lower-tech crowd, a good rule of thumb is to allow 50 to 90 percent of the length of time it takes to do the interval for your recovery. For example, if you're running 1,000-meter repeats in 3:20, you would run slowly for 1:40 to 3 minutes between intervals.

//// Don't Max Out Your $\dot{V}O_2$max Workouts

Two related mistakes that marathoners sometimes make in training are running intervals too fast and running intervals too frequently. Let's consider why you should avoid these errors.

RUNNING INTERVALS TOO FAST

A common mistake among marathoners is to do speed work too hard. The idea that running your intervals harder will make you run better is appealing, and it seems logical. It's also incorrect. Running your intervals faster than the optimal zone will do two things—build up a high degree of lactate in your muscles and shorten the duration of your workout. Both of these effects are counterproductive for marathoners.

The marathon is an aerobic event. More than 99 percent of the energy you use in the marathon is supplied by your aerobic system. As we saw earlier in this chapter, during the marathon, you run slightly below your lactate threshold pace; therefore, you don't

(continued)

accumulate much lactate in your muscles and blood. In fact, when lactate levels are measured at the end of a marathon, they are only slightly above resting levels.

There's no reason, then, for marathoners to do training that builds up high levels of lactate, such as intervals run at 1,500-meter race pace or faster. Running intervals at this pace produces high levels of lactate and improves your ability to produce energy using the glycolytic system (what you probably think of as running anaerobically) and to buffer high levels of lactate. None of these adaptations is relevant to the marathon. Running intervals much faster than 3,000- to 5,000-meter race pace also produces a smaller stimulus to improve your $\dot{V}O_2$max.

RUNNING $\dot{V}O_2$max SESSIONS TOO FREQUENTLY

Another common mistake among marathoners is trying to include too many $\dot{V}O_2$max sessions in their marathon training programs. As discussed previously in this chapter, the most important adaptations for marathon success are a high level of endurance, a fast pace at lactate threshold, and the ability to store a large quantity of glycogen in the muscles and liver. $\dot{V}O_2$max sessions are definitely a secondary consideration for a marathoner. Intervals require large amounts of physical and psychological energy, which can be better used doing more specific marathon training. $\dot{V}O_2$max sessions have their place in marathon preparation, but they should be included sparingly.

Integrated Training: Training at Marathon Race Pace

Your goal for the marathon is to be able to maintain your goal race pace for 26.2 miles. The physiological demands of this task require a high lactate threshold, excellent capacity to store glycogen, well-developed ability to burn fat, and so on. Each of the various types of training that we have discussed so far focuses on improving a specific aspect of your physiology for the marathon. Now we'll discuss a type of training that integrates the various physiological attributes as specifically as possible for the marathon race.

Long runs at marathon race pace directly prepare you for the demands of the race. The principle of specificity of training states that the most effective way to prepare for an event is to simulate that event as closely as possible. The closest way to simulate a marathon, of course, is to run 26.2 miles at marathon pace. Unfortunately (or perhaps fortunately), long runs at marathon pace are very hard on the body. If you run too far at marathon pace, the required recovery time will negate the benefits of the effort. Similarly, if you do long runs at marathon pace too often, you will greatly increase your likelihood of self-destructing through injury or overtraining.

The training programs in this book include one or two runs in which you'll run 12 to 15 miles of a longer run at goal marathon race pace. These runs are the most specific marathon preparation that you'll do. The intention is to stress your body in a similar way to the marathon but to limit the duration so that your required recovery time is held to a few days. On these runs, use the first few miles to warm up, then finish the run with the prescribed number of miles at marathon race pace. In addition to the physiological and psychological benefits these runs impart, they're an excellent opportunity to practice drinking and taking energy gels at race pace.

Where should you do your marathon pace runs? Races of the appropriate distance are ideal—you'll have a measured course, plenty of aid stations, and other runners to work with. As with doing tempo runs in races, though, be sure to limit yourself to the day's goal and run them no faster than is called for.

If you can't find a race of suitable length in which to do your marathon-pace runs, try to run at least part of them over a measured course so that you can get feedback about your pace. A reasonable way to check pace is to do 1 or 2 miles in the middle of a road race course that has markers painted on the road. Similarly, many bike paths have miles marked. Your entire run needn't be over a precisely calibrated course, but try to include at least a few stretches where you can accurately assess your pace, and then rely on perceived exertion or heart rate during the other parts of the run.

Given the opportunity for regular splits and frequent fluids, a track would seem to be an ideal locale for marathon-pace workouts, but bear in mind the reason for these runs. The purpose is to simulate marathon conditions as closely as possible. This means running on a road, not doing endless repeats of a 400-meter oval. Learn your goal marathon's topography and attempt to mimic it on your marathon-pace runs. Many runners do this when preparing for courses with obvious quirks, such as Boston, but the principle applies for all marathons. Pancake-flat courses such as Chicago also take their toll because your leg muscles are used exactly the same way from start to finish.

Wear your marathon shoes when doing at least one of these workouts, even if you'll be racing the marathon in flats. You want to have at least one run of 15 miles or so in your race-day shoes to learn whether they provide enough support when you start to tire and whether they blister you.

Structuring Your Training Program: Periodization

Now that we've discussed the types of training that help improve marathon performance, the next step is to develop your overall training plan. You need to prepare so that you're at your best on marathon day. Systematically structuring your training to bring you to your desired end point is called *periodization*. The challenge in developing a periodized training plan is to decide how many hard sessions to do, which types of sessions to do, and when to do them.

A useful framework is provided by organizing your training into macrocycles, mesocycles, and microcycles. These concepts are used for preparing training programs in a wide variety of sports and have been used extensively in track and field.

1997 Chicago Marathon. Road running more closely simulates the conditions of the marathon course than running on a track.

For a marathoner, a macrocycle is the entire training period leading up to the marathon. You'll likely have two macrocycles per year, each consisting of 4 to 6 months. Both of your macrocycles may culminate with a marathon, or you may have one goal marathon for the year and a second macrocycle leading up to a goal race at a shorter distance. Runners doing more than two marathons in a year will probably still have only two macrocycles per year. Multiple marathoners can only do a partial buildup for some of their marathons.

A macrocycle is divided into several mesocycles, each of which has a specific training objective. For a marathoner, a mesocycle may last from 4 to 10 weeks. For example, the first mesocycle in marathon preparation will almost always be a high-volume base training block of at least 4 weeks. As the race approaches, the priorities in your training shift. Each shift in priorities is reflected in a new mesocycle.

Each mesocycle is divided into several microcycles. A microcycle is a series of days that make up a shorter block of training. Microcycles can be anywhere from 4 days to 2 weeks long. Often, the most effective training pattern is with a microcycle pattern of 8 to 10 days. In this book, we realize that the rest of your life revolves around a 7-day week, so we've made a practical compromise on the ideal. We'll use the terms *microcycle* and *week* interchangeably. (Just for kicks, see what happens next Friday at the office when you say to a coworker, "Boy, I thought this microcycle would never end.")

Let's consider a runner whose annual training plan centers around two marathons per year. She would train for the marathon for 12 to 18 weeks and taper for 3 weeks culminating in the race, followed by 5 to 8 weeks to recover before starting focused training for the next target race. This indicates a minimum of 20 weeks for a marathoner's macrocycle.

Now, let's consider the training objectives in preparation for the marathon. The macrocycle will generally be divided into five mesocycles (table 2.3). The first mesocycle will focus on increasing mileage and improving pure endurance. This will likely be the longest mesocycle in the program and may last as long as 10 weeks. The second mesocycle will focus on improving lactate threshold, with further improvement of pure endurance as a secondary objective. The third mesocycle will focus on race preparation and will include tune-up races. The fourth mesocycle will include a 3-week taper and the marathon. The fifth and final mesocycle in a marathoner's macrocycle will consist of several weeks of recovery.

Table 2.3   Typical Marathoner's Macrocycle

Mesocycle	Primary objective
1	Increasing mileage to improve pure endurance
2	Improving lactate threshold
3	Race preparation
4	Taper and the marathon
5	Recovery

Your 7-day microcycle will typically consist of three hard training sessions. This is the maximum number of hard sessions that most distance runners can respond to positively. A few runners can handle four hard sessions per week, and some runners can handle only two. Considering that there are at least five categories of hard training sessions that you can do, it takes a good deal of intelligent planning to come up with the optimal training program for you. The training schedules in this book are structured around five mesocycles per macrocycle and three hard training sessions per microcycle.

Tune-Up Races

Training provides a variety of stimuli that lead to adaptations that improve your marathon performance. Training also gives you the confidence that comes with setting and achieving challenging training goals. However, training doesn't completely prepare you for the marathon. An additional component to successful marathoning can be gained only by racing.

Tune-up races are important benchmarks of your fitness and prepare you mentally for the rigors of racing. Because less is at stake, even the toughest workout isn't as mentally demanding as a race. After all, in a race, when you're competing against other runners, there's a fine margin between relative success and relative failure. Similarly, in a race you're committed to finish (or you should be) whether you're having a good day or a lousy day; in a workout, if things aren't going well, you can always stop early with your pride relatively intact. The all-out aspect of racing provides a mental hardening that's necessary to run a good marathon. When runners do no premarathon tune-up races, they have greater anxiety leading up to the marathon.

Tune-up races serve two purposes. First, they provide feedback on your fitness, reducing an element of uncertainty about your marathon preparation. Second, they make you go through the nerves of racing, helping to reduce anxiety in the last few days and hours before the marathon. When you're at your limit in the marathon, feeling tired, wondering whether you can hang on even though there are still 10 miles to go, it helps to have been through the demands of racing at shorter distances. Even though the ultimate test (the marathon) is crueler, the preparation gained from shorter races is priceless.

By tune-up races, we mean all-out efforts, not races in which you give less than your best, such as races you use as the setting for a tempo run or marathon-pace run. Tune-up races can vary in length from 5 miles to 25 km, depending on their training purpose. Races of 5K or shorter are less specific to marathon success, and races of 30K or longer require too much recovery.

Tune-up race distances can be divided into two categories. Races of 15 km to 25 km take at least 5 days to recover from, and you must place them strategically in your training program. These races provide the greatest physiological and psychological benefit. Therefore, prepare for these races with a mini-taper of 4 to 6 days. You can't afford to taper any longer than 6 days because the tune-up race isn't your primary goal and you need to keep training for the marathon. A tune-up race of 15K to 25K really represents a training block of at least 10 days, consisting of 4 to 6 days of tapering, the race itself, and several days recovery before the next hard training session.

The second category of tune-up race distances is 5 miles to 12K. These races take less out of you and require less tapering and fewer recovery days than races of 15K or longer. You can approach tune-up races of 5 miles to 12K in two ways. First, you can train through them and treat them as an all-out effort done while fatigued. This will provide an excellent training stimulus as well as a mental challenge that will help steel you for the marathon. Racing when tired, however, brings the danger of believing that your finishing time and place represent your current fitness level. If you typically race 10K in 32:00 but run 33:10 in a tune-up race, you could interpret the result as meaning that you're not in shape, and you might start to train harder or become discouraged. It's important to put the result in the context of the situation.

The other way to approach a tune-up race of 5 miles to 12K is to do a mini-taper and give yourself a couple of recovery days. This is the appropriate approach if you're using the race to assess your fitness level or as a confidence booster leading up to the marathon. Table 2.4 indicates how close to a tune-up race you can do a hard workout without going into the race fatigued. Although you won't see the benefits of the workout in this week's race, you should be recovered enough so the workout doesn't detract from your race performance.

Table 2.4 Balancing Hard Workouts and Tune-Up Races

Type of workout	Minimum no. days before tune-up race
$\dot{V}O_2$max interval	5
Tempo run	4
Long run	4

Tempo runs are the easiest to recover from because they don't break down the body as much as other forms of hard training. Long runs require at least 4 days of recovery to put in a good race effort, although replenishing glycogen stores generally requires only 48 hours. Interval workouts put the body under the most stress and require the longest time to recover from.

Now you know what physiological traits are needed to run a good marathon and how to train to improve those traits. More so than with any other popular distance, though, success in the marathon depends not only on what you do to your body but also on what you put in your body. Proper nutrition and hydration are critical when training for and running a marathon. They're the subjects of the next chapter.

3

Nutrition and Hydration

This chapter looks at two critical but often misunderstood factors in marathon preparation and racing—nutrition and hydration. Why are these matters critical? Because the two factors that typically conspire to make you slow in the last few miles of the marathon are glycogen depletion and dehydration. By understanding the role of nutrition for marathon preparation and racing, you can develop strategies to optimize your marathon performance.

This chapter discusses the importance of staying well hydrated and how to prevent dehydration; the roles of carbohydrate and fat as the primary fuels for endurance exercise, and how to prevent glycogen depletion; the role of protein for endurance athletes; the need to maintain normal iron levels; and nutritional considerations for racing the marathon. Understanding the information in this chapter is an essential component of your marathon preparation.

The Importance of Hydration

Staying well hydrated is vital to successful marathoning during training and racing. Becoming dehydrated negatively affects your running performance and also slows your ability to recover for the next workout. Your blood and other fluids help to remove waste products and to bring nutrients to tissues for repair. Replacing lost fluids as quickly as possible after running, therefore, will speed your recovery.

Let's take a look at the physiology of dehydration. When you sweat, the following chain of events occurs:

- Your blood volume decreases, so
- less blood returns to your heart; therefore,
- the amount of blood your heart pumps with each beat decreases, so
- less oxygen-rich blood reaches your working muscles; therefore
- you produce less energy aerobically, and
- you must run at a slower pace.

These effects are magnified on a hot day because one of your body's major responses to increase cooling is to send more blood to the skin to remove heat from the body; this process means that even less blood returns to the heart to be pumped to the working muscles. The result is a higher heart rate for a given pace and an inability to maintain the same pace as on a cool day. Looked at in another way, dehydration also reduces your body's ability to maintain your core temperature because less blood is available to be sent to your skin and your sweat rate decreases. Struggling to maintain a fast pace on a hot day becomes more dangerous as you become progressively more dehydrated and can lead to heatstroke.

The need to drink during the marathon is obvious. But staying well hydrated is also important during training. Don't just rely on your thirst—your body's thirst mechanism is imperfect. Marathoners sometimes become chronically dehydrated without realizing it. Interestingly, this seems to happen most often in the winter, when the need to drink isn't as obvious. But whenever you're running high mileage, you need to replace a large amount of fluid daily, even if you're training in minus-10-degree conditions.

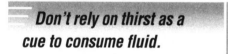

Don't rely on thirst as a cue to consume fluid.

It's also easy to become dehydrated because monitoring your fluid level takes such regular attention. You can't just sit down and drink a half gallon of fluid at one sitting and assume you're fully hydrated. It takes time for your body tissues to absorb water. If you replace a little less fluid than you lose each day, after a few days you'll run poorly but may not know why.

Studies have found that dehydration of 2 percent of body weight leads to about a 6 percent reduction in running performance. For years, the general wisdom has been that running performance is affected by dehydration only when you lose more than 2 percent of your body weight. Recently, however, Ed Coyle, PhD, a former competitive runner and now professor of exercise physiology at the University of Texas at Austin, has provided evidence that even a small amount of dehydration causes a decrease in running performance. This is because any reduction in blood volume will reduce the amount of blood returning to your heart.

It's not unusual to lose 3 pounds of water per hour when running on a warm day. At this rate, during a 2-hour run you would lose about 6 pounds. For a 140-pound runner, this would represent more than a 4 percent loss in body weight and more than a 12 percent decrement in performance. The effect increases as the run progresses, so this runner wouldn't be any slower the first few miles but would likely slow by up to a minute per mile by the end of the run. Staying well hydrated, then, can be the difference between training hard enough to provide a strong stimulus for your body to improve or just going through the motions in training and never reaching your potential.

How Much to Drink

For any marathoner training in warm conditions, preventing dehydration must be a high priority. How much you need to drink to stay well hydrated during your marathon preparation depends on a number of factors, including the heat and humidity, your body size, how much you're training, and how much you sweat.

Your baseline fluid needs when you're not training are about 4 pints per day. On top of that, you need to add your fluid losses from training and other activities. Weigh yourself before and after running and calculate how much weight you lost, then drink with the objective of bringing your weight back up to normal. Because you don't retain all of the fluid that you drink, becoming fully hydrated typically requires drinking an amount of fluid equivalent to about $1\frac{1}{2}$ times the amount of weight that you lost. For example, if you lost 3 pounds during a training run, you would need to

© Ray Malace

Keep water at your desk and drink frequently throughout the day.

drink about $4\frac{1}{2}$ pounds of fluid ($4\frac{1}{2}$ pints) during the next several hours to be sure that you're fully rehydrated.

If you add $4\frac{1}{2}$ pints to make up for the fluid lost during training to the 4 pints you require as a baseline, that makes a total fluid requirement of $8\frac{1}{2}$

pints for the day in this example. This is a large amount of fluid, and consuming this much during the day requires a strategy, particularly for those with normal jobs. Keeping a water bottle at your workstation is a must. You'll regain fluids most effectively if you discipline yourself to drink regularly throughout the day. Try to avoid waiting until shortly before training to replace your fluids—you can't rush the process, and so you'll go into your workout either bloated from too much fluid ingested too quickly or dehydrated from not having enough fluid.

How much you should drink during your runs is discussed under "Marathon Race-Day Nutrition and Hydration" later in this chapter.

What to Drink

Water and carbohydrate-replacement drinks are excellent for maintaining hydration during running. The advantage of replacement drinks with 4 to 8 percent carbohydrate is that they're absorbed as quickly as water and also provide readily usable energy. The carbohydrates can help your performance during workouts lasting longer than 1 hour. The exact carbohydrate concentration that's best for you will depend on your stomach's tolerance and how warm it is during training and during your marathon. On a cool day, you may want to use a carbohydrate content of 6 to 8 percent, whereas on a warm day, when fluid is more critical than extra carbohydrate, you may want to stay in the 4 to 6 percent range. Sports drinks should also contain between 250 and 700 mg of sodium per liter to enhance glucose and water absorption and improve fluid retention.

Attempting to do high mileage or high-intensity training in hot weather is a physiological challenge that requires you to be flexible with your training schedule. By planning your training, you can minimize the impact of hot weather. Start each workout fully hydrated by making rehydration a priority after the previous day's run. Run at the time of day when the weather is the least taxing on your body. On a hot, humid day, slow your pace from the outset rather than waiting until your body forces you to slow.

/// **Alcohol and Caffeine**

Most running books just tell you to avoid alcohol and caffeine. That's neither realistic nor helpful advice for the majority of people who regularly enjoy coffee, tea, beer, wine, or spirits. The real issue is determining how much of these beverages you can drink before they have a significant effect on your running performance.

ALCOHOL

Alcohol (ethyl alcohol) primarily affects your brain. One or two drinks temporarily lead to reduced tension and relief from stress but also cause dehydration. The night before your marathon, reduced tension is a good thing, but as discussed earlier, any amount of dehydration is detrimental to running performance. With this in mind, it's best to limit yourself to one or, at the most, two beers or one glass of wine the night before the marathon. Take in enough extra fluid to make up for the dehydrating effect of the alcohol. Drink an extra ounce of water for each ounce of beer and an extra 3 ounces of water for each ounce of wine that you drink. The same guideline holds for the night before a long run.

CAFFEINE

The International Olympic Committee considers caffeine a banned drug, but the maximum allowable limit in the urine has been set high enough that you would need to consume about eight cups of percolated coffee to fail a drug test. A cup of coffee or tea on the morning of the race is fine. In fact, if you're used to having a cup of coffee each morning, abstaining from coffee could have a detrimental effect on your performance because of the withdrawal effects of caffeine deprivation.

Caffeine has a diuretic effect similar to that of alcohol. If you're used to drinking coffee, then the diuretic effect is lessened. If you're not used to coffee, then have an extra ounce of fluid for each ounce of coffee you consume; regular coffee drinkers can make up for the caffeine with somewhat less fluid.

Caffeine is a banned drug because it may have performance-enhancing effects in some situations. Several studies have found performance-enhancing benefits from caffeine ingestion, several others have found no effect of caffeine ingestion on endurance performance, and at least one study found caffeine ingestion to be related to reduced performance. The differences in these results may be at least partly explained by differences in individuals' responsiveness to caffeine.

The two effects of caffeine that may boost performance for marathoners are a glycogen-sparing effect and its effect as a central nervous system stimulant. Ingesting caffeine mobilizes fatty acids that allow you to use more fat and less glycogen at a given pace, meaning that your glycogen stores last longer. Instead of you hitting the Wall at 23 miles because of glycogen depletion, caffeine ingestion could theoretically allow your glycogen stores to last the full marathon distance.

As a central nervous system stimulant, caffeine also increases arousal. This effect would seem to be more important for sprinters than for marathoners, who generally want to stay calmly focused throughout the event. Because of the tendency for caffeine to stimulate the central nervous system for a couple of hours followed by a rebound effect, it's usually wise for runners to avoid caffeine before competition. If you take caffeine before the marathon, the potential exists for this rebound effect to kick in about 2 hours into the race, when you're getting fatigued anyway. Unless you've practiced taking caffeine before your longest training runs, the risk of a negative impact on performance is too great to warrant taking caffeine (except possibly for one cup of coffee) before the marathon.

Hope You Like Carbs

The main fuels for endurance exercise are carbohydrates and fats. Proteins also provide a small amount of energy. Carbohydrates supply the majority of energy during exercise, and fats supply the bulk of the remainder. If you want to run 26.2 miles at a good pace, you had better like carbohydrates because they'll be the mainstay of your diet during day-to-day training and especially in the few days before the marathon.

Even if you're a gaunt marathoner, your body has a large stockpile of energy in the form of fat. A 140-pound runner with a body-fat level of 6 percent still carries around 8.4 pounds of fat. Each pound of fat supplies 3,500 calories of energy, so this individual has more than 29,000 calories stored as fat.

For the purposes of fast marathoning, of course, what matters are your carbohydrate, not fat, stores, and your carbohydrate reserves are much more limited. If you do a good job of carbohydrate loading, you can store about 2,000 to 2,500 calories of glycogen (the body's storage form of carbohydrate).

When you run, your body burns a mixture of carbohydrate and fat. The harder you run, the higher the proportion of carbohydrate you use; the slower you run, the higher the proportion of fat you use. During walking, more than half of the calories you burn are provided by the breakdown of fat. As your pace increases, you use proportionately less fat and more carbohydrate. An easy recovery run may be fueled by 65 percent carbohydrate and 35 percent fat. If you race the marathon, approximately 75 to 90 percent of the fuel you use is supplied by the breakdown of carbohydrates. For those jogging the marathon, the proportion of carbohydrate used would be somewhat lower.

Carbohydrate is a more efficient energy source than fat. The breakdown of fat requires more oxygen per calorie released than does carbohydrate. Because fat doesn't produce energy aerobically as efficiently as carbohydrate does, you can't run as fast burning just fats. Your body uses several strategies to keep you from running out of carbohydrate stores. One of these strategies is to use relatively more fat as your carbohydrate stores become low. Anyone who has hit the Wall knows the joys of this "strategy." A problem with glycogen depletion is that there aren't warning signs that it's going to occur until it's too late. When you have to slow suddenly in a marathon, the culprit is probably glycogen depletion, not dehydration, which tends to affect you more slowly.

You can prevent carbohydrate depletion by glycogen loading. Glycogen loading (also known as carbohydrate loading) is the practice of manipulating your diet and training to increase your glycogen stores.

Marathoners can almost double their muscle glycogen stores by doing a long run 7 days before a race, then eating a low-carbohydrate diet for 3 days, followed by a high-carbohydrate diet (70-80 percent of calories from carbohydrates) for the 3 days before the race. The long run depletes your body's glycogen stores, and the 3 days of low carbohydrate intake keep them low. This triggers a mechanism in your body to store as much glycogen as

> *You can train your body to store more glycogen.*

possible. When you eat a high-carbohydrate diet during the last 3 days before the marathon, therefore, your body stores an extra supply of glycogen.

This classic approach to glycogen loading has fallen out of favor as we've learned more about tapering for marathons. Carbohydrate depletion recently has been shown to suppress the immune system, so the classic glycogen depletion and loading regime increases your risk of getting sick when you can least afford it. Also, a 20-miler 1 week before your marathon carries too much risk, in the form of lingering fatigue or soreness, for the benefits it brings to your carbo loading. (Besides, what marathoner wants to avoid carbs for 3 days?)

The good news is that glycogen stores can be elevated to similar levels without the long run and low-carbohydrate phases of the original glycogen-loading diet. All you need to do is eat a normal diet up until the last 3 days before the race and taper your training program to about half your normal training load. Then eat a high-carbohydrate diet the last 3 days and do a short, slow run on those days. Your body will store glycogen to almost the same level as if you did the whole glycogen-depletion-and-loading regimen.

Rice, pasta, bread, sweet potatoes, pancakes, bagels, potatoes, corn, and raisins are excellent sources of carbohydrates. Many of the world's best marathoners eat rice for their prerace meal because it provides plenty of carbohydrates and is easy to digest. Expect to gain a couple of pounds and feel slightly bloated when you glycogen load because your body stores 2.6 grams of water for every gram of glycogen. The added weight is just extra fuel to help get you through the marathon, and the stored water will help to prevent dehydration as the marathon progresses.

If you eat a normal runner's diet, with about 60 percent of your calories from carbohydrate, you probably store about 1,500 to 2,000 calories of glycogen in your muscles. If you glycogen load, however, your muscles have the capacity to store between 2,000 and 2,500 calories of glycogen. Each mile that you run burns about 90 to 140 calories, depending on your weight and metabolism, and 75 to 90 percent of those calories are supplied by carbohydrate. If you do a great job of loading, you'll have just about enough glycogen for the marathon.

Glycogen loading is also important before your long runs. Make sure to eat a high-carbohydrate diet the day before your long run so that you have plenty of fuel to go the distance. Carbohydrate loading before your long runs will help ensure that you have high-quality long runs, which will increase your confidence for the marathon.

How Much Carbohydrate Do You Need in Your Daily Training Diet?

Your daily carbohydrate requirement depends on your weight and how much you're training. If you're averaging an hour to an hour and a half of training per day, you need approximately 7 to 8 grams of carbohydrate per kilogram (3-3½ grams per pound) of your body weight per day. If you're training for 2 hours or more per day, you need approximately 9 to 10 grams of carbohydrate per kilogram (4-4½ grams per pound) of body weight per day.

As an example, say Gary is running 80 miles per week and weighs 154 pounds (70 kg). His average daily training time is about 80 minutes. Gary's daily carbohydrate requirement is 490 to 560 grams (70 × 7 to 70 × 8). Each gram of carbohydrate supplies 4.1 calories, so Gary's calorie supply from carbohydrate should be 2,000 to 2,300 per day.

Tips to Replenish Your Glycogen Stores

With a typical runner's high-carbohydrate diet, you probably have enough glycogen to get you through a 20- to 22-mile long run or a hard interval workout. After a long run or a long interval workout, therefore, your glycogen stores are depleted. It typically takes 24 to 48 hours to completely replenish your glycogen stores. When you do two long or hard workouts in a row, therefore, you risk going into the second workout with partially filled glycogen stores, becoming depleted, and having a bad workout. The frequency with which you can train hard is determined by your recovery rate between workouts, and this will be increased greatly by replenishing your glycogen stores quickly.

Here are strategies you can use to increase your rate of glycogen replenishment.

• Don't wait. Your body stores glycogen at a faster rate during the first hour after exercise, so have a carbohydrate drink with you when you finish your long runs or other workouts. Bring along some easy-to-digest carbohydrate foods as well. To speed glycogen resynthesis, take in about 1 gram of carbohydrate per kilogram of body weight (a little under half a gram per pound) in the first 15 minutes after the workout, and another gram per kilogram of bodyweight during each of the following 3 hours.

• Increase your intake of carbs. After a glycogen-depleting workout, increase your carbohydrate intake to approximately 10 grams per kilogram of body weight (4½ grams per pound) during the next 24 hours.

• Eat high–glycemic index foods. The glycemic index of a food is determined by the effect it has on your blood glucose level. High–glycemic index foods cause a large increase in blood glucose levels, whereas low–glycemic index foods have a lesser effect. During the first few hours after a workout, your glycogen stores will be replenished more quickly if you eat high–glycemic index foods, such as potatoes, rice cakes, bread, bagels, and crackers.

The Role of Protein for Marathoners

Conventional wisdom indicates that strength-trained athletes such as weight lifters need lots of extra protein to build muscle but that the protein needs of endurance athletes are the same as for sedentary folks. Over the past 10

John Keston

Fastest Marathon: 2:52:32
Marathon Career Highlights: World record, 70-and-over division of 3:00:58.

Photo courtesy of John Keston

If you think competitive marathoning is exclusively a young person's game, consider John Keston.

Keston began running at age 55 after being diagnosed with hypertension and allowed himself time to build a solid base before considering the marathon. "My initial mileage was about 20 miles a week, and I spent 5 years increasing to 60 a week, after which I felt capable of running a marathon," he says. "This regimen—a very gradual increase in mileage and speed work—although not specifically planned, worked for me." Without a competitive background, Keston experimented with a variety of races to find his best distance and thinks that running races from the mile up helped him as a marathoner because "I was essentially a seasoned runner."

When he ran 2:58 just a few months before his 70th birthday, Keston knew what his next goal should be: break the 70-and-over record of 3:01:14 and, if possible, become the first runner over the age of 70 to break 3:00. His subsequent experience shows the importance of having a challenging, meaningful goal when confronted with the marathon's inevitable setbacks.

Starting in January 1995, Keston wound up running a string of multiple marathons that would hobble nearly any runner half his age. Food poisoning before his first attempt at the 70-and-over record slowed him to a 3:14. By June of that year, Keston had run five more marathons, all between 3:01 and 3:07 (and all of which were course records in his age group).

"In 1996, thinking I was past being capable of breaking the record, I began the year running shorter races," he says. "But in the back of my mind was the nagging desire to go for the marathon record." Keston again embarked on a marathoning spree and again came agonizingly close. "My last serious effort was to be the Twin Cities Marathon in October," says Keston, a classically trained thespian. "I sang 'The Star Spangled Banner' to start the race, walked to the start line and broke the existing record by just 16 seconds, running 3:00:58." It was his tenth marathon in the last 20 months.

(continued)

John Keston *(continued)*

Keston attributes his ability to meet his goal to intelligent recovery between attempts and the pull of meeting the task he had set himself. "I didn't have too much time between each effort," he says. "I got lots of rest and cut back on long, sustained training efforts but kept up a regimen of shorter speed sessions twice a week. I stayed motivated because I believed I could accomplish my goal and I had worked so hard to achieve it."

Even though he came to his record attempt without decades of wear and tear already in his legs, Keston says that he still needed to make concessions to age. A few months before breaking the record, he switched from daily running to alternating a hard running day with walking the following day.

"I run 5 to 18 miles one day, always with some form of speed work, tempo run, intervals, and so on," he says. "The following day, I will not run but walk 3 miles in the morning and 2 or 3 miles in the evening. I still get stiff and have the natural, good soreness of the hard workouts, but the walking days clear this and set me up for another hard effort the following day. Stretching—particularly on the walking days—is often and sustained, and I incorporate a weight training session, with special attention to my quads and hamstrings."

years, however, studies have clearly shown that endurance athletes have elevated protein needs. As a marathoner, your body needs protein to repair damaged muscles, to make red blood cells to deliver oxygen to your muscles, to make mitochondria in your muscles to produce energy aerobically, to maintain a strong immune system, and to make enzymes and hormones that keep your body functioning normally.

Sedentary individuals need about 0.8 to 1.0 gram of protein per kilogram of body weight per day (0.35-0.45 gram of protein per pound per day). Endurance athletes have elevated protein needs because of their greater wear and tear on muscle tissue and red blood cells, need for more mitochondria, and so on. Several formulas are used for calculating the protein needs of endurance athletes, but a typical guideline is 1.2 to 1.4 grams of protein per kilogram of body weight (0.55 to 0.65 gram of protein per pound of body weight) per day. Table 3.1 presents daily protein requirements for marathoners.

Table 3.1   Daily Protein Requirements for Marathoners

Weight (lb)	Weight (kg)	Protein required (g/day)
100	45	55–65
120	55	66–78
140	64	77–91
160	73	88–104
180	82	99–117
200	91	110–130

Chances are that most marathoners meet or exceed their protein requirements through a typical American diet. Runners who are vegetarians or who greatly restrict their meat intake may not meet their protein needs. If you're a vegetarian, it's not difficult to meet your protein requirements, but it does require some knowledge and planning.

Eating too much protein can also have negative consequences for your running performance. If you eat too much protein, you may not be consuming enough carbohydrates, so such a diet would reduce your energy levels. Your body would use the excess protein as energy by removing the amino groups and oxidizing the resulting carbon skeleton. This process requires the removal of waste products, which stresses the kidneys and can lead to dehydration.

The Importance of Iron

Iron is vital to running performance. Despite this importance, many runners don't monitor their body's iron levels. Even many physicians don't understand the complete role of iron for endurance athletes.

Iron is necessary for producing hemoglobin in your red blood cells. Oxygen attaches to hemoglobin for transport in your blood to your muscles. If your hemoglobin level is low, less oxygen reaches your muscles, which means that your muscles can't produce as much energy aerobically. The result is that your $\dot{V}O_2max$ and lactate threshold are reduced, and you can't maintain as fast a pace. In addition, iron is a component of many other substances in the body, such as enzymes in your muscle cells for aerobic energy production, so low iron levels may cause low energy levels.

For many years, top athletes and coaches have recognized the benefits of a high red blood cell count; this awareness has led to the illegal practices of blood doping and, more recently, use of synthetic erythropoietin (EPO) to increase red blood cell count. EPO is a hormone the body produces naturally that determines the body's level of red blood cell production. When EPO levels rise through natural means or through injection of synthetic EPO, red blood cell production and hemoglobin levels increase. The result is that the runner can produce more energy aerobically and, therefore, maintain a faster pace.

Though a few athletes try to artificially achieve a high red blood cell count, the typical marathoner needs to ensure that she or he doesn't have a low red blood cell count or low iron stores. Low iron levels may be the most prevalent nutritional deficiency in American marathoners. With iron deficiency anemia, your iron stores are gone and your hemoglobin level is reduced. With iron depletion, on the other hand, your iron stores are low but not gone, and your hemoglobin is still normal. Although anemia is more detrimental, both of these conditions can negatively impact your running performance.

Why Do Marathoners Tend to Have Lower Iron Levels?

Runners tend to have lower iron levels than sedentary folks for many reasons: increased blood volume, low iron intake, foot strike hemolysis, iron loss through sweat and urine, and iron loss through the gastrointestinal (GI) system. For marathoners, the iron losses tend to be higher than for those doing shorter races, primarily because of higher training volumes. Let's look at each of these factors.

Increased Blood Volume

Endurance athletes have more blood than normal people. This adaptation allows the stroke volume of the heart to increase, which allows $\dot{V}O_2max$ to increase. This is a good thing. The iron in a runner's red blood cells, therefore, is diluted in a greater volume of blood. If the runner's red blood cell mass doesn't increase as much as the blood volume, then hemoglobin concentration will decrease and may incorrectly indicate an iron deficiency. This is a natural phenomenon that any sports doctor will recognize but that your local general practitioner may not.

Low Iron Intake

Many endurance athletes have low iron intakes. Low iron intake can be a problem for vegetarians and runners who eat red meat less often than once a week. The typical high-carbohydrate, low-fat, low-cholesterol runner's diet often includes little or no red meat. Red meat contains heme iron, which is more easily absorbed than plant sources of iron. Runners who don't eat meat can obtain sufficient iron through dietary sources but only by carefully selecting their foods.

Foot Strike Hemolysis

Foot strike hemolysis is the breakdown of red blood cells when the foot hits the ground. Foot strike hemolysis is potentially a problem for marathoners who run high mileage on asphalt or are heavier than most runners.

Iron Loss Through Sweat and Urine

A relatively small amount of iron is lost through sweat and urine, but for high-mileage runners training in hot, humid conditions, this iron loss may add up. For marathoners living in the South or training through the summer in preparation for a fall marathon, sweat may be a significant source of iron loss. More research is needed to determine the magnitude of iron losses in sweat.

Iron Loss Through the GI System

Loss of iron through the GI tract (primarily the stomach or large intestine) is a problem for some marathoners. In a recent study following 11 runners over a competitive season, GI bleeding was evident in 17 of 129 stool samples after training and in 16 of 61 stool samples after racing. The bleeding is fairly minor each time, but there may be a cumulative effect over years of running.

All of the preceding factors in combination make it important for marathoners to monitor their iron intake and their iron levels. The highest risk occurs in premenopausal female runners, whose iron intake often doesn't meet their needs.

How Do You Know If You Have Low Iron?

If you have low iron, first, you'll be dragging. Your heart rate may be elevated, and your enthusiasm for running will have sunk. These symptoms tend to come on gradually, however, so you may not suspect that you have low iron levels until they've had a large impact on your training. You can confirm your suspicions only with a blood test. You should find out your hemoglobin level (the iron in your red blood cells) and your serum ferritin level (your body's iron stores).

Normal hemoglobin concentration ranges from 14 to 18 grams per deciliter (g/dl) of blood for men and 12 to 16 g/dl of blood for women; for an endurance athlete, the lower end of normal should be extended by about 1 g/dl because of his or her larger blood volume. For a male marathoner, then, a hemoglobin level between 13.0 and 13.9 g/dl could be considered in the low end of the normal range and would be similar to a level of about 14.0 to 14.9 g/dl for an untrained man who doesn't have a marathoner's elevated blood volume. Similarly, a woman marathoner with a hemoglobin level between 11.0 and 11.9 g/dl would be a bit lower than optimal but would be similar to a level of about 12.0 to 12.9 g/dl for an untrained woman.

Normal reference serum ferritin levels are 10 to 200 nanograms per milliliter (ng/ml) for women and 10 to 300 ng/ml for men. Conflicting schools of thought exist on the relationship between ferritin levels and running performance. One opinion is that ferritin levels aren't directly related to performance, but if your ferritin level falls, eventually your hemoglobin and performances will decline too. Low ferritin, therefore, can be viewed as an early warning sign.

The other school of thought is that ferritin reflects the iron stores that the body can use to make enzymes for oxidative energy production; therefore, they have a direct impact on performance. The optimal level of serum ferritin seems to differ among individuals. Dick Telford, PhD, of the Australian Institute of Sport, has found that the performance of some runners seems to be affected when their ferritin levels drop below 50 ng/ml, whereas others perform fine if their ferritin levels remain above 25 ng/ml. Telford says that even with iron supplementation, some runners have difficulty raising their ferritin levels above 50 ng/ml.

David Martin, PhD, who has been in charge of testing elite distance runners for USA Track and Field since 1981, says that in his experience with runners, training and racing performances are usually affected when ferritin levels drop below 20 ng/ml and that when those athletes increase their ferritin levels above 25 ng/ml, they experience a rapid turnaround in performance. These experiences indicate that a ferritin level between 25 and 50 ng/ml may be normal or low depending on your individual physiology but that a ferritin level below 25 ng/ml is a definite red flag for a runner.

How Much Iron Do You Need?

According to the National Academy of Sciences' 1989 Recommended Daily Allowances (RDA), premenopausal women need about 15 milligrams of iron a day, whereas postmenopausal women and men require 10 milligrams of iron a day. Iron requirements haven't been established for high-mileage runners, so all that can be said with confidence is that marathoners need at least the RDA. As with any mineral, too much iron can be a health hazard. In fact, the typical American man is more likely to get an iron overload than to be iron deficient.

How Can You Prevent Iron Depletion?

As with other running problems, such as injuries, the best strategy is to avoid low iron in the first place. Good food sources of iron include liver, lean meat, oysters, egg yolk, dark green leafy vegetables, legumes, dried fruit, and whole-grain or enriched cereals and bread.

Dr. E. Randy Eichner, chief of hematology at the University of Oklahoma Health Sciences Center, offers these tips to prevent iron deficiency:

- Eat 3 ounces of lean red meat or dark poultry a couple of times a week.
- Don't drink coffee or tea with meals because they reduce iron absorption.
- Eat or drink foods rich in vitamin C with meals to increase iron absorption.
- Use cast-iron cookware (particularly for acidic foods like spaghetti sauce).

Include good sources of iron in your diet.

Although these recommendations may seem like subtle changes in diet, they can have a powerful effect on your iron levels. For example, you'll absorb three times as much iron from your cereal and toast if you switch from coffee to orange juice with breakfast. Eichner and Martin recommend taking iron supplements, in the form of ferrous sulfate, ferrous gluconate, or ferrous fumarate, only if necessary after making the recommended dietary changes.

Supplements and Other Ergogenic Aids

Ergogenic aids are substances that may enhance athletic performance. In *The Ergogenics Edge*, Melvin Williams, PhD, classifies ergogenic aids as nutritional aids (e.g., vitamins, minerals, protein supplements, carbohydrate supplements, bee pollen, ginseng, etc.), pharmacological aids (drugs such as anabolic steroids and amphetamines), or physiological aids (e.g., human growth hormone, EPO, creatine, and glycerol) (Williams 1998). Most supposed ergogenic aids have no scientific evidence to support their use and will do nothing to improve your running performance.

The multimillion-dollar supplement industry is poorly regulated, with the result that many unsubstantiated claims are made. The advent of unregulated Internet sites pushing supplements with advertisements written as though they're the results of scientific studies has made it even harder for runners to know what works. It doesn't help when famous athletes endorse these products. The manufacturer tells the athlete wonderful things about the supplement, and the athlete gets paid to build credibility for the product by repeating those wonderful things. As a result, many people waste a few dollars on products that neither harm nor help performance.

Taking supplements that you know little about also carries a risk, as they may contain harmful or illegal substances. Many athletes who have failed drug tests for the steroid nandrolone have claimed that small amounts of the substance or of a precursor of nandrolone must have been in one of the supplements they were taking. Of course, almost everyone who fails a drug test claims the result is false, but the nandrolone claim contains enough credibility that investigators are looking into its relation to a variety of supplements.

Are there any legal pills you can pop that will help your running performance? The answer is yes, and the list is short. We could spend page after page discussing the supplements that don't work. In *The Ergogenics Edge*, Williams discusses 61 types of supplements and drugs that claim to improve athletic performance. Thirty-nine of those claim to improve aerobic endurance, which, if true, would improve marathon performance. Imagine how fast you would run if you took all 39! In reality, you would be a lot poorer and would still need to eat a healthy diet to get the nutrients you need. Let's look at supposed ergogenic aids by category.

Nutritional Aids

The many nutritional supplements available on the market can be put into the following four categories:

1. those that have been clearly shown to enhance endurance performance;
2. those with no evidence from well-controlled scientific studies that they enhance endurance performance;
3. those that enhance performance only if you have a nutritional deficiency; and
4. those that require more research.

Category 1 includes only carbohydrate supplements and fluid. We have already discussed these topics in depth.

Category 2 includes almost all nutritional supplements that make miraculous claims, including ginseng, bee pollen, and various herbs and plant extracts.

Category 3 includes most vitamins and minerals that have an established RDA. If you fall below the RDA for a prolonged time, you'll develop a nutritional deficiency that could inhibit your running performance and your ability to recover. All of the vitamins and minerals you need can be obtained from foods. Vitamin and mineral supplements are expensive, and relying on them for your vitamin and mineral needs is simply an admission that the quality of your overall diet is poor.

Within category 4, preliminary evidence exists that antioxidants can help marathoners and other endurance athletes. Antioxidants work by neutralizing oxygen free radicals, which are formed during aerobic metabolism. Free radicals damage cell membranes and other parts of muscle cells. Antioxidant supplementation, therefore, reduces the damage caused by free radicals. Antioxidants may also help maintain immune function after strenuous exercise. The most commonly used antioxidants are beta carotene (precursor to vitamin A), vitamin C, vitamin E, and selenium.

Studies on the benefits of antioxidant supplementation have had mixed results—some show links between antioxidant supplementation and reduced muscle damage, whereas others show no benefit. Similar mixed results have been reported for the role of antioxidants in maintaining immune function. In one study, runners who took 600 milligrams of vitamin C a day for 3 weeks had more than 50 percent fewer head colds after the Comrades ultramarathon than did runners taking a placebo.

As more evidence accumulates, it's prudent to take only moderate doses of antioxidants. Large doses of one vitamin or mineral may lead to decreased absorption of other nutrients, decreased immune function, or both. For example, studies have found that very high doses of vitamin E, vitamin D, or zinc reduce immune function.

Colostrum is a substance that's currently receiving a great deal of attention, and although preliminary evidence suggests that it may provide benefits for endurance athletes, more research is needed. Additionally, new substances and combinations of substances are being introduced to the market each week, almost all of which will be of no benefit to your athletic performance.

Pharmacological and Physiological Aids

Of the pharmacological and physiological ergogenic aids that have been shown to have a positive effect on athletic performance, almost all have been banned by the International Olympic Committee and many other sporting bodies. Within the realm of legal pharmacological or physiological ergogenic aids, the only ones that may provide benefits for an endurance athlete are moderate amounts of caffeine or glycerol. Despite manufacturers' claims, other legal physiological ergogenic aids, such as carnitine, coenzyme Q_{10}, choline, and inosine, haven't been consistently shown to enhance endurance performance.

The effects of caffeine were discussed earlier in this chapter. That leaves glycerol, a product that our bodies produce naturally. Glycerol supplementation increases total body water stores. This may be an advantage for a warm-weather marathon because if you start the race with more stored fluid, then the effects of dehydration won't affect you as soon in the race. Although several sports drinks on the market contain glycerol, it's still open to debate whether glycerol leads to enhanced performance during warm-weather competitions. (Glycerol supplementation isn't advisable for shorter races in cool conditions because the weight of the extra fluid you carry would be detrimental to performance.)

Marathon Race-Day Nutrition and Hydration

So you've followed the advice in this chapter and eaten properly and stayed well hydrated throughout your months of preparation. Guess what—your work isn't done yet. Your strategies for taking calories and fluid on race day can have a strong influence on your marathon performance.

Let's assume that you've done a good job of glycogen loading during the previous several days and that you're well hydrated. Before the race, you want to take in between 200 and 500 calories of mostly carbohydrates to top off your glycogen stores. It's best to get these calories in 3 to 4 hours before the race. This shouldn't be a big deal for races with late starts, like New York City, which begins a little before 11:00 A.M., or Boston, with its noon start. But for a race like Chicago, which starts several hours earlier, you may have to get up a bit on the early side, eat something, and then try to doze a while longer. (Good luck with that on race morning!) You should also take in about a pint of fluid to replace fluids lost overnight and ensure that you're fully hydrated.

Even if you carefully carbohydrate load for several days leading up to the marathon, you don't have much of a buffer against glycogen depletion. The solution is to take in additional calories during the race.

How much you need to drink during the marathon depends on your body size, the heat and humidity, and your sweat rate. The maximum amount you should drink during running is the amount that can empty from your stomach. Research has shown that most runners' stomachs can empty only about 6 to 7 ounces of fluid every 15 minutes during running, representing about 24 to 28 ounces per hour. If you drink more than that, the extra fluid will just slosh around in your stomach and not provide any additional benefit. You may be able to handle more or less than the average, however, so experiment with how much liquid your stomach will tolerate.

During training, it's relatively easy to stop and drink as much as you want whenever you feel like it. All that's required is a bit of planning and perhaps a few containers strategically placed the night before your long run. During the marathon, however, it's very difficult to drink 6 to 7 ounces of fluid at an aid station without stopping. In fact, a study by Tim Noakes, MD, and colleagues found that most runners drink less than 16 ounces per hour when racing. Another study found that runners lose, on average, 3.2 percent of body weight during a marathon. As we saw earlier in this chapter, a loss of more than 3 percent of body weight leads to a loss of more than 9 percent in performance. The average marathoner, therefore, runs the marathon slower than his or her potential because of the effects of progressive dehydration during the race.

Drinking 28 ounces per hour of a 4 percent solution will supply 32 grams of carbohydrate, whereas an 8 percent solution will supply 64 grams of carbohydrate. Each gram of carbohydrate contains 4.1 calories, so you'll be taking in 130 to 260 calories per hour. If you run the marathon in 2:45, therefore, you'll take in about 350 to 700 calories during the race. During the marathon, a typical 140-pound male burns about 100 calories per mile. Of those 100 calories, about 80 are supplied by carbohydrate and the remaining 20 by fat. The carbohydrates you consume during the race, therefore, supply enough carbohydrate fuel to last an extra 4 to 9 miles! Even if you take in only half this amount, you'll substantially increase your chances of reaching the finish without running out of glycogen.

An alternative method of taking in carbohydrate during the marathon or your long runs is to use energy gels. Energy gels are convenient because they come in small packets that you can carry with you. Depending on the brand you choose, each gel packet contains between 80 and 130 calories of carbohydrate. Energy gels are the consistency of pudding and are best described by the brand name "Gu." You must follow gels with a couple of sips of fluid to wash them down, so the best time to take an energy gel is shortly before an aid station. As always, don't wait until race day to try an energy gel. Practice taking gel packets while running at marathon race pace.

If you run the marathon in over 4 hours on a warm day and drink large amounts of plain water during the race, you may be at risk of hyponatremia. This is a condition caused by unusually low sodium levels in your blood; a large proportion of your body fluid is replaced with water, thereby reducing your body's sodium content. The symptoms of hyponatremia are weakness, disorientation, and seizures. Hyponatremia typically occurs only toward the end of ultramarathons or Ironman triathlons, but it can occur in the marathon on hot days for slower runners who consume only water. The simple way to avoid hyponatremia during a hot-weather marathon is to consume fluids containing at least 250 milligrams of sodium per liter.

Can You Take In Enough Fluid During the Race to Prevent Dehydration?

The answer to this question is straightforward: compare the amount of fluid you consume during the marathon to the amount you're likely to lose. On a cool day, you'll likely lose 2 to 3 pounds of water per hour during the marathon, whereas on a warm day the figure is probably 3 to 4 pounds per hour. On a truly hot day, with temperatures above 80 degrees, you may lose 5 pounds of fluid per hour. We already estimated that a typical runner's stomach can absorb about 28 ounces per hour, which is a little bit less than

2 pounds. On a cool day, therefore, you can just about balance your fluid losses with fluid taken in during the marathon. On warm or hot days, you'll incur a steady, progressive fluid deficit, and the farther you run, the greater your fluid deficit will be.

How to Drink on the Run

It's imperative, then, to practice drinking while running at close to marathon race pace until you get good at it. It makes sense to slow a bit at the aid stations, but if you're competitive, you won't want to lose time to the runners around you. By practicing drinking on the run, you can greatly improve your proficiency at this skill.

If you're an elite runner, you can usually arrange to have squeeze bottles at the aid stations along the course. This is optimal but obviously not readily available to everyone. Non-elites can help themselves by choosing marathons where friends or family members can meet you regularly along the way and give you bottles. Still, the majority of marathoners must master the paper cup.

Practice drinking while running at or near marathon race pace.

A convenient way to practice drinking from cups is the round-and-round-the-track method—simply set up some cups at the local track and practice drinking every couple of laps. The advantage of the track is convenience. The disadvantage is that, if you're running intervals, you'll be breathing so hard that you'll get to experience the dubious thrill of getting water up your nose. Of course, if you can master drinking at faster-than-marathon race pace, then drinking during the marathon will be a snap.

Another convenient way to practice drinking on the run is the road-loop method. Back your car to the end of the driveway, put a few cups of the beverage you'll drink during the marathon on the back of your car, and head out for a repetitive loop run, grabbing a cup every time you pass your car.

Race-Day Technique

If volunteers are handing out fluids during the race, try to make eye contact with one and point at the cup so that you don't surprise him or her. (If the cups are on a table, eye contact with the cup generally won't help.) If volunteers are offering both water and a sport drink, begin yelling your preference as you approach the aid station so that the right volunteer hands you a cup.

Slow slightly and try to move your arm back while you grab the cup so that you don't hit the cup with your full running speed. Squeeze the top of the cup closed so that all of the liquid doesn't slosh out, and take a swig. This will help prevent fluid from going up your nose when you tip the cup up to drink. The trick is to breathe normally. Always take a couple of normal breaths between swigs. When you're done drinking, accelerate back to race pace.

Unless you're an elite marathoner, the best strategy on a warm and humid day is to stop and drink at the aid stations. Water stops in a marathon are often every 5K or every 2 miles, so there are about 8 to 12 stops. If you stop for 10 seconds at each station, you'll add about 1 to 2 minutes to your time. If you run through the stops while drinking, you'll slow a little anyway, so stopping isn't going to add much time, and stopping helps to ensure that you take in enough fluid to fight off dehydration. On a warm day, an extra minute or 2 at the water stations can repay you with 10 to 20 minutes gained by the finish of the marathon.

What and when you eat and drink play an important role in how you adapt to training for a marathon. As we've seen, neglecting proper nutrition and hydration will mean not reaping the full benefits of your hard work. The same is true for not paying attention to easy days and other aspects of managing recovery from taxing training. Let's look at what to do to maximize your chance of marathon success during the many hours each week when you're not running long or hard.

chapter

4

Balancing Training
and Recovery

As we saw in chapter 2, every time you do a hard workout, you provide
a stimulus for your body to improve in some way, such as your lactate
threshold, fat-burning ability, VO_2max, and so on. Any one workout,
though, provides only a mild stimulus for improvement; it's the sum of
your workouts over time that determines the total stimulus to improve a
specific component of your fitness. For example, if you do one tempo run
in the few months before your marathon, you provide a mild stimulus for
your lactate threshold to improve. If you do six tempo runs in 8 weeks,
you provide a strong repetitive stimulus for your lactate threshold to
improve.

The training stimulus, however, is only half of the formula for performance improvement. To improve, your body must recover from training
and adapt to a higher level. By learning to manage your recovery, you'll
optimize your training. If you manage your recovery so that you can do
hard workouts more frequently or so that the quality of your hard
workouts consistently improves, then you'll provide a greater stimulus
for your body to improve its capacities.

Recovery from training is important, both from day to day and over the
course of your marathon-preparation program. Poor management of
your recovery can lead to overtraining, which simply overwhelms your
body's ability to respond positively to training. In addition, tapering your
training during the last several weeks before the marathon is critical to
reaching the starting line in peak fitness and with maximal energy
reserves. In this chapter, we'll review all of these important factors in
marathon success.

Recovery and Supercompensation

One of the realities of running is that if you do a hard workout today, you won't be a better marathoner tomorrow. In fact, tomorrow you'll just be tired. Hard training causes immediate fatigue, tissue breakdown, dehydration, and glycogen depletion. Depending on the difficulty of the training session (and other factors discussed in this chapter), you'll require from 2 to 10 days to completely recover from a workout.

At some point, however, the fatigue of each workout dissipates and you adapt to a higher level. To optimize your training, you need to find the correct balance between training and recovery for you. Training provides the stimulus for your body to adapt, but recovery is when you allow your body to adapt and improve. Your training session also provides a stimulus for your body to adapt to a higher level, which is called supercompensation.

> *To optimize training, find the correct balance between training and recovery.*

Effectively managing your recovery means answering two questions:

1. How many days after a workout do you reap the benefits of that workout?
2. How much time should you allow between hard workouts or between a hard workout and a race?

Let's try to answer those questions.

Turning Genes On and Off

The intensity, duration, and frequency (number of sessions per week) of your training all influence the rate at which your body adapts. The adaptations in hormone levels, fat-burning ability, capillary density, and so on that result from endurance training occur because of repeated training bouts rather than as a result of one workout in isolation. It's as though your body must be convinced that you're really serious about training before it makes the physiological adaptations that let you reach a new level.

The process of adaptation begins with your genes. Training provides stimuli (for example, glycogen depletion) that turn specific genes on or off. By altering the expression of genes, training changes the rates at which your body makes and breaks down specific proteins. For example, endurance training turns on genes for the production of mitochondrial protein. More endurance training leads to more mitochondria in your muscles so that you can produce more energy aerobically. Your muscles and cardiovascular system adapt over days and weeks to the cumulative effects of repeated training.

Kristy Johnston

Fastest Marathon: 2:29:05
Marathoning Career Highlights: First place,
1993 Houston and 1994 Chicago marathons.
Second place, 2000 Olympic marathon trials.

Brian J. Myers © Photo Run 2000

For most of the last decade, Kristy Johnston has been one of America's top marathoners, often beating women with arguably more talent, thanks to her clear goals, focused preparation, and sound recovery.

Johnston is a pure marathoner. Although she has run solidly at other distances, such as a 1:12 half marathon, "I plan my shorter races around the marathon," she says. For her, tune-up races are an important part of marathon preparation, but still just a part, and one that needs to be kept in perspective. "I take 2 to 3 days before the race easy, but I don't treat them as a huge deal," Johnston says. "I have the attitude that I will go into the race to do my best for that day. I will probably get beat by some people who I think should never beat me, but I know the marathon is my ultimate goal."

Johnston also uses tune-up races for other aspects of marathon preparation. "I use the race to practice things about the race coming up," she says. "Maybe race preparation, new sports drink/gel stuff, pace . . . just race experience. I try to put in a few races that will reflect something about the marathon I'll be running, such as heat, hills, time of day. Sometimes, I'll decide to run a local race because I have a tempo run planned and I feel like getting out there with some other people."

As a language arts teacher to seventh and eighth graders, Johnston's days during the school year are filled with responsibilities and energy drains other than running. ("They're busy, like having a room full of Jack Russells who haven't been to the doctor for their operations," she says about her students.) She's usually at school by 6:30 A.M., gets home to run at 4 P.M., and is asleep before 9 P.M. To accommodate this schedule, "Weekends are all about sleep and running," she says. Other than a Wednesday $\dot{V}O_2$ max session, nearly all of Johnston's hard training occurs on the weekends—a 7- to 9-mile tempo run on Saturday and a long run on Sunday. She maintains the quality on back-to-back hard days by taking two consecutive easy days before and after what she calls "the weekend attack."

Johnston also intelligently plans long-term rest, which has no doubt increased her consistency over so many years. "I think I do a pretty good job of separating training

(continued)

Kristy Johnston *(continued)*

from recovering," she says. "I see some people finish a marathon, and the next day, they're out for a 10-mile run. I'm out for a 10-day party. I couldn't maintain my hard training if I didn't give myself the mental and physical break after each race. I take a minimum of 3 weeks of no running after a marathon, even if I bomb. The bomb tells me I was probably overtrained anyway. It does no good to punish myself for a poor performance."

She's also a testament to the value of at-home support for one's marathoning. Her husband, Chris Fox, is now a leading masters runner and with a 27:53 10,000-meter best, represented the United States in that event in the 1995 World Championships. "He's been at the highest level of running, so he knows all of the little things that make training life possible," Johnston says. "He sets out my water bottles for long runs, he runs with me when I'm too tired to get out the door, he keeps the house better than I do when I'm not working or training—he sees the big picture.

"We succeed together," she adds, "and when we fail together, well, we head to Key West for a week and get drunk together."

Factors Affecting Recovery Rate

Runners vary greatly in how long it takes them to recover from and adapt to a workout. Differences among runners in recovery time and rate of improvement are determined by genetics and lifestyle factors. Your genetics determine your predisposition to adapt to training; some of us are programmed to adapt more quickly than others. Lifestyle factors, such as diet, quantity and quality of sleep, general health, age (we tend to recover more slowly with age), gender (women tend to recover more slowly because of lower testosterone levels), and various life stressors (such as work and relationships), all influence how quickly you recover from and adapt to training. Because so much variation exists among runners in how many workouts they can tolerate in a given period, you shouldn't copy your training partner's running program. Only through experience will you learn how much training you can handle.

As an example, figure 4.1, adapted from Tudor Bompa's *Periodization* (1999), details two runners who do the same workout and experience the same amount of initial fatigue but who recover at different rates. Rachel (represented by the solid line) recovers more quickly than Karen (represented by the dashed line). Rachel will be able to recover from and adapt positively to more high-quality workouts in a given period and will, therefore, improve more quickly than Karen. Rachel would also require a shorter taper before a race than Karen.

Only through trial and error will you know how much training your body can positively adapt to in a given time. Successful marathoning requires that you go through this self-discovery process intelligently and systematically.

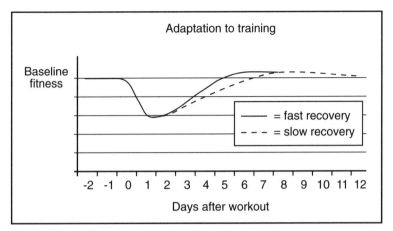

Figure 4.1 Two runners' rates of recovery.

Determining this balance can be tricky because it can be hard to isolate variables. For example, if your job is much more stressful than the last time you trained for a marathon, your rate of recovery might be slower. You must find the correct balance of training stimulus and recovery for your specific circumstances over the long weeks that constitute marathon training.

Time Required for Recovery and Supercompensation

Unfortunately, the scientific literature doesn't provide clear evidence of the amount of time required to realize the benefits of an individual training session. Personal experience and discussions with many runners and coaches indicate that 10 days is an adequate amount of time to recover from and reap the rewards of most hard training sessions. Given that any one workout provides only a small fitness benefit—on the order of magnitude of less than 1 percent—but that a workout can cause severe short-term fatigue, it's wise to err on the side of caution and allow enough time to fully recover from training before a race. For the marathon race itself, complete recovery from training is critical for success. Marathon tapering generally requires a full 3 weeks and is discussed later in this chapter.

//// Does Massage Improve Recovery?

Running causes muscle tightness and damage to muscle fibers. Your muscle fibers need time for repair and recovery before they can work well again. If you train hard before allowing your muscles to recover properly, then you're likely to have a subpar workout on sore and tired muscles, and your risk of injury will increase.

Sports massage is designed to help overworked muscles become ready to train again. Many serious marathoners use sports massage to speed recovery and prevent injuries. Some get these treatments weekly, whereas others wait until their legs and

(continued)

back scream for it. Sports massage feels great, but does it work? Does it really improve recovery?

The answer is that we don't really know. The few studies that have been done on the benefits of massage have shown mixed results. This may be due to poorly controlled study designs or differences in the types of massage used.

There's no denying, though, the value that some of the world's best marathoners place on regular massage. Certainly, regular massage doesn't impair their recovery. If you can afford massage, anecdotal evidence suggests that it will help you to recover more quickly from hard marathon training. To be effective, sports massage should be "pleasantly uncomfortable"; that is, it shouldn't be gentle. An experienced massage therapist will provide a relaxing experience and effective treatment at the same time.

Table 4.1 shows typical times to reap the benefits of three major types of workouts. The third column indicates typical amounts of time to recover from a workout of each type. For example, the table indicates that you should allow 3 to 5 days between tempo runs or between a tempo run and a tune-up race. You don't, however, need to allow 3 to 5 days between a tempo run and a long run or interval workout. That's because each type of workout uses different combinations of energy systems, so complete recovery from one type of workout isn't necessary before you do another type of workout.

Table 4.1 Minimum Time Between Hard Workouts and Tune-Up Races

Type of workout	Sample workout	Days before tune-up race or next similar workout
Tempo run	4 mi @ 10 mi race pace	4
Long run	17–20 mi	4
$\dot{V}O_2$max intervals	6 × 800 @ 3K race pace	5

Although you won't see the benefits of this week's workout in this weekend's race, if you do the workout early enough in the week you should recover enough for it not to have a detrimental effect on your race performance. Table 4.1 acknowledges that we often do a tune-up race when the fatigue of previous training is reduced rather than when supercompensation has occurred. You generally can't afford the time required to be optimally rested for tune-up races. Marathoners should allow only enough rest and recovery to obtain optimal results for the marathon itself and possibly for one tune-up race.

Of the major types of workouts, tempo runs are the easiest to recover from because they don't break down the body as much as the other forms of hard training. Tempo runs are neither fast enough to cause substantial muscle damage nor long enough to totally deplete your muscles of glycogen.

Long runs seem to cause the most variability in recovery time among runners, although replenishing glycogen stores generally requires only 24 to 48 hours. Some runners are able to recover relatively quickly from long runs, whereas others are wiped out for days after one. The variability in recovery time depends on the genetic and lifestyle factors discussed previously and on the type of courses you train on (downhills cause more muscle damage and greater recovery time).

Interval workouts put your muscles and cardiovascular system under the most stress and generally require the longest recovery time. Later in this chapter, we'll discuss strategies that you can use to speed your recovery.

Regardless of the type of workout involved, the pattern of workout and recovery is basic to effective training. Generally known as the hard/easy principle, this dictates the structure of your training over the weeks and months leading up to the marathon. Let's investigate the rationale for following the hard/easy principle.

The Hard/Easy Principle

Conventional wisdom calls for following the hard/easy principle of training, which is typically interpreted to mean that a hard effort is always followed by one or more recovery days. A recovery day may consist of an

The conditions of your training courses will affect your recovery time.

easy run, a light cross-training session, or total rest. During your marathon preparation, however, it's sometimes necessary to violate this training pattern and do back-to-back hard days. The appropriate interpretation of the hard/easy principle is that one or more hard days should be followed by one or more recovery days. Let's investigate the physiological rationale for following the hard/easy principle and look at two situations in which you should do back-to-back hard training days.

Reasons to Follow the Hard/Easy Principle

The hard day/easy day training pattern follows from the physiological dogma of stimulus and response—hard training provides a stimulus for your body to improve, but rest is then needed to allow your body to recover and adapt to a higher level. Three reasons to follow the hard/easy principle are to prevent glycogen depletion, to prevent illness, and to minimize the effects of delayed onset muscle soreness (DOMS).

Preventing Glycogen Depletion

As discussed in chapter 3, your body can store only a limited amount of glycogen. With a typical runner's high-carbohydrate diet, you probably have enough glycogen to get you through a 20- to 22-mile long run or a hard interval workout. It takes about 24 to 48 hours to completely replenish your glycogen stores. When you do two hard workouts in a row, therefore, you risk going into the second workout with partially filled glycogen stores, becoming depleted, and having a bad workout. Although glycogen depletion is potentially a problem on the second hard day, with a bit of planning it needn't be an insurmountable problem. Three hard days in a row, however, would very likely lead to glycogen depletion and a prolonged recovery period. By following the hard/easy principle, you give your body time to build up your glycogen stores so you are prepared for the next hard workout.

Preventing Illness

After high-intensity exercise, your immune system is temporarily suppressed, creating an open window during which you're at increased risk of infection. Studies indicate that the immune systems of healthy, well-trained runners are typically suppressed only following exercise lasting more than 1 hour at about marathon race pace or faster. Immune system suppression after high-intensity running has been found to last from 12 to 72 hours. The clear implication is to not do another hard training session until your immune function recovers from the previous hard session or race. Allowing at least one easy day before the next hard workout provides a minimum of 48 hours of recovery, which is typically enough time for your immune system to return to full strength.

Minimizing the Effects of DOMS

Contrary to many runners' beliefs, high levels of lactate (lactic acid) in your muscles aren't what make you sore for several days after a hard effort. Essentially all of the lactate you produce in a race or workout is eliminated from your body within a few hours. Rather, DOMS is caused by microscopic muscle damage that occurs from eccentric (lengthening) muscle contractions, such as when you run downhill. During downhill running, your quadriceps muscles contract eccentrically to resist the pull of gravity and keep your knees from buckling. The resulting muscle damage leads to inflammation, which causes soreness. It takes 1 to 2 days for this process of muscle damage/inflammation/pain to reach a peak, and the effects can last for up to 5 days. While you're experiencing DOMS, your muscles need time to repair. The damaged muscles are also weaker, so any workout done before the soreness goes away not only will be painful but also will likely not be intense enough to improve your marathon fitness.

The physiology of DOMS favors a 2 hard day/2 easy day approach because it takes 1 to 2 days for DOMS to kick in, then it takes another couple of days for the soreness to dissipate. By doing back-to-back hard days, you may sneak in your second workout before soreness and muscle weakness develop. You would then have 2 days to recover before the next hard effort.

When to Do Back-to-Back Hard Days

We've seen several reasons why you should follow the hard/easy principle in your training and that a hard day doesn't always have to be followed by an easy day. A pattern of 2 hard days in a row followed by 2 (or more) recovery days may actually allow you to handle and recover from, more high-quality training. Let's look at two specific situations in which you should do back-to-back hard days.

During weeks that you race, you need to train but also to rest for the race. In *Daniels' Running Formula*, renowned exercise physiologist and coach Jack Daniels, PhD, recommends back-to-back hard days during race weeks rather than alternating hard and easy days (Daniels 1998).

For example, say you're following a strict hard/easy schedule and have a race on Saturday. If you did a long run on the previous Sunday, then you would run hard Tuesday and Thursday and easy on the other days. Doing a hard session on Thursday, however, doesn't make sense because you would still be tired from that effort for Saturday's race. If, however, you do back-to-back harder workouts on Tuesday and Wednesday, as detailed in figure 4.2, you would still get your hard sessions in but would have an extra day to recover for the race. Although this modification still doesn't provide the optimal amount of time to recover for Saturday's race, it's an intelligent compromise that allows you to get your high-quality training while also racing reasonably well.

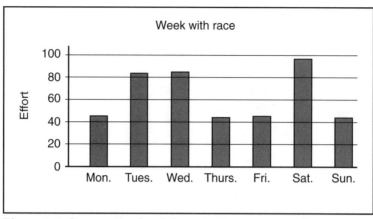

Figure 4.2 Consecutive hard days during a race week.

Another time when you might do 2 hard days in a row is if your weekly schedule is dictated by the Monday-to-Friday workweek. If you're too busy or fatigued during the week to get in regular high-quality training, then you'll want to take advantage of the weekend and squeeze in 2 hard days. This situation is detailed in figure 4.3. Hard days on Saturday and Sunday followed by recovery days on Monday and Tuesday provide a strong training stimulus and 2 full days to recover before the next hard effort on Wednesday. Easy days on Thursday and Friday then leave you well rested for another weekend of hard training. Four of the 5 weekdays become recovery days, and you still get in three hard training sessions per week.

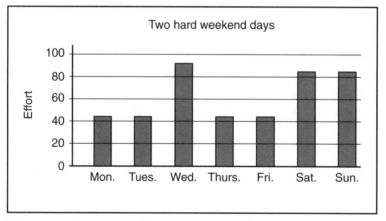

Figure 4.3 Consecutive hard days on weekends.

This brings us to the time-honored tradition of racing on Saturday and doing your long run on Sunday. If you race 10K or less, you'll dip into your carbohydrate stores but (assuming that, like most runners, you generally eat a lot of carbs) will most likely not come close to fully depleting your glycogen stores. By eating your normal high-carb diet, you'll be reasonably topped up with glycogen and ready to handle your long run on Sunday morning. If Saturday's race is longer than 15K, however, you'll have severely depleted your glycogen stores and may find yourself at less than your best for Sunday's long run. If you race more than 15K on Saturday, then skip the long run on Sunday. In that situation, you'll be better off by postponing your long run until you've recovered from the race.

/// Consecutive Hard Sessions of the Wrong Kind

An old school of thought is to do several hard days in a row "to get used to running on tired legs." Does this idea make sense?

As we've seen, the best way to prepare for marathon conditions is to do high-quality long runs and tempo runs. If you run a 22-miler at 40 seconds per mile slower than goal marathon pace, starting relatively fresh, you'll provide a more specific stimulus to improve your marathon performance than if you start the run fatigued and struggle to run 1½ minutes per mile slower than goal marathon pace. At least once every 3 weeks, give yourself the chance to do your long run fresh. You'll feel great on these runs, thereby leading not only to a better effort but also to positive psychological reinforcement.

Doing an interval session or tempo run on tired legs makes no sense whatsoever. The objective of interval training (e.g., 6 × 1,000 meters at 5K race pace) is to improve your maximal oxygen consumption. The objective of tempo runs (e.g., 5 miles at 10-mile race pace) is to improve your lactate threshold. If you run these workouts while tired, you'll either do them more slowly than optimal or you'll have to cut back the volume of the workout (e.g., do fewer intervals or a shorter tempo run). In either case, you'll provide less of a stimulus to improve than if you had started the workout relatively fresh.

So far, we've considered only the pattern of hard training and recovery within a week. Just as important is the pattern of hard efforts and recovery over the course of your marathon preparation. Week after week of hard training can eventually lead to staleness or overtraining. To adapt optimally, it's best to have several hard training weeks followed by a recovery week. The longer training schedules in the second section of this book regularly incorporate recovery weeks.

There are several patterns that you can follow. The correct pattern for you depends on how hard you're training, your body's ability to adapt to training, and the sum of other stressors in your life. The most commonly used pattern is 3 hard weeks followed by a recovery week. During the early buildup phase of marathon preparation, some runners can handle 4 high-mileage weeks followed by 1 recovery week. In other cases, 2 hard weeks followed by 1 recovery week is optimal. Again, through trial and error you'll have to find the pattern that's best for you.

As a general rule, your recovery weeks should include 75 percent as much training volume as your hard training weeks. For example, if your hard weeks consist of 60 miles per week, then you would run 45 miles during your recovery week. Be sure to reduce the quantity and the intensity of your hard sessions during your recovery week. For example, cut the distance of your long run as well as the pace per mile, and schedule a session of strideouts rather than a $\dot{V}O_2$ max session during a recovery week.

Recovery Days (or, Easy Days)

So far in this chapter, we've discussed the necessity of incorporating recovery into your training schedule. Following the hard/easy principle, 1 or more hard days are always followed by 1 or more easy days. Easy training days are more appropriately called recovery days because their purpose is to allow you to recover for your next hard effort.

So what constitutes a recovery day? As with most aspects of running, the answer depends on your physiology. Recovery days should be less difficult than hard sessions in the volume (distance) and the intensity of training. In some cases, a recovery day should be a day of rest or a day of cross-training.

The most common training mistake marathon runners make is training too hard on recovery days. If you train too hard on a scheduled recovery day, then you'll be a bit tired for your next hard day and that workout won't go as well as planned. If you're like most runners, you'll be ticked off, and you'll run your next scheduled recovery day a bit harder. So begins a vicious cycle in which your recovery days are done too hard and the quality of your hard days declines. The result is mediocre performances in training and racing. Just as it takes discipline to push through a tempo run when you feel bad, so does it take discipline to train easily when you feel good on a planned recovery day.

The other mistake that marathoners often make is to try to squeeze in too much distance on recovery days. Early in your training program, when the marathon is still more than 10 weeks away, it probably doesn't hurt to add a couple of extra miles to recovery days because the overall intensity of training tends to be rather low. When you're into the last 10 weeks of training, however, you have hard sessions with specific purposes. If you go into your hard days tired from too many slow miles on your recovery days, then your overall progress will be compromised.

Your recovery days shouldn't impose additional training stress on your muscles or your nervous system. You should try, therefore, to minimize the pounding on your legs on those days. Running on soft surfaces on your recovery days will reduce the cumulative impact your legs and back experience over the course of the week. When you consider that your recovery days occur when you're the most tired and when your muscles are the most fatigued and least resilient, it makes sense to take it easy on your muscles on those days. This also implies avoiding hill running on your recovery days not only because running uphill is likely to require more effort than is optimal for an easy day but also because downhill running tends to induce muscle damage, and you certainly don't want to incur additional muscle damage on a recovery day.

//// *Recovery Considerations in the Real World*

At his peak, Bill Rodgers used to say that nobody working a full-time job would beat him in the marathon. He knew that even if they could string together training to match his around the constraints of regular employment, the extra rest and attention to detail that his schedule allowed would give him an edge on race day.

Of course, you're probably not trying to win Boston, nor do you likely have the luxury of quitting your job for the sake of your running. Still, you can hasten your recovery from hard workouts by regularly paying attention to these matters at work.

◆ Hydration. Always have a water bottle at your workstation, and commit to draining it several times a day.

◆ Calories. Keep healthful foods at work so that you can graze throughout the day as opposed to getting so famished that you hit the vending machines in desperation.

◆ Posture, part I. Make sure that your computer screen is at eye level and not too far away so that you don't sit with your head tilted and thrust forward all day.

◆ Posture, part II. Even if your computer is set up ideally, it's still easy to sit with a slumped upper body when you're at a desk all day. Sit with your head, shoulders, and hips aligned, and with a slight curve in your lower back. Good posture at work translates into fewer biomechanical woes on the run.

◆ Move. Get up and walk around at least once an hour to lessen the strain on your lower back and hamstrings. If the smokers in your office are allowed to leave their desks throughout the day to tend to their habit, then you should be able to stand and stretch your legs to tend to yours.

Using a heart monitor is a good way to prevent yourself from training too hard on your recovery days. (See chapter 2 for in-depth information about training by heart rate.) If you keep your heart rate below 75 percent of your maximal heart rate or 70 percent of your heart rate reserve plus your resting heart rate, you'll let your body recover to allow high-quality workouts on your hard training days.

For example, say your resting heart rate is 50 beats per minute and your maximal heart rate is 185 beats per minute. If you train by maximal heart rate, then you would want to keep your heart rate below 139 (185×0.75) on your recovery days. Heart rate reserve is your maximal heart rate minus your resting pulse. In this example, then, your heart rate reserve is 135. If you train using this more complicated but more precise method, you would want to keep your heart rate below 145 (resting heart rate of 50 + [135×0.70]) on your recovery days.

The lower-tech way to determine your appropriate recovery training intensity is to run approximately 2 minutes per mile slower than your 10-mile to half marathon race pace. For example, if you run the half marathon in 1:18, or just under 6:00 per mile, then your recovery runs should be done at roughly 8:00-per-mile pace.

In some situations, cross-training is the best type of exercise on recovery days. For marathoners who come out of Sunday long runs feeling beat up, cross-training is the safest option for training on Monday. Your recovery is enhanced by the increased blood flow, but there's no additional pounding on your legs and back. Cross-training is discussed in chapter 5.

Avoiding Overtraining

Overtraining is a danger for any motivated marathoner. In striving to improve your performance, you progressively increase the volume and intensity of your training. At some point, you hit your individual training threshold. When you exceed that threshold, positive adaptation stops, negative adaptation occurs, and your performances in training and racing suffer.

Individual training thresholds vary greatly among runners. Former American record holder Jerry Lawson trains comfortably at 140 miles per week, whereas some runners struggle to maintain 40-mile weeks. Similarly, some runners can handle 2 hard days of training in succession, whereas others need 3 easy days after each hard workout. Your individual training threshold also changes with time. Lawson couldn't always handle such big mileage, but he increased his mileage as his capacity to withstand the stress increased.

Defining Overtraining

It's important to clarify what overtraining is and isn't. Fatigue for a day or 2 after a hard training session isn't overtraining. In fact, it's a necessary step in the process of recovery and development. When training stress is applied in the appropriate dosage, then you improve at the optimal rate. If your training stress is above the optimal level, you may still improve, but you'll do so at a slower rate. Only above a higher threshold (your individual training threshold) does true overtraining occur.

> **Fatigue for a day or 2 after a hard training session isn't a sign of overtraining.**

What's much more common than overtraining is overreaching. This is the zone between optimal training for improvement and the point at which performance decreases. Unfortunately, this zone is where many marathoners spend much of their time.

Overreaching occurs when you string together too many days of hard training. Your muscle fatigue is most likely from glycogen depletion, and you simply need time for metabolic recovery. A few days of moderate training combined with a high-carbohydrate diet should quickly remedy the situation. Overreaching can also be caused by dehydration, lack of sleep, or other life stressors on top of your normal training. In all of these cases, your body should rebound quickly when the extra stress is removed.

Repeated overreaching eventually leads to overtraining syndrome, which is thought to be regulated by the hypothalamus. Located at the base of the brain, the hypothalamus controls body temperature, sugar and fat metabolism, and the release of a variety of hormones; it's essentially your master control center for dealing with stress. When your hypothalamus can't handle the combination of training and other stressors in your life, the result is overtraining. The symptoms are fatigue, reduced immune system function, disturbed sleep, decreased motivation, irritability, and poor athletic performance. Overtraining occurs when your training and life stressors exceed your body's ability to adapt.

Overtraining is caused by poor planning and not heeding your body's feedback. In the July 1998 issue of *Medicine and Science in Sports and Exercise*, Carl Foster, PhD, presented a new technique to help athletes detect and avoid overtraining. The technique is based in part on evidence that horses progress following a hard/easy training program but become overtrained when the workload on the easy days is increased. (Stick with us here; this has applications for running.)

The hypothesis is that overtraining is related to both the difficulty of training (the training load) and the "monotony" of training. To assess the former, an athlete rates the difficulty of a training session on a scale from 1 to 10 and then multiplies this number by the total number of minutes of the training session. Monotony of training is the variation (or lack thereof) in the difficulty of training from day to day. Monotonous training typically consists of 1 moderately hard day after another, whereas varied training consists of a mix of hard days, easy days, and the occasional rest day.

Training strain is the combined effect of the training load and the training monotony. Foster found that training strain can predict overtraining-related illness and injury. In a study with 25 endurance-trained athletes, 84 percent of illnesses were preceded by an increase in training load above the athlete's individual training threshold, while 77 percent of illnesses were preceded by an increase in training monotony. Training load and training monotony combined (training strain) explained 89 percent of illnesses among these athletes. Almost half of the peaks in training above these athletes' individual strain thresholds resulted in illness.

These results suggest not only that training load is a useful predictor of overtraining-related illness but also that training monotony is a contributing factor. This is the best evidence to date that mixing recovery days into your training program is necessary for optimal improvement without breaking down.

Tables 4.2 and 4.3 present sample weeks with almost identical training loads. Training schedule A (table 4.2) is an example of a low-monotony week. There are 3 days (Tuesday, Wednesday, and Sunday) with a training load greater than 500, 1 day (Friday) between 300 and 500, and 3 days (Monday, Thursday, and Saturday) under 300. Following this schedule, you would get in high-quality training with adequate recovery, and you could expect your fitness to steadily improve.

Table 4.2   Training Schedule A: Low Monotony

	Workout	Effort (1–10)	Duration (min)	Training load
Monday	6 mi	4	45	180
Tuesday	7 × 1,000 m	8	65	520
Wednesday	10 mi	6	75	450
	Weights	7	45	315
Thursday	6 mi	4	45	180
Friday	Tempo run	7	50	350
Saturday	4 mi	3	35	105
Sunday	15 mi	6	125	750
Total load				2,850

Training schedule B (table 4.3) is an example of a high-monotony week. Every day of the week has a training load between 300 and 500. Following this schedule, you would be training fairly hard all the time and would never feel particularly fresh for your next workout. Foster's results suggest that continued training in this way would be more likely to lead to overtraining syndrome than following training schedule A. Because it includes fewer high-quality training efforts, training schedule B would also lead to a slower rate of improvement than training schedule A.

Try recording your training this way for several months and see if you can detect your individual strain threshold. If you can find the combination of training load and monotony that puts you over the edge, then you can keep your training strain below that threshold for optimal training and optimal marathon performance.

Breaking Out of Overtraining

If you're truly overtrained, you need to take immediate action. The first step is to see a sports physician to check that you don't have an illness that mimics the symptoms of overtraining. The possibility always exists that excessive fatigue is caused by something worse than running. Also ask the physician

Table 4.3   Training Schedule B: High Monotony

	Workout	Effort (1–10)	Duration (min)	Training load
Monday	8 mi	5	66	330
Tuesday	6 × 1,000 m	7	60	420
Wednesday	9 mi	6	70	420
Thursday	6 mi	4	45	180
	Weights	7	45	315
Friday	Tempo run	7	50	350
Saturday	8 mi	6	60	360
Sunday	12 mi	5	100	500
Total load				2,875

to check your hemoglobin and ferritin levels to see whether your iron levels are normal (see chapter 3).

Unless you have a particularly severe case of overtraining, 3 to 5 weeks of greatly reduced training should bring your energy level back to normal. It appears that reducing training intensity is more important than reducing training volume in breaking out of overtraining syndrome. Reducing your training intensity so that you're doing only easy aerobic running is the most important step in breaking out of overtraining.

You should, however, also reduce your training volume. The correct amount to reduce your training volume depends on your individual circumstances and how deeply entrenched in overtraining you've become. As a rule of thumb, reducing your mileage by 50 percent should be enough to allow your body to recover. In addition, if you've been training twice a day, it will be necessary to reduce to one training session a day. Your body needs time to recover. For the first several weeks, it's also helpful to have at least 1 day a week off from training.

In some cases of overtraining syndrome, a contributing factor is an imbalance between calories consumed and calories used. When you have a caloric deficit for a prolonged period in combination with hard training, your body's hormonal system undergoes modifications that are associated with overtraining syndrome.

According to Suzanne Girard Eberle, MS, RD, author of *Endurance Sports Nutrition* (2000), you could be a candidate for metabolic imbalance even if your weight remains steady. "Your weight may stay the same or only slightly decrease because your metabolic rate drops as your body attempts to adjust to fewer calories," she notes. "Frequent colds, slow recoveries from workouts,

Reducing training intensity will help you recover from overtraining.

nagging injuries, chronic fatigue, and, for women runners, the loss of menstrual periods are the true red flags that you're not consuming enough calories to meet the energy demands of training and racing."

Increasing caloric intake while simultaneously reducing training load will eliminate the caloric deficit and should allow your hormonal system to return to normal.

Tapering for Optimal Marathon Performance

Training provides the long-term improvements in fitness that are necessary for marathon success. As you're no doubt aware, though, training also tends to leave you a bit tired most of the time. As we've noted, despite much of the popular running literature, this doesn't mean that you're overtrained—a moderate amount of residual fatigue is fine during the many weeks of training in preparation for the marathon. The periodic recovery weeks in your training schedule are designed to reduce, but not totally eliminate, the accumulated fatigue of training.

When the marathon approaches, however, you need to cut back your training for a more prolonged period so that you're optimally rested for the marathon. The challenge during the last several weeks leading up to the marathon is to find the best balance between continued training to get into the best possible racing shape and resting to eliminate the fatigue of training.

A review published in the *International Journal of Sports Medicine* examined more than 50 scientific studies on tapering to find out whether tapering works and how to go about it (Mujika 1998). The review concluded there's no question that tapering works. Various studies have found improvements in performance of up to 16 percent when athletes taper their training before competition, with most studies finding improvements of 3 to 5 percent. In a marathon, a 3 percent improvement in speed would be the difference between running 2:31 and running 2:26, and a 5 percent improvement would result in 2:23.

> **Tapering before the marathon will help you be optimally rested.**

So the potential gains from tapering are substantial. What's the most effective way to cut back your training before the marathon?

How Long Should You Taper?

Several studies investigating the relationship between racing performance at various distances and taper duration concluded that the optimal length of taper is from 7 days to 3 weeks. For the marathon, the general consensus is to taper for a minimum of 2 weeks and that 3 weeks are optimal. Too short a taper will leave you tired on marathon day, whereas tapering for too long will lead to a loss of fitness. When you consider that any one workout will give you less than a 1 percent improvement in fitness but that a well-designed taper can provide an improvement in race performance of several percent, it's wise to err on the side of tapering too much rather than not enough. For the marathon, a well-designed 3-week taper will leave you optimally prepared and recovered for the race.

How Should You Reduce Your Training to Improve Racing Performance?

The scientific evidence indicates that the key to effective tapering is to substantially reduce your mileage while maintaining the intensity of your training. Reducing the amount that you run reduces accumulated fatigue to improve your marathon performance, while interspersing high-intensity efforts maintains your fitness. How much to reduce your mileage depends on your current training volume and your overall health. In general, older runners tend to require slightly more time to taper than younger runners.

The optimal amount to reduce training is still open to debate. Guidelines for cutting back your mileage, based on research, discussions with elite marathoners and coaches, as well as personal experience, are as follows:

* Third week premarathon: 20 to 25 percent
* Second week premarathon: 40 percent
* Marathon week (6 days before race): 60 percent

For example, a marathoner would reduce her mileage by 20 to 25 percent in the third week before the race, by 40 percent the following week, and by 60 percent during race week. For race week, the 60 percent mileage reduction is for the 6 days leading up to the marathon.

Three weeks before your marathon is arguably the most important time for a successful taper. This is the week that many marathoners do too much because the marathon still seems a long way off. If you work too hard during this week, however, you may find yourself feeling flat with 2 weeks to go and struggling to rest up as quickly as possible for the race. It's much better physiologically and psychologically to allow your body to start to freshen up during this week.

Marathoners tend to progressively decrease their training efforts during their marathon taper. That method presents two problems. First, by steadily decreasing training effort over the 3 weeks, they risk a small loss in fitness before the marathon.

The larger concern, however, is psychological. The steady reduction approach doesn't provide any psychological reinforcement. Marathoners generally need reminders that they're still fit, or their confidence may become shaky. The more effective approach to tapering is to intersperse harder efforts within an overall trend of recovery. Figure 4.4 shows a 3-week marathon taper in which harder efforts are included every few days. This type of taper will leave you fit, rested, and confident for the marathon.

Based on the optimal tapering criteria we've just discussed, here's a sample tapering schedule for a marathon (table 4.4). This tapering program

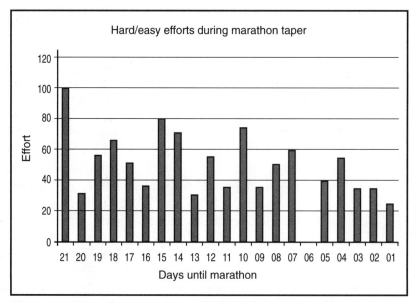

Figure 4.4 Marathon tapering with the right amount of hard efforts.

is taken from the 18-week training schedule in chapter 9 of this book. Following this schedule, your mileage would have peaked at 70 per week, and you would have run your last 20-miler on Sunday before the start of the taper. Let's go through this schedule day by day to see the rationale for each day's training.

Week 1 starts with 2 recovery days to recover from the long run on Sunday. The second day includes eight repetitions of 100-meter strideouts to improve

Table 4.4 A Sample 3-Week Marathon Taper

	Weeks to goal		
	2	1	Race week
Monday	Rest or cross-training	Rest	Rest
Tuesday	7 mi w/ 8 × 100 m strides	8 mi w/ 8 × 100 m strides	5 mi a.m. 4 mi p.m.
Wednesday	12 mi	5 mi	7 mi w/ 2 mi @ marathon pace
Thursday	6 mi w/ 6 × 100 m strides	8 mi w/ 3 × 1,600 m @ 5K race pace	5 mi
Friday	5 mi	5 mi	5 mi w/ 6 × 100 m strides
Saturday	8-10K tune-up race	7 mi w/ 8 × 100 m strides	4 mi
Sunday	17 mi	13 mi	Goal marathon
Weekly mileage	56	46	30 (6 days prerace)

your leg turnover. Wednesday's workout is a 12-miler to provide a mild endurance stimulus. Thursday and Friday are recovery days, leaving you well rested for Saturday and your last tune-up race before the marathon. Sunday is a 17-miler to again provide a mild endurance stimulus to help maintain the adaptations from your previous long runs.

Week 2 starts with 3 recovery days, with Tuesday including a few strideouts to enhance your leg turnover. Thursday calls for your last workout at close to $\dot{V}O_2$max pace. This is done 10 days before the marathon to allow time for recovery and supercompensation. Friday and Saturday are recovery days, with Saturday again including a few strideouts to enhance your leg turnover. The week ends with a 13-miler on Sunday, once again providing the body with a reminder to maintain the adaptations built up over many weeks of long runs.

Marathon week is all easy recovery with the exception of Wednesday. Wednesday is a dress rehearsal for the marathon. Wear the shoes, socks, shorts, and so on that you'll wear in the marathon. This is your last chance to check that everything is right for the race. After an easy 3 miles, run 2 miles at marathon race pace, then 2 more miles easy. You should feel reasonably fresh but will probably not yet feel fully rested. If you have any tight muscles, there's still time to get a massage, stretch, or see a physical therapist to get your legs ready for race day.

In chapter 3, we discussed the importance of carbohydrate loading for the marathon. It's vitally important that your muscles and liver be optimally stocked with glycogen when you reach the start of the race. Of similar importance is arriving at the starting line fully hydrated. See chapter 3 for in-depth information on these topics.

In this chapter, we've looked at how ensuring adequate recovery allows you to get the most from your long runs and hard workouts. Successful marathoning, however, often involves more than just running. Just as true recovery days can mean the difference between adequate and optimal progress in your training, supplemental training, such as flexibility work and strength training, can help you get the biggest bang for your marathon-training buck. Let's look at the most useful nonrunning exercises for marathoners.

Supplemental Training

This chapter focuses on several important aspects of training that can make the difference between mediocrity and marathoning excellence. First, we consider 2-a-day workouts and when they're a beneficial training strategy (as well as when they're counterproductive). The rest of the chapter discusses four types of supplementary training that often get lumped into the category of "cross-training" but that really deserve to be treated separately.

The first of these is core stability training, which is a vitally important but often overlooked aspect of training, particularly for marathoners. Next, we look at the importance of flexibility for marathon performance and how to improve it. Third, we discuss various forms of aerobic cross-training that will enhance your cardiovascular fitness and reduce your likelihood of incurring injuries. Finally, we look at whether strength training is beneficial for marathoners and how to incorporate it into your overall training program.

Doing Doubles

Marathoners have a tendency to start running twice a day before their weekly mileage warrants it. Doing doubles sounds like serious training, so runners often assume it must be better marathon preparation. The reality is quite different; as you increase your training mileage in preparation for a marathon, you should resist the urge to switch from single runs to doubles.

In chapter 2, we discussed the various training adaptations that are specific to improving your marathon performance. Marathon training focuses on endurance-based adaptations such as depleting your glycogen reserves to provide a stimulus for your body to store more glycogen and training your muscles to utilize more fat at a given speed. You'll provide a greater stimulus for these adaptations through a single 12-mile run than by doing a 7-miler and a 5-miler at the same pace.

It might sound counterintuitive, but runners preparing for shorter races should run more doubles at a given level of weekly mileage than marathoners. Runners focusing on 5Ks, for example, should start adding doubles when their weekly mileage gets above 50. That's because the 5K specialists' main training emphasis is high-quality interval sessions, and more frequent, shorter runs will help keep their legs fresh for these workouts.

For marathoners, the basic guideline is to not do double workouts until you've maximized the amount you're running in single workouts. If you're preparing for a marathon and are running less than 75 miles a week, then you shouldn't regularly be running doubles. If you're running less than 75 miles a week, by the time you get in your long run and a midweek medium-long run, there's no reason to double more than once or twice a week to get in the remaining miles. It's better to get in longer runs and give your body 22 or 23 hours of recovery between runs.

> **Do not add double workouts until you've maximized your single workouts.**

Once you get above 75 miles a week, however, double workouts have a definite role in your marathon program. As with any other aspect of training, doubles should be introduced gradually. Start by adding one double per week and then another, as you gradually increase your mileage. The schedules in part II of this book incorporate this approach to adding doubles.

When Doubles Aren't Worth It

The minimum time for an added second run should be 25 minutes. If you run less than that, it's hardly worth the extra time and effort—both physiologically and in taking time from your busy life—to change, get yourself out the door, stretch, shower, and so on. That's especially the case if a too-short, not-crucial run means cutting into precious sleep time. In some situations, it's wiser to add cross-training to your program than to increase your risk of injury with more miles of running. Various options for cross-training are discussed later in this chapter.

How, then, should you introduce doubles into your program? The training schedules in this book add second runs to a day's training for specific reasons. One main category of second runs is on hard days. An easy run in the morning will loosen you up for an evening $\dot{V}O_2$max session or tempo run. Similarly, 30 minutes of easy running in the evening will help you recover from a morning tempo run or tune-up race.

Gezahenge Abera

Fastest marathon: 2:07:54
Marathon Career Highlight:
2000 Olympic Marathon Champion

Ethiopia's Gezahenge Abera shows that when forecasting Olympic marathon outcomes, it's best to look beyond the obvious favorites to relative newcomers to the distance who are rapidly improving.

Although Abera came to the 2000 Olympic marathon with a sub-2:08 best, he wasn't picked by many to medal, much less win. Just 22 years old in Sydney, Abera was running only his sixth marathon, but he was on the part of the performance–improvement curve that all marathoners dream about—from a 2:17 debut at altitude in 1998, to 2:13 early in 1999, to 2:07 late that year. Before Sydney, Abera was best known for placing second in the three-way sprint that decided the 2000 Boston race. More significant, though, was his 1999 Fukuoka win, in which he not only set his PR but won against a small, international field, similar to the situation in Sydney.

Abera also shows that even the majority of the most talented runners in the world face a learning curve when they come to the marathon. Incidents such as Ondoro Osoro breaking 2:07 and winning the 1998 Chicago race in his first marathon are the exceptions, not the rule. If your debut marathon falls short of your expectations, don't assume you're not cut out for the event.

Abera follows the program that has brought success to so many Ethiopians—group training at high altitude of up to 12,000 feet, with an emphasis on high-quality long runs and tempo runs. His coach, Dr. Yilma Berta, has also advised 1996 women's Olympic champion Fatuma Roba. Long runs are about 35 kilometers in length and are not leisurely strolls. After she won the Olympic race, Roba said that on the day of the long run the women in the group were given a 5- to 10-minute head start over the men. The women were instructed not to let the men catch them, while the men were told to catch the women. Most of the high-altitude training occurs over very hilly terrain.

Abera alternates stints at high altitude with bouts of sea-level training, where he can hone his speed. At both Fukuoka and Boston, he was involved in sprints for

(continued)

Gezahenge Abera *(continued)*

the win past the 26-mile mark. At Sydney, he took the lead earlier but still with less than 5 kilometers to go. Finishing speed might not be as crucial for non-elite marathoners as for Abera and shouldn't be a main focus of your training, but as Abera's ability to accelerate late in the race shows, it shouldn't be ignored if you want to run your fastest marathon.

Finally, Abera illustrates the importance of running well tactically. At Fukuoka, he misjudged the finish and had to mount a furious sprint to claim the win. At Sydney, he ran patiently over a hilly course on a very windy day, marshalling his resources for one big push late in the race and not fronting the pack before then. Running your best marathon almost always means knowing the course you'll be running and making concessions to the weather when warranted.

A second main use of doubles in the schedules is on recovery days. When your mileage increases to where your recovery days call for more than 8 miles of running, it's time to switch those days to easy doubles. It's easier on your body, and your recovery will be enhanced if you do two runs of 5 miles rather than a single 10-miler. Avoid the temptation to add mileage to your recovery days for the sole purpose of boosting your weekly mileage. Extra mileage on these days is counterproductive because your recovery will be less complete for your subsequent hard days.

The schedules may also call for an easy second run on the day of your medium-long run. These runs will provide an incremental training stimulus by depleting your carbohydrate stores and training your muscles to rely more on fat at a given speed. It's preferable to do the second, short run in the evening after a medium-long run in the morning. If your schedule is such that you'll be doing your medium-long run in the evening, be sure to run very easily in the morning. As we discussed in chapter 2, medium-long runs bring you the most benefit if they're done at a good pace, so don't let a short morning run detract from the medium-long run's quality. A better-quality medium-long run is preferable to a double in which the medium-long run is a slog.

The schedules never call for a second run on the day of your weekly long run. This is a perfect example of mileage for mileage's sake because an evening run after your long run will only slow your recovery. As soon as you finish your long run, your objective switches to recovering as quickly as possible for your upcoming hard training days.

Core Stability Training

Long-distance running develops muscular endurance in specific leg and hip muscles and is wonderful for your cardiovascular system, but it tends to make some muscles strong and tight while others remain weak. Modern lifestyles, which often consist of sitting for long periods, exacerbate these problems. Core stability training—also called proximal stability training because proximal means close to the center of the body—can eliminate these imbalances, thereby preventing injuries and reducing the degree to which your form deteriorates as you fatigue during the marathon. Core stability training consists of strengthening your abdominals, hips, lower back, and gluteal (butt) muscles using a series of exercises. You don't need a gym or machines, just the dedication to stick with the exercises.

When you run, your trunk acts as a fixed base while your legs work as levers relative to that base to propel you forward. If the torso and pelvic muscles that form your fixed base are weak or fatigue quickly, then you can't maintain an efficient body position while running. By improving the strength and muscular endurance of your pelvis and torso, you provide a more stable base of support for your legs to work from. This improvement will allow you to maintain your stride length throughout the marathon; part of the reason that many marathoners slow as the race progresses is that their stride shortens as they tire.

In addition, runners often have weak abdominal muscles, which allow the pelvis to rotate forward and put more stretch on the hamstrings (figure 5.1). This is a less efficient position for your running and also increases your risk of lower back problems. Proximal stability exercises strengthen the abdominal muscles and work on other stabilizer muscles of the pelvis and trunk. By improving the position of your pelvis, you create a more stable base.

This line of thinking has been around for decades in a variety of sports, but Australian great Rob DeCastella was one of the first to recognize the benefits

Figure 5.1 (*a*) Rotated pelvis position; (*b*) good pelvis position.

for marathon runners. DeCastella had excellent core stability, which contributed to his low incidence of injury as well as the annoying habit he had of maintaining his speed and running form throughout the marathon. A typical example of Rob's ability to maintain form and therefore speed during the marathon was his mastery of the 1986 Boston Marathon. There, he went through the relatively easy first half in 1:03:38 and, alone, ran the much more demanding second half just 35 seconds slower to finish in a then–course record of 2:07:51.

Core stability training should generally be done three times a week. You can do this type of training year-round. For examples of core stability training, we recommend *Stronger Abs and Back* (1997) by Greg and Dean Brittenham.

Flexibility Training

Marathon training takes a toll on the body. One of the greatest costs of all that mileage is a loss of flexibility. Improving your natural range of motion can improve your running technique and increase your stride length while reducing your risk of injury.

Tight muscles provide resistance that limits your ability to stride out. Stretching not only increases your muscle length but also improves the length of the connective tissue surrounding the muscle fibers. Your regular stretching routine before and after running helps to maintain your flexibility but is unlikely to improve it. To achieve gains in flexibility, include one or two training sessions of at least 30 minutes per week devoted to flexibility exercises or yoga.

Always do your stretching when your muscles are warmed up. A warm muscle stretches more easily and greatly reduces the likelihood of injury while stretching. If you're doing a specific flexibility training session, then walk, jog, or cycle for 5 minutes or so to improve the blood flow into your muscles. If you're doing a normal training run, then warm up for 5 minutes and stretch before starting the run. We know that you've probably heard this advice before and that you probably know some good runners in your area who pride themselves on never stretching, but there's no getting around the facts: even a small amount of stretching before running will improve the flow of your running and help to improve your running form. After running, try to allow a minimum of 10 minutes for stretching your major muscle groups.

Stretching should be firm enough to create adequate tension in the muscle but gentle enough that your muscles can relax. If you stretch aggressively, your muscles will tighten in a protective reflex to prevent straining or tearing muscle fibers. You need to stretch gently and consistently to obtain improved length in the muscle and surrounding connective tissue.

There are several schools of thought on how long to stretch and how many times to repeat a stretch. The traditional recommendation is to hold a stretch for at least 30 seconds and to do each stretch once or twice. Recent evidence suggests that stretching may be equally, or even more, effective if you hold the stretch for 10 to 15 seconds and repeat the stretch three times.

Be sure to breathe while you stretch. Some runners inadvertently hold their breath while stretching, thereby reducing stretching's effectiveness.

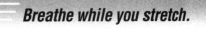

Breathe while you stretch.

Two important areas for marathoners to focus on are the hip flexors and hamstrings. Your hip flexors (primarily iliopsoas and rectus femoris) are the muscles that lift your thigh relative to your hip. These are some of the strongest muscles in the body, and they tend to become short and inflexible in runners. Improving the flexibility of your hip flexors increases your thigh's ability to move back relative to your pelvis, thereby allowing your stride length to increase.

Tight hamstrings restrict your stride length by preventing your thigh from swinging forward completely. The combination of tight hip flexors and tight hamstrings causes the familiar marathoners' shuffle. Stretching your hamstrings consistently (a slow, but steady process) will allow your stride to increase to its natural length.

Sport Stretch (1998), by Michael Alter, provides an excellent series of stretches for runners.

Core stability training and flexibility exercises are easy to skip when you're tired and your main training goal is getting in your long run and tempo runs. These extra sessions, however, will provide refreshing variety to

Stretch gently after your muscles have warmed up.

your training. Together, these two types of training make a powerful combination to increase your stride length and maintain efficient running style throughout the marathon. When scheduling your training, count time for these sessions as an integral part of your workout.

Cross-Training

Predictable training errors, such as increasing mileage or adding speed work too quickly, lead to the majority of running injuries. Just as the risk of coronary artery disease can be reduced through regular exercise, so can the risk of running injuries be reduced through modifying risk factors. One way to do this is to reduce pounding on your legs and back by substituting cross-training for a portion of your running.

Cross-training reduces your risk of injury.

The primary reason to cross-train is to provide additional cardiovascular fitness without increasing the repetitive wear and tear associated with running. Cross-training indoors can also be useful when the weather or pollution levels prevent you from running outside. Unfortunately, many runners cross-train only when injured and then return exclusively to running as soon as the injury recovers. Sure, cross-training is highly effective for maintaining fitness during times of injury but that shouldn't be the only time that most runners do it. If you're careful about increases in mileage and intensity, the surfaces you run on, and the like, and you still can't consistently reach the level of weekly mileage you'd like, then you should incorporate cross-training into your training program year-round.

No form of cross-training is a perfect substitute for running because our bodies adapt very specifically to training. Though you will gain cardiovascular benefits from cross-training, your neuromuscular system will gain little because the movement patterns are different in cross-training activities. That's okay, however, because cross-training should be viewed as a supplement to, not a replacement for, your running. Use cross-training in place of recovery runs and, if necessary, in place of a portion of your general aerobic conditioning. The advantage of using it for recovery training is that the increased blood flow improves your recovery without increasing the cumulative impact forces on your body.

Apples and Oranges?

But won't your racing performances suffer if you replace some of your running with cross-training? The specificity-of-training principle states that your body adapts very specifically to the type of training that you do. That's why you won't have much success as a runner by doing all your training on the bike or in the pool. But if the majority of your training is running, can you enhance your running performance by doing other types of aerobic workouts? Let's see what the research says.

A 1993 study published in *Medicine and Science in Sports and Exercise* investigated the effects of 5 weeks of increased training intensity through running and cycling compared to solely running in moderately trained runners (Mutton et al. 1993). Both groups increased their $\dot{V}O_2$max values from 55 to 58 milliliters per kilogram per minute and improved their 5K times by more than 90 seconds. These results indicate that in moderately trained runners, similar improvements in running performance can be attained by increasing running training or adding cross-training.

In a 1995 study published in the *European Journal of Applied Physiology*, Carl Foster, PhD, and colleagues investigated the effects of increasing training volume via additional running versus an equal increment of cross-training. Thirty reasonably well-trained runners were divided into two groups. One group (run + run) increased their running mileage by 10 percent; the other group (run + swim) added an equivalent amount of swimming to their training. After 8 weeks of increased training, the run + swim group improved their 2-mile race performance by 13 seconds, whereas the run + run group improved their 2-mile time by 26 seconds. In addition, the run + run group members' lactate threshold improved, but the run + swim group's didn't. The results of this study suggest that reasonably well-trained runners can improve their running performance through cross-training, but the improvement is likely to be less than through increased running.

Perhaps the best study on cross-training for runners was published in the February 1998 issue of *Medicine and Science in Sports and Exercise* (Flynn et al. 1998). Twenty well-trained distance runners increased their training for 6 weeks by adding three workouts per week. One group (run + run) added running workouts, whereas the other group (run + cycle) added cycling workouts. Both groups improved their 5K times by approximately 28 seconds (from 18:16 to 17:48) after the 6 weeks of increased training.

These results clearly show that runners can improve performance by increasing training using cycling workouts. Other cross-training activities that work the large-muscle groups of the legs (such as stair climbing, in-line skating, rowing, deep-water running, and cross-country skiing) would likely lead to similar improvements, whereas activities less similar to running (such as swimming) wouldn't.

Although the evidence suggests that cross-training can lead to improved performance in moderately trained or even well-trained runners, no scientific evidence exists concerning cross-training for elite runners. A 1994 review of cross-training studies in *Sports Medicine* concluded that though cross-training is beneficial for moderately trained athletes, the specificity-of-training principle likely becomes more critical the higher the level of performance (Tanaka 1994). So don't worry about having to give up your stair climber to Khalid Khannouchi the next time you're at the health club.

For all but the elite, then, it appears that if you increase your training volume by cross-training, you can improve your running performance. The improvement, however, won't be as large as if you had increased your mileage. This point goes right to the heart of the mileage versus injury trade-off. Sure, you would improve more by increasing your running, but you would also increase your risk of injury. The challenge for marathoners is to manage that trade-off by running as much as you can handle before the risk of injury shoots up.

There are many ways to cross-train, including cycling, water running, in-line skating, rowing or kayaking, cross-country skiing, stair climbing, and swimming. Let's look at the plusses and minuses for marathon runners of the various types of cross-training.

Cycling

Cycling offers many options in that you can ride a bike outdoors, use your bike on a training stand indoors, or use an exercise bike at home or at a gym. An advantage of cycling is that it works the cardiovascular system while eliminating the impact forces that cause most running injuries. You can therefore add cycling to your training program with little risk of bringing on typical running injuries. An advantage of cycling compared to other cross-training options is that you get to cover ground and feel the wind in your hair, just as in running.

The downsides of cycling are the risk of getting squashed by a car, the large amount of time required compared to running, and developing a short running stride. The first downside is all too possible, particularly for runners with good cardiovascular fitness but poor bike-handling skills; to keep your heart rate up, you'll likely have to maintain speeds that could put you in danger. In a low-traffic area, cycling outdoors is a great option, but if you're limited to cycling in an urban area without bike paths, then you may want to stay with the more boring indoor options.

Riding indoors can be a surprisingly satisfying experience because you can concentrate on your workout without distractions or dangers like traffic lights and cars. Although the maximum time a sane person should sit on a bike indoors is about an hour, when injured, Scott laid claim to the dubious achievement of a 3-hour, 40-minute ride in his garage. (Having an extensive CD collection helps.) During times of injury, an indoor bike can also be used for lactate threshold training.

To get a similar workout to running requires about three times as long on a bike. But because the main rationale for recovery runs is simply to increase blood flow through the muscles, you can replace a 30-minute recovery run with about 45 minutes on the bike.

Because cycling is highly repetitive and uses a limited range of motion, it presents a danger of shortening your stride. You can minimize this concern by walking and then running slowly for several minutes after cycling and then stretching your hamstrings, quadriceps, and hip flexors. Also, be sure to keep the bike in an easy enough gear, with RPMs of at least 90, so that cycling doesn't detract from your running turnover.

Water Running

Unfortunately, a number of running injuries are aggravated by some types of cross-training. Fortunately, with most running injuries, you can safely run in the water. Deep-water running with a flotation vest provides an excellent training stimulus and simulates land running more closely than most other cross-training options. Running in the water is a total body exercise that works your legs, trunk, and arms and positively stresses your cardiovascular system.

Several studies have verified that runners can use deep-water running to maintain fitness. Investigators from Florida State University coerced a group of trained male runners to run in the water while another group continued regular training. The runners were tested for $\dot{V}O_2$ max, lactate threshold, and running economy before and after 6 weeks of water running. The water-running group fully maintained their aerobic fitness during the 6 weeks (Wilber et al. 1996). Similarly, a study by Ed Eyestone (yes, the Olympic marathoner) and colleagues at Brigham Young University found no change in 2-mile run time after runners trained in the water for 6 weeks (Eyestone et al. 1993). There's little question, then, that water running is an effective method for runners to stay fit.

Water-running technique is an area of some debate. Some coaches insist that you should try to simulate land running form as closely as possible. Though that's a nice ideal, the most important consideration is to maintain your training intensity to the highest degree possible; if your form needs improvement, so be it.

Regardless of your running form, your stride rate will be slower during water running because of the increased resistance of moving your legs through water. If you try to simulate land running too closely, your stride rate will be even slower. For that reason, don't worry if you don't bring your leg behind your body to the same degree as in land running; just find a happy compromise with decent form and a reasonable rate of leg turnover.

Some athletes move forward while running in the water and (very slowly) do laps during their workouts. Whether you move forward or remain relatively still depends on subtle changes in body position. Try to maintain a relatively upright posture during water running; this posture will work your trunk muscles and result in only a slight tendency to move forward through the water.

You won't be able to achieve as high a heart rate running in the water as when running on land. A study from Karolinska Institute in Stockholm found that heart rate is 8 to 11 beats per minute lower for the same oxygen uptake when running in the water compared to normal running (Svedenhag and Seger 1992). This study also found that on average maximal heart rate is 16 beats per minute lower during all-out water running compared to land running. Lower heart rates during water running are primarily because of the pressure of water on the body; the water pressure makes more blood return to the heart so that more blood is pumped with each heartbeat.

A useful rule of thumb is that heart rates during water running are about 10 percent lower than during land running. For example, if you get your heart rate up to 140 beats per minute in the water, that's roughly equal to 154 beats per minute during normal running. In addition, the temperature of the water affects your heart rate during deep-water running—your heart rate will be lower in cool water and higher in warm water. Interestingly, two studies have found that women have slightly lower heart rates and oxygen consumption than men during deep-water running. This is thought to be because of women's generally higher body fat content and resultant greater buoyancy as compared to men.

The Karolinska study found that perceived exertion is higher during water running for a given heart rate or level of oxygen consumption. In other words, to get a beneficial workout in the water, you'll feel that you're working harder than during land running. (We can speak from experience that perceived effort at a heart rate of 140 in the water is much higher than for a heart rate of 154 running on land.)

For this reason, if you're injured and replacing land running with water running, you'll need to emphasize interval workouts in the water. If you do only steady water-running sessions, your effort won't be high enough to maintain your fitness. Interval sessions in the water, however, give you brief breaks, both physical and mental, that allow you to work harder and obtain a superior workout. Another plus is that time passes relatively quickly when you're doing intervals, whereas steady water running is terribly boring. Even if you're using water running on your recovery days while marathon training, to get in a halfway decent workout you'll probably have to concentrate on maintaining intensity more than if you were going for an easy run around the block.

In-Line Skating

Advantages of in-line skating for cross-training are that it's fun, it gets you outside with the wind in your hair, and it has some similarities to a running stride. Disadvantages are the time it takes to develop reasonable skill and the safety factor. You may reduce your risk of running injuries by adding in-line skating to your training program, but you could end up with a few scrapes and bruises instead. Once you master it, though, in-line skating can be an effective form of cross-training. After a series of running injuries, Olympic 10,000-meter runner Steve Plasencia successfully used in-line skating to maintain his fitness and reduce his injury risk for several years while continuing to compete at a world-class level. You can use in-line skating for recovery training and general aerobic conditioning.

Rowing or Kayaking

Rowing or kayaking on the water is a wonderful whole-body exercise that requires a fairly high degree of skill. If you know how to do it, rowing or kayaking is a great replacement for recovery training and a portion of your aerobic conditioning. Rowing on a machine, such as a Concept II rowing ergometer, is much more forgiving—if your technique is poor, you stay dry. Rowing has the added benefit of strengthening your back, shoulders, and arms. When starting out, ask someone who knows what they're doing to show you the correct technique because improper rowing technique can put a large amount of strain on your back.

Cross-Country Skiing

Cross-country skiing is the only form of exercise that provides cardiovascular benefits equal to, or even slightly better than, those associated with running. The whole-body nature of cross-country skiing really works the cardiovascular system, and some of the highest $\dot{V}O_2$max values have been recorded in cross-country skiers.

As with rowing, if you know how to do it, cross-country skiing is pretty much the perfect form of cross-training. Unfortunately, cross-country skiing also requires skill. As can be the case with cycling outdoors, highly trained runners with no experience or little coordination may not be able to go fast enough for long enough while skiing to get in a good workout. As Bob Kempainen famously showed while preparing for the 1992 Olympic marathon trials, cross-country ski machines are a good option too but are not as much fun as gliding along the snow.

Stair Climbing

Stair climbing is hard work and provides a great cardiovascular workout. Unfortunately, the stresses of stair climbing are close enough to those of running that the reduction in injuries from substituting stair climbing for a portion of your running may not be that great. For this reason, stair climbing is not recommended during recovery from most running injuries. If you're healthy, however, stair climbing can substitute for recovery runs. The same is true of increasingly popular elliptical trainers, which can also be used when you're injured.

Swimming

Swimming is a wonderful form of cross-training that works the cardiovascular system with absolutely none of the jarring stresses of running. To get in a decent workout requires some skill, but with a little bit of instruction, even a dyed-in-the-wool marathoner can quickly build up to 30 or 40 laps. Swimming isn't as similar to running as some of the other cross-training options, but if most of your training still consists of running, that doesn't really matter. Swimming is a great way to increase your recovery and your general aerobic fitness without increasing your risk of a running-related injury.

Resistance Training

Resistance training using weights, bands, or your own body weight can correct muscle imbalances and prevent injuries. We've already discussed core stability training, which is a type of resistance training with a specific purpose. Other types of resistance training will get your arms and shoulders in shape, which don't get much benefit from running, and strengthen your leg muscles. Done correctly, weightlifting can reduce your risk of injury by strengthening the connective tissue, including tendons and ligaments. Weightlifting may even improve your running economy so that you use less oxygen at a given pace.

If done to excess, however, weightlifting will make you muscle-bound, tighten up your muscles, leave you injured, and give you extra bulk that you might not want to be carrying around come the 23-mile mark. Marathoners, after all, want to be the classic vertical hyphen, with no extra baggage—Tegla Loroupe and Moses Tanui probably don't get asked for help too often on moving day. Resistance training does have a role, however, in a marathoner's overall training program.

To Lift or Not to Lift?

Whether weight training can improve marathon or other endurance performance is still open to debate. A 1988 study by Dr. R.C. Hickson and colleagues at the University of Illinois at Chicago investigated whether adding strength training to an endurance training program would improve endurance performance. The investigators had eight well-trained cyclists and runners add weight training to their exercise programs. The subjects performed three to five sets of four leg exercises, three times per week for 10 weeks. Leg strength increased by 27 percent on parallel squats, 37 percent on knee extensions, and 25 percent on knee flexion during the 10 weeks. The weightlifting, however, didn't result in any change in the subjects' $\dot{V}O_2$max. Short-term endurance was measured by having the subjects cycle and run as hard as possible for 4 to 8 minutes. When retested after weight training, the subjects had increased their time to exhaustion by 11 percent during cycling and 13 percent during running (Hickson et al. 1988).

The effects of weight training on the subjects' running performances, however, were less clear-cut. Two of the eight subjects were injured from the heavy resistance training and were unable to complete the post–weight training 10K run. Of the other six subjects, their 10K times improved from an average of 42:27 before weight training to 41:43 afterward. Though this improvement was not statistically significant, it does suggest that weightlifting had some positive impact on running performance.

A 1994 study from the department of kinesiology at the University of New Hampshire, however, strongly supports weightlifting for distance runners. Exercise physiologist Ron Johnston found improvements in running economy after a 10-week weight training program. In this study, 12 trained female distance runners were split into groups for 10 weeks of training. The experimental (run + lift) group continued to run and added a three-times-a-week strength training regimen consisting of 14 exercises working the upper body, abdominals, and legs. The control group just ran.

The run + lift group improved their upper-body strength by 24 percent and leg strength by 34 percent. $\dot{V}O_2$max and oxygen consumption at lactate threshold didn't change in either group. The most interesting finding was that running economy improved significantly in the run + lift group but didn't change in the run-only group. Running economy improved by more than 2 percent at the three running speeds used in the study. Johnston explains, "Strength training improves running economy either due to a reduction in wasted motion, or because stronger legs allow runners to rely more heavily on their more economical slow-twitch muscle fibers" (Johnston et al. 1997).

As discussed in chapter 2, running economy determines how fast you can run at a given level of oxygen consumption. Because the amount of oxygen consumption that you can maintain during a race is determined by your lactate threshold, your running economy really dictates how fast you can race. An improvement of 2 percent in running economy translates to a 2 percent increase in race speed, which represents an improvement of more than 3 minutes for a 2:40 marathoner.

If you decide to lift weights, get advice from a coach or trainer who understands that you are weightlifting to improve your running, not to look good at the beach. If you decide to weight train your legs, schedule your weight sessions so that they're not right before or after a hard running workout. If you run before or after work, lunchtime is an excellent opportunity to get in high-quality lifting sessions that won't detract from your running.

Lifting for the Long Run

An early study by biomechanists Peter Cavanagh, PhD, and Keith Williams, PhD, found that most runners naturally use the most economical stride length for a given speed (Cavanagh and Williams 1982). This led to the belief that runners shouldn't alter their stride length. That advice is correct for the short term, but that doesn't mean that you can't or shouldn't attempt to improve your body to make it a more effective running machine. Over months and years, you can increase your stride length by improving your strength and flexibility. The gains per stride will be small, but when multiplied over thousands of strides, the benefits can be substantial.

//// **What If You Hate to Lift?**

If lifting weights isn't for you, then try another form of resistance training—hill training. During hill running, your body weight is the resistance. A 1985 study suggests that running hills can produce improvements in running economy similar to those that occur through "normal" resistance training. In this study, 16 elite male runners improved their running economy by 1 to 4 percent per year through a combination of long-distance running, intervals, and hills. Other studies that included just long-distance running and intervals found no improvement in running economy, which indicates that the hills were probably what led to the improvements.

Running uphill requires that your legs propel your body weight upward against gravity. Moreover, they do so under conditions that more closely replicate racing conditions than does even the most well-designed weight machine. Anecdotal evidence for the benefits of hill running comes from the Kenyan and Ethiopian runners of today and goes back to coaching legend Arthur Lydiard and the great New Zealand runners of the 1960s and 1970s. The best runners in the world run hills day after day. Of course, genetic factors separate elite runners from recreational runners, but it certainly appears that hill training is an important element that, unlike your genes, you can influence. Another advantage of hill running over lifting weights is that you simultaneously build your cardiovascular system.

Resistance training can improve running performance by increasing the force that your slow-twitch muscle fibers develop. This requires relatively low resistance and high repetitions. Lifting to increase muscle size is counterproductive to endurance (and particularly marathon) performance. During endurance training, you work to increase the capillary density and mitochondrial content of your muscles. When muscle size is increased, the capillary and mitochondrial density of the muscle is reduced. It's important, therefore, that you design your resistance training to avoid gains in muscle size.

Resistance training should generally take place two times a week. With this frequency you will see steady improvements in strength but will not compromise the rest of your training program due to excess fatigue. As discussed previously, core stability training should be done more frequently.

In this chapter, we've looked at several types of training that build on the solid foundations of marathon preparation we discussed in chapters 2 to 4. But let's not hit the road just yet. The training schedules later in this book are based on your having picked a challenging but reasonable marathon goal and progressing systematically toward it. In the next chapter, we'll look at the types of goals to pick and how to evaluate your progress toward your goal.

6

Tracking
Your Progress

This chapter focuses on evaluating your marathon preparation. Other than the fact that it seems that all you do lately is run, how do you know if you're progressing toward achieving your marathon goals? To evaluate your progress, first you must set goals. Only then are you able to monitor your progress toward achieving them.

First, we'll look at how to set motivating goals and how to monitor your progress without becoming obsessed with trivia. An important aspect of monitoring your progress, of course, is evaluating your fitness. We'll look at several methods you can use to monitor your fitness as your training continues.

One stumbling block in meeting your goal can be your running form. The marathon is notorious for exposing a runner's weaknesses. Though you may be able to get away with weak gluteals or tight shoulders in a 10K, in the marathon these weaknesses will become magnified as the race progresses. We'll look at the most common running form errors among marathoners and learn how to correct them.

Finally, we'll look at how to overcome roadblocks in your marathon preparation. It's rare that everything goes perfectly during the many weeks of getting ready for the marathon. How you respond to the inevitable hurdles such as head colds, strained muscles, and snowstorms will have a major influence on your marathon performance and your peace of mind.

Setting Goals

Goal setting is critically important for marathon success. Well-defined goals will help you get through the weeks and months of rigorous preparation.

Crystal-clear goals also will help you to persevere during the marathon, particularly during the mind-numbing stretch from mile 16 to mile 24.

> *Your goals must be meaningful and motivating.*

Goal setting involves two steps—identifying what you want to accomplish and then developing a plan to achieve it. Goal setting is an individual process. Your goals must be meaningful and motivating to you.

The Three Goals for Marathoners

As a marathoner, you need to set three types of goals: your marathon career goal, your goals for your next marathon, and a series of short-term process goals. Your marathon career goal is the level you ultimately hope to achieve. It may be to run a certain time, to qualify for Boston, or to make the Olympic team. Your career goal provides long-term direction but does little to provide day-to-day motivation for your training. Your career goal is very personal, and if you share it with others, their reaction may be that you're bragging. Let your career goal fuel the fire of your training, but share it with only a select few confidants.

Your goals for your next marathon—your outcome goals—establish the framework for your training. Those goals may be to run a personal best time or to better an earlier time on the same course, or they might be tactical goals, such as to run the second half of the marathon as fast as the first half. Once you've set your goals for your next marathon, you start the process of determining how to reach those goals. Your training plan should be designed so that your fitness and mental preparation logically progress to help you reach your goals.

Within your training program, you should establish a set of process goals. Process goals are specific tasks that you perform that contribute toward reaching your goal for the marathon. By focusing on these stepping-stones, you'll greatly increase your chances of reaching the outcome that you want. Examples of process goals are weekly mileage, getting in a certain number of core stability or flexibility sessions, and times for tempo runs and interval sessions. Process goals can also cover areas such as mental preparation, nutrition, and tactics. For example, a runner whose mind tends to drift may establish a mental process goal of concentrating well during an entire 5-mile tempo run. She may evaluate whether she reached that goal by checking the consistency of her mile splits. A nutritional goal may be to prevent becoming chronically dehydrated by drinking at least 3 liters of fluids each day. A runner who tends to start too fast and die during the marathon may set a tactical goal of running the first 10 miles of his long runs at 7:20 per mile and then picking it up to 7:00 pace.

What's a Good Goal?

Sport psychologists have conducted a large number of studies investigating the relationship between goal setting and successful athletic performance.

Follow these guidelines for setting motivating goals that will help you to achieve your potential in the marathon.

• Your goals should be specific and measurable. Vague goals can't possibly motivate you. If your goals aren't measurable, you won't know if you've reached them. For example, if you say, "My goal is to be more dedicated to training," what does that mean? But if you say, "My goal is to run at least 5 days per week for the next 12 weeks," then you'll know for sure whether you achieved that goal, and you'll have benchmarks along the way to help you monitor your progress.

• Your goals should be challenging. Goals that are too easy aren't motivating. Your process goals should require you to exceed yourself in some way, such as in training volume or the consistency of your training. Similarly, your goals for your next marathon should present a motivating challenge. If you've run 2:48 and set a goal to break 2:50 in your next marathon, how motivating is that? An appropriately challenging goal may be to run 2:45 or perhaps 2:40.

• Your goals should be realistic. Wildly optimistic goals that you don't believe you can ever reach are also not motivating. Your goals should be challenging yet achievable. You need to evaluate your current level as a marathoner and how much you believe you can improve. If you've run 40 miles a week during preparation for your previous marathons, then don't set a goal of averaging 80 miles a week this time around. A goal of 50 miles a week would be challenging but also realistic enough to provide day-to-day motivation for your training. Likewise, if your best marathon time is 3:06, don't set a goal of breaking 2:40 for your next race. Put your physical, mental, and emotional energy into a realistic goal, such as breaking 3:00, and you'll maximize your chance of performing at your best.

• Your goals should be set within a stated time frame. Establish firm dates for achieving your goals. Nothing beats a deadline for focusing your creativity and energy toward achieving a goal. (Ask any book author.) Goals without a time frame tend to remain stuck in the future.

//// The Benefits of Logging On

Your training log is an important tool for recording your process goals and monitoring your progress toward achieving those goals. Daily training feedback is an important factor in helping you stay motivated. The information you put in your training diary can help you identify how you respond to specific types of training and other individualized factors contributing to success. Besides the details of your training sessions, record your resting heart rate each morning, the number of hours and quality of your sleep, and your general energy level. You will find this information extremely useful later in determining your body's ability to successfully adapt to training.

Evaluating Your Fitness

During your marathon preparation, your confidence will tend to rise and fall on the basis of how you feel from day to day. To really know how fit you are, you need an objective measure to help you monitor your progress. By checking your progress, you can fine-tune your training to maximize its effectiveness. There are several ways to track your fitness in preparation for the marathon. We will look at two lab tests plus four workouts that you can do on your own.

Maximal Lactate Steady State

The maximal lactate steady state (MLSS) test is the most accurate test you can do to predict marathon performance. In this test, an exercise physiologist finds the fastest pace that you can run while the lactate level in your blood remains steady.

The test isn't easy. In the lab where Pete works, they usually perform it only on male marathoners who run under 2:40 and female runners who break 3:00. During the test, you run on the treadmill for 20 minutes at your usual marathon race pace, and the tester pricks your finger every 5 minutes to measure your blood lactate level. You are given 30 minutes of rest, and then you run for 20 minutes at a pace that is 10 seconds per mile faster. If your lactate level is steady during the second run, then you come back a week later and run 20 minutes at a still faster speed. This process continues until the speed is identified at which your lactate rises continuously during the 20-minute run. The previous speed is your MLSS pace, the fastest pace you can run without a continuous increase in lactate levels. Most marathoners need to do three 20-minute runs before their MLSS pace is identified.

According to exercise physiologist and coach Jack Daniels, PhD, good marathoners can typically run the marathon at 2 to 3 percent slower than their MLSS pace. For example, if your MLSS pace is 10 miles per hour, we would predict that you can run the marathon at 9.7 to 9.8 miles per hour, which represents a pace of 6:07 to 6:11 per mile and a marathon time of 2:40 to 2:42. In Pete's experience, this test is remarkably accurate in predicting marathon performance. Although the MLSS test interferes with the marathoner's training, the test itself is an excellent training session.

Lactate Threshold

As we saw in chapter 2, your lactate threshold pace is the running speed at which lactate starts to rapidly accumulate in your muscles and blood. The lactate threshold test is similar to the MLSS test in that blood lactate levels are measured at progressively faster running speeds. The advantage of the lactate threshold test, however, is that the test is done in one session.

Typically, you run for 5 minutes at five to seven different speeds. The speeds are selected so that you reach your lactate threshold on the fourth or fifth repetition. Because distance runners' lactate thresholds are usually very close to their 15K to half marathon race pace, you can select the speeds for the test using your race pace for these distances. For example, if your 10-mile race pace is 5:27 per mile (11 miles per hour), then you would do the first stage of the test at 9.5 miles per hour and increase the treadmill speed by half a mile per hour for each subsequent stage so that you reach your estimated lactate threshold pace on the fourth repetition. You could then repeat the test several weeks later to track your progress.

The disadvantage of the lactate threshold test is that it isn't as accurate as the MLSS test in predicting marathon performance. Sometimes the results predict marathon performance quite precisely, but in other cases the prediction may be off by as much as 10 minutes. Even in those situations, the lactate threshold test is useful to measure over time. An improvement in lactate threshold pace almost invariably represents an improvement in your ability to run the marathon.

Tune-Up Races

The simplest way to monitor your fitness is just to enter a race during your marathon preparation. The longer the race, the better indication you'll get of your marathon fitness, but the more time you'll need for recovery. If you train through the tune-up race, your performance will likely be several percent slower than if you had rested for the race. Tune-up races every 2 to 3 weeks during marathon preparation are great motivators and excellent workouts, and they provide feedback on the effectiveness of your training program. The schedules in part II of this book call for several tune-up races in the couple of months before your marathon. Just remember to take into account different courses and weather conditions in comparing your pace in different races.

Time Trials

Time trials are an excellent way to assess your fitness over time. The advantages over a tune-up race are that you can do time trials whenever they best fit your schedule, and you can run the same course each time. An improvement of several seconds per mile is an indication that your training program is working. If your times stay the same or get worse, you simply may not be training hard enough, or, more likely for most marathoners, you may be worn out from overtraining. In that situation, you'll need to step back and interpret the time trial results within the overall context of your training.

If weather conditions change substantially between time trials, however, then it's difficult to know how to evaluate your performance. For example, if you run an 8-mile time trial on a hot day in July and record a time of 44:52 and then repeat the time trial on a much cooler day in September and run 43:10, the improvement may be because of improved fitness, the cooler conditions, or some combination of both. Because several variables changed, you can't say for certain why your time improved. Similarly, if you run a time trial on a calm day and then repeat it a few weeks later on a windy day, you may find that your time gets worse despite an improvement in fitness.

If getting to a race isn't feasible at the points in the training schedules that call for tune-up races, then run time trials on those days. Runners vary greatly in how close to a maximum effort they can give in such situations, though, so this will probably add another variable in evaluating the meaning of your results.

Heart Rate at a Set Pace

Another way to evaluate your fitness is to wear a heart monitor and check your heart rate at your goal marathon pace. For example, you could do a thorough warm-up and then run 2 miles on a track at your goal marathon pace and check your heart rate during the second mile. As you get fitter, you would expect your heart rate to go down by several beats per minute. For example, 12 weeks before the marathon, your heart rate at your goal marathon race pace may be 160 beats per minute. As your fitness improves, you would hope to see your heart rate at that pace decrease several beats per minute, perhaps to 155 to 157 beats per minute.

When interpreting heart rate results, you need to account for temperature and wind conditions. As with time trials, a windy or hot day will make it more difficult to interpret your results. If it's windy, your heart rate will be elevated several beats per minute when you run into the wind. Your heart rate will also be slightly lower when running with the wind, but this reduction isn't as great as the elevation that comes from running into the wind, so your overall heart rate for a given pace will be higher on a windy day. On a hot day, your body sends blood to your skin to help with cooling, and your blood volume is reduced as you become dehydrated from sweating (see chapter 3). These factors increase your heart rate at a given pace. When you run on a hot day, therefore, your heart rate could be 5 to 10 beats per minute higher than on a cool day. Keep this factor in mind when comparing your heart rate under different environmental conditions.

Marathon-Pace Runs

The training schedules in chapters 8 to 10 call for one or two medium-long runs at your goal marathon pace. Using these to evaluate your progress can be highly subjective, especially because you have so few examples to judge from. These runs are also subject to the many variables that can affect the information you get from your tune-up races, time trials, and runs at a set heart rate. Still, these workouts should give you a sense of how your training is progressing and whether your goal is a good one. When they go well, they're tremendous confidence boosters because you'll have run roughly half your race at goal pace while in the midst of heavy training.

How's Your Running Form?

When you watch elite marathoners, you see a wide variety of running styles. This can lead to the conclusion that running technique isn't important for marathon success. Not so. Certain characteristics are common to the styles of almost all successful marathon runners. The closer that your form adheres to these ideals, the more efficiently you run and the less susceptible you are to injury and fatigue. Because good form goes a long way toward helping you meet your goals, it's worth the effort to periodically assess your running style and, if needed, work to improve it.

Your running style is determined by your biomechanics, including the lengths of your bones, your muscle and tendon flexibility, the strength and endurance of various muscles, and the coordinated contraction pattern of your muscles and the resulting movement of your limbs. Running requires a complex series of perfectly timed muscle contractions. The movement and positioning of your legs, trunk, arms, and head all combine to determine your unique running style.

There are three reasons to evaluate your running form: to reduce the likelihood of injuries, to minimize wasted energy, and to eliminate obvious imperfections. Reducing the likelihood of injuries usually isn't a straightforward process; it requires a personal approach, often requiring working with a physical therapist who's familiar with the characteristics of long-distance runners. Although fine-tuning running technique to improve running economy requires an exercise physiology lab, it's often possible to refine a runner's style to increase the likelihood of marathon success. Similarly, many marathoners have obvious imperfections in their running form that become magnified as fatigue sets in over the course of the marathon. Eliminating obvious imperfections can improve the flow of your running, thereby reducing the likelihood of your tightening up and slowing down over the course of the marathon.

Proper running technique helps prevent injury and fatigue.

At the lab where Pete works, dozens of marathoners and other runners come in for evaluation of their running style. Some have long, frustrating injury histories, whereas others are simply looking for a performance edge. These athletes are videotaped from the back, side, and front while running on a treadmill, and then while running outside. They're taped while wearing their training shoes as well as with their racing flats because sometimes a runner will have excellent form in training shoes but shows definite areas for improvement in poorly supportive racing flats.

The same imperfections in running form show up again and again. Many of these problems are caused by lifestyle factors, such as driving too much or sitting in front of a computer all day. Other problems are caused by muscle tightness or muscle weakness. Still others are caused by the runner simply not realizing how he or she looks while running. The basic components of an economical running style are identical for men and women. The subtle differences are because of the average woman's wider pelvis, which tends to increase the angle of the femur for correct knee alignment. Runners are often surprised to see how they look on the video, particularly in slow motion. Let's review the most common running form problems and how to correct them.

Tight Shoulders, Neck, and Upper Back

Upper-body tightness is by far the most common technique problem in runners. It generally stems from spending too much time sitting slumped in front of a computer or at a desk, and driving. These modern-day situations tend to leave your shoulders, neck, and upper back tight. This leads to holding the shoulders up, giving the impression of having a short neck; holding your arms out from the sides of your body (in an abducted position); or both. Holding your shoulders up keeps your arms from being able to swing freely forward and back. As a result, you use a side-to-side movement of the arms, which is wasted motion. (Some movement of the arms across the chest is normal). If your arms are out from the sides of your body, then you're using energy to hold them in that position. To see the effect on your marathon performance, try standing for more than 2 hours while holding your arms out from your sides. This is unnecessary fatigue. Similarly, try holding your shoulders up for over 2 hours. Tightness in the shoulders feeds into the arms and vice versa.

To correct tight shoulders, neck, and upper back requires eliminating the cause. Short of quitting your job, you can minimize the effects of sitting at a desk by taking short breaks every

Running with a tight upper body.

Stacey Cramp

15 to 20 minutes. This will give the muscles a chance to relax and help to eliminate chronic tightness. Your workstation setup can also have a major effect on your accumulated muscle tightness. If your monitor or keyboard is a few inches too high or too low, this can have a major effect on your posture and muscle tightness over the hundreds of hours that you spend in work position. Similarly, check your driving posture in your car. A change in seat position can often reduce back strain.

A variety of stretches are helpful to loosen up tight shoulders, neck, and upper back. For an excellent series of stretches for each of these areas, see *Sport Stretch* (1998), by Michael Alter. Do these stretches before each run so that you start the run with relaxed shoulders and arms. During your runs, remind yourself to keep your shoulders low and relaxed until this new habit becomes automatic. One good way to check this is to concentrate on having your wrists pass your waist as you run.

Head Forward of Body

Head forward of the body is common among office workers who sit in front of computers much of the day. Your head should be directly over your body. If your head is forward of your body, your neck and upper-back muscles must constantly contract to keep your head from falling forward. This makes those

Stacey Cramp

Holding the head too far forward.

muscles chronically tight and fatigued. Your head may be forward of your body because of tight upper-back and neck muscles and generally poor posture.

A simple correction can be to move your computer monitor closer to your chair—some people lean forward all day long trying to read their monitors.

Generally, correcting a forward head requires stretching, relaxation, and conscious correction. You need to stretch the muscles at the top of your back and the back of your neck. For an excellent series of stretches for this area, see *Sport Stretch*. Simply lying on your back and gently tucking your chin can relax and gently stretch your neck muscles. You also need to consciously focus on running with your head over your body. Your training partners can give you feedback so that you know when you have it right. This is a problem that you can definitely conquer with a bit of determination.

Tension in Arms

Arm tension is often related to having tight shoulders or a tight neck and upper back, but sometimes it's just a bad habit. To check whether your arms are tight, observe whether the angle at your elbows changes during the course of a stride. When you have tension in your arms, the elbow tends to stay locked in one position. When your arms are swinging freely, the angle at the elbow opens and closes with the momentum of the forearm. Similarly,

Stacey Cramp

Running with arm tension.

your hands should be relaxed. Don't hold a fist when you run because doing so will cause you to tighten your arms, shoulders, and neck.

To reduce tension in your arms primarily requires relaxation and conscious correction. You need to retrain your arm muscles to relax. Tension in the arms often stems from tension in the shoulders, so stretching and relaxing your shoulders (see preceding paragraphs) may help you to relax your arms. Stretch and relax your shoulders and arms before each run so that you get used to the feeling of flowing along with your arms swinging freely at your sides. You also need to remind yourself (or have a running partner remind you) to relax your arms. At first, your muscles may tighten up again during the run, but they should gradually stay more relaxed throughout your runs. This is very important during the marathon because tension in the arms often results in general tightness and muscle fatigue by the 20-mile mark.

/// Drills to Improve Form

You've probably seen sprinters doing various combinations of high-knee running, butt kicks, skipping, and the like. These drills are great for distance runners, too. First, they can improve your coordination and running form. Second, they lead to gains in strength endurance that can allow you to maintain your stride length throughout the duration of a race. Drills up a moderate slope provide even greater resistance; by concentrating on high-knee lift, a complete toe-off, good arm drive, relaxed neck and shoulders, and so on, you'll improve your ability to hold good running form.

The key aspects of drills are to exaggerate various aspects of the running stride and to concentrate on maintaining your form as you begin to fatigue. Do drills when you're warmed up but still fresh—there's no use trying to improve your coordination and technique when you're already tired. Allow plenty of rest between drills, and visualize yourself completing each drill with perfect form.

Forward Lean at Waist

Some runners lean forward at the waist without realizing it, whereas others lean forward on purpose in the belief that it's correct running style. Poor posture while sitting can also contribute because too much time in the wrong sitting position will flatten the small curve that should be in your lower back, and your upper body tips forward over your waist. Running upright requires little effort from your back and trunk muscles. When you lean forward at the waist, however, your trunk and quadriceps muscles work overtime to keep you from falling forward. The result is early fatigue and sore muscles.

Eliminating an excessive forward lean requires activation and strengthening of your gluteal (butt) and abdominal muscles, and conscious correction. Conscious effort can help to correct this problem in some cases. Others will require a series of strengthening exercises from a physical therapist or athletic trainer. If you have this problem, be sure to read the section in chapter 5 on core stability training.

Stacey Cramp

Leaning forward at the waist.

Instability in Trunk

If you watch a film of the best marathoners in the world and speed it up, you will see that their torsos are stable and their legs and arms move relative to this stable base. This is a very efficient running style. When your trunk twists, energy is wasted because that energy isn't used for forward propulsion. Instability in the trunk is typically caused by weak lower abdominal and gluteal muscles.

Reducing trunk instability requires activation and strengthening of your gluteal (butt) and lower abdominal muscles, and conscious correction. You'll need a series of strengthening exercises from a physical therapist or athletic

Stacey Cramp

Trunk instability.

trainer. Again, be sure to read the core stability training section in chapter 5 if you have this problem.

Excessive Vertical Movement

Some vertical movement of your body is necessary during running because with each step you're alternately airborne and earthbound. The optimal amount of vertical motion is greater for shorter races in which you're moving more quickly and with a greater stride length. The best marathoners have a small amount of vertical movement in their strides. You can best observe this by watching the height of their shoulders and head from the side. If you have excessive vertical movement, then you're wasting energy fighting gravity that could be used to help you move forward.

Excessive vertical motion can be reduced by improving your core strength and stretching your calf muscles. Some runners also improve simply by seeing how much they bounce up and down and then thinking about gliding along when they run. Excessive vertical movement is more common among novice runners. With running experience, the extra motion is usually reduced.

Excessive movement vertically.

Overstriding

Very few runners overstride. Scientific studies have shown that the vast majority of runners naturally select their optimal stride length. Runners almost always select the most economical stride length for a given speed. Somehow, we all have a built-in ability to select the most economical stride length. The few runners who overstride often do so because someone has told them to increase their stride length. The only way to naturally increase your stride length is to increase your strength and flexibility so that your optimal stride length increases. Running with a longer-than-optimal stride length just wastes energy.

To correct overstriding, try running barefoot. It's almost impossible to overstride when running without shoes. If you haven't run barefoot for many years, then take it easy at first because it's easy to strain a calf muscle, the Achilles tendon, or the small muscles in the feet. A few hundred meters of barefoot running several times a week will help you find the optimal stride length for you.

Overstriding while running.

Stacey Cramp

Splayed Feet

Feet that point away from a line of forward motion as you land and push off slow you down—some of the energy you generate with each stride is being directed elsewhere than toward your forward progress. The degree to which your feet splay is determined partly by your genetics, such as if your leg bones aren't well aligned. The problem can also have fixable causes. If your gluteals (butt muscles) are weak and tight, or your hip flexors are tight, then your feet will tend to point to the outside as you run.

Look at videotape or photos of you running. Check whether your feet are pointed in the direction of your motion. (You can also check this for a few strides after running through a puddle or when running on snow.) If your toes are pointed away from a line of forward motion, work on strengthening and stretching your gluteals and stretching your hip flexors.

Overcoming Roadblocks

Part of the challenge of the marathon is that preparing for it takes so long and the training required is so demanding that roadblocks along the way to your goal are nearly inevitable. It's important not only to organize your training and life so that as few impediments as possible crop up but also to deal with the ones that nevertheless occur. The most common roadblocks are injuries and illnesses, bad weather, and outside commitments. Let's consider each of these intrusions into your marathon preparation.

Stacey Cramp

Running with splayed feet.

Victah Sailer © Photo Run 1999

Joe LeMay

Fastest Marathon: 2:13:55
Marathon Career Highlights: First place, 1999 California International Marathon. First American (13th place), 1999 Boston Marathon.

Joe LeMay shows that with dedication and the occasional compromise, a runner can achieve high-mileage training and marathoning success while working full-time.

LeMay works 40 hours a week as the e-mail administrator for a small software firm in Connecticut. The job is a 40-minute drive from LeMay's house. LeMay regularly logs (and documents on his Web site, www.joelemay.com) 130-mile weeks. Where does he find the time and energy?

Here's how LeMay describes a typical workday: "I get up just after 6:00. I get out the door between 6:30 and 6:45 and get in anywhere from 9 to 12 miles in the morning, finishing by 7:45 to 8:00. I get to work by a little after 9:00. I work until 6:00, then run for another hour. That's 18 to 21 miles for the day right there. I'll usually leave work then, by 7:00 or 7:30. When I go to the track, I try to leave work on time and get the workout done by 8:00. I get home around 8:00. I make dinner for my wife and me and we end up eating around 9:00. It's a tight schedule. Sometimes I get almost 8 hours of sleep, but usually it's about 7."

LeMay's weekends usually aren't much more carefree. "I sleep the same amount," he notes. "I might be able to get in a nap in the middle of the day if I'm lucky. Usually I have to go somewhere and do something. I try to avoid it, but there's always some family gathering or some social event I'm obligated to for some reason. I really hate all the driving—I just want to stay home and rest. Sometimes almost all of Saturday is spoken for in training anyway: morning run, massage, weights, a couple hours of free time, then the afternoon run."

Obviously, to sustain such a schedule for most of the year, LeMay is highly motivated by his marathon goals. Your mileage may vary, so to speak, but if you're serious about your marathon, setting aside some of the distractions in your life to concentrate on your training in the few months before will pay off on race day.

Even with his near-monastic lifestyle, LeMay has to make compromises. "I'd sure like to get more," he says about sleep. "I'd also like to take more time stretching and warming up for my workouts. The way things are, I have to just get out the door in the morning." Bear in mind, though, that LeMay usually runs more than 2 hours a day. You'll probably be averaging less time training, even at the peak of marathon preparation, so you should be able to find the time for a few good stretching and supplemental exercise sessions per week.

To save time, LeMay says, "I usually do my second run from work. That way, when I get home, I'm done. If I go home first, I'll waste a lot of time reading the mail, et cetera, before heading out the door." LeMay says that if he had a shorter commute, he would try to incorporate his running into it to save even more time. "My dream has always been to live within 10 miles of where I work, so I can run there," he says.

While at work, LeMay is ever conscious of tending to his marathoner's body. "I always have a bottle of water or Gatorade nearby," LeMay says. "I try to drink plenty. I try to stretch as much as possible. I try to sit straight. I'm always careful walking around and up and down stairs to not trip. I avoid crowds so I don't catch anything."

Again, not many people want to—or can—live like this all the time, but nearly all marathoners would benefit from adopting some of LeMay's ways.

Injuries and Illnesses

Injuries and illnesses are best caught early. Successful marathoners have the ability to recognize an injury or illness at an early stage before it becomes serious. Returning to training after an injury or illness requires careful analysis—too much too soon will result in additional time off. During this period, it's important to avoid the factors that caused the injury or illness in the first place, such as worn-out shoes, running on concrete, overtraining, or a lack of sleep.

If you're forced to miss more than a few days of training, then you need to decide whether to try to catch up or revise your marathon goal. This decision will be influenced by how much time you missed, how long you've been preparing, and how many weeks are left until your marathon. Missing 2½ weeks of preparation when you have 16 weeks to go is no big deal, but missing that amount of time during the last 2 months of preparation will likely require you to modify your goal.

Table 6.1 provides guidelines for when you may need to revise your goals after an injury or illness. Typically, if you've lost less than 10 days of training, then you can safely start back where you should have been on the schedules. If you've missed $\dot{V}O_2$max workouts, however, you may need to slow your pace during your next few $\dot{V}O_2$max sessions to reflect the lost time.

Mother Nature

In general, you'll just have to deal with bad weather. Sometimes, however, Mother Nature dishes up a blizzard or 100+ degree weather that's counter-

Table 6.1   Making up for Lost Time

Number of days missed	8 weeks or more until marathon	Less than 8 weeks until marathon
<10	Resume schedule	Resume schedule
10 to 20	Resume schedule	Revise goal
>20	Revise goal	Revise goal

productive to continued healthy training. If you can, find a treadmill indoors or choose an appropriate cross-training activity for a couple for days until the weather becomes bearable.

As with other factors influencing your marathon preparation, weather might necessitate some not-minor changes in your life. For example, you might have to alter your normal schedule so that you can get in reasonable training early in the morning during oppressive summer heat. Or if your area has been snowed under for weeks, you'll probably need to find a few well-paved stretches where you can safely do multiple laps to get in your miles.

Try to anticipate weather when picking your marathon goal. If you don't run well in the heat and live in a sultry climate, it makes little sense to plan for a September marathon because your hardest training will have to occur during the least conducive weather of the year. Similarly, Boston in April can be a tough goal if you live in an area where winter running is a daily challenge.

The Real World

There's really no excuse for outside commitments to regularly interfere with your marathon preparation. Put more gently, don't set an ambitious marathon goal when you know the rest of your life will be busier than usual. Once you've picked your marathon and have decided how long you'll prepare for it, try to anticipate and eliminate factors that would significantly interfere with your training.

Of course, regardless of how focused you are on your training, you're going to have the occasional day when meeting your training goal is exceedingly difficult, if not impossible. A sick child, unsympathetic boss, or traffic accident all have a way of dashing plans for a high-quality tempo run. If necessary, juggle the days in the training schedule you're following so that you get in the most important workouts while still allowing for adequate recovery. A good rule of thumb is that if you can do 90 percent of the planned training schedule, then your preparation is going well.

By now, you should have a thorough understanding of what your marathon preparation should consist of and why. We've looked at the physiological requirements of successful marathoning; how to improve your ability to meet those requirements; and several aspects of managing your training that will allow you to get the most from your workouts, such as proper nutrition, supplemental training, and improving your running form. Unfortunately, all of this seemingly endless work can be wasted with the wrong race-day strategy. What to do the day of and during your goal marathon is the focus of the next chapter.

7

Race-Day Strategy

Your overall preparation for the marathon occurs over several months. During that time, you meticulously plan and diligently train so that you're in peak condition for the race. To do your best, however, you also need to have a plan for the marathon itself. That plan is the focus of this chapter. How much should you warm up for the marathon, and what should that warm-up consist of? How should you handle the first few miles, the first half of the race, the long stretch up to 20 miles, and the final 6 miles and 385 yards? Let's take a look at race-day strategies that help you get everything out of your months of preparation so that you cross the finish line exhausted but satisfied.

Warming Up

Warming up for any race is important. The purpose of a warm-up is to prepare your body to run at race pace. This involves increasing your metabolic rate, your body temperature, and the circulation of blood (and thus oxygen) to your muscles. The warm-up activates your aerobic system to work optimally from the start of the race.

There's a downside, however, to warming up for the marathon. One of the challenges in the marathon is to reach the finish line before becoming glycogen depleted. In chapter 3, we emphasized the importance of carbohydrate loading before the marathon and taking in carbohydrate during the marathon to help ensure that you don't run out of carbs before the finish. But during a warm-up, you burn a mixture of carbohydrates and fat, thereby slightly reducing your glycogen stores. The key, then, is to find the minimum amount of warm-up necessary to prepare your body to handle race pace as soon as the starter's gun is fired so that you save as much of your precious carbohydrate reserves as possible for the 26.2 miles ahead.

The optimal warm-up for the marathon depends on the level of the marathoner. For beginners, whose main goal is to finish, no warm-up is necessary. They can warm up during the first couple of miles of the race. For more serious marathoners, who will attempt to run the distance significantly faster than their normal training pace, the optimal warm-up consists of two runs of about 5 minutes each, with some gentle stretching in between.

You should start warming up about 30 to 40 minutes before the start of the race. Start your first warm-up run slowly, and gradually increase your pace so that you finish at about 1 minute per mile slower than marathon race pace. Next, stretch for about 10 minutes, including loosening up your shoulders and neck. Follow that with another 5 minutes of running, this time gradually picking up the pace until you reach marathon pace for the final 30 seconds or so. Then stretch a bit more.

> **Start warming up 30 to 40 minutes before the race.**

That's it. Try to time your warm-up so that you finish no more than 10 minutes before the race starts. If you warm up too long before the race, you'll lose some of the benefits of the warm-up yet will have still used up some of your carbohydrate stores. The ability to time your warm-up like this is an advantage of running a smaller marathon, as compared to a mega race, where you're more likely to be herded to your starting position long before the race begins.

Before the start of the Olympic marathon, the athletes do a bit of nervous jogging around, but almost no one does more than 10 minutes of easy running plus one or two accelerations up to race pace. This is enough of a warm-up for these runners to handle 5:00-per-mile pace for the first mile. A similar routine will get you to the starting line prepared to handle your goal marathon race pace.

Your Pacing Strategy

In chapter 6, we discussed the importance of setting goals for your marathon. Assuming that you have a time goal for the marathon, how should you go about trying to achieve that time? Some marathoners go out hard and then try to hang on as well as possible in the second half. Others try to run an even pace throughout. A few take it easy early on and then run the second half faster. Let's consider the physiology of the marathon and the implications for your optimal pacing strategy.

In chapter 2, we saw that your marathon pace is very close to your lactate threshold pace, which is determined by your oxygen consumption at your

Khalid Khannouchi

Fastest Marathon: 2:05:42
Marathon Career Highlights: World record in winning 1999 Chicago Marathon. Won 1997 Chicago Marathon in debut at the distance.

Victah Sailer © Photo Run 1999

The world's fastest marathoner had to be talked into running his event.

By the mid-1990s, Khannouchi—then a Moroccan, now an American—had become a dominating figure on the U.S. road-racing scene, but he hadn't run a marathon. In fact, he didn't want to, saying that he "was afraid to go to the marathon." His wife/coach/agent, Sandra, however, knew from his races and training that he would be a great marathoner, and she persuaded him to try 26.2 miles at the 1997 Chicago Marathon. She told him that if she was wrong, he could blame her.

She was right, of course. So right, in fact, that Khannouchi won his debut in 2:07:10, at the time a world best for a first-timer. In 1998, despite an injury, Khannouchi ran nearly as fast to place second. At his annual Chicago pilgrimage the next year, Khannouchi really popped one, breaking the world record by 23 seconds to finish in 2:05:42. That's 4:48 per mile for 26.2 miles.

Khannouchi is known for finishing his marathons very quickly, an ability he comes by via preparation. "You must train according to how you want to run the race," he says. "If you want to finish slow, do your long run slow." Khannouchi says that on his hardest long runs (of 22 to 23 miles), he runs the beginning miles at 15 seconds per mile slower than marathon pace, the middle miles at marathon race pace, then 3 miles working down toward 10K pace and a final 2 miles on the track even faster, trying to finish at 4:30 pace.

"A normal marathoner can try the same thing, but all training does not work for everyone," Khannouchi says. He adds, "You have to build gradually to this kind of run. You can't go from a slow run to this kind of long run without a buildup. Have at least five long runs to build up. In the first run, do only the last mile at 10K pace, et cetera."

Khannouchi is also known for running outstanding times at shorter races, even 5K, while in a marathon buildup. He treats these solely as tune-ups that he doesn't rest

(continued)

Khalid Khannouchi *(continued)*

for—he does two speed workouts the week before a race and doesn't reduce his mileage in the few days before it. "Khalid has a sense of competition," Sandra says. "When he gets in a race, his competitive spirit will push him to his limit even though he is tired. His pride drives him to win. He likes to win, while losing makes him stronger." Sandra viewed his loss at a 5-miler soon before he set the world record at Chicago as a good sign because of the motivation it would provide.

After some of his marathons, Khannouchi has been a bit hobbled. "He has a tendency to get hurt because he has weak tendons and ligaments," Sandra says. "It takes at least 6 days to get rid of sore muscles. Khalid puts everything into his racing. He takes a long time to recover because he likes to be completely recovered so that he'll last longer in the sport. The body deserves to rest." At first, Khannouchi doesn't run—"doesn't think about running, just relaxes," Sandra says—and then builds back gradually. He starts with easy running, adds fartleks, and doesn't return to track workouts until the fourth week after a marathon at the earliest.

lactate threshold and your running economy. If you run faster than your lactate threshold pace, then lactate accumulates in your muscles and blood; this occurrence deactivates the enzymes for energy production and makes you slow down. When you exceed your lactate threshold pace, you also use more glycogen, so your limited glycogen stores are depleted more quickly than necessary.

These basics of marathon physiology indicate that the best strategy for the marathon is relatively even pacing. If you run much faster than your overall race pace for part of the race, then you'll use more glycogen than necessary and will likely start to accumulate lactate. If you run much slower than your overall race pace for part of the race, then you'll need to make up for this lapse by running faster than the most efficient pace for another portion of the race. The optimal pacing strategy, then, is to run nearly even splits, taking into account the idiosyncrasies of the course you'll be running.

> *Relatively even pacing is the optimal pacing strategy.*

Most runners shouldn't try to run dead-even splits, however, because during the marathon you'll gradually fatigue your slow-twitch muscle fibers and will start to recruit more of your fast-twitch A fibers to maintain your pace. Unfortunately, these fast-twitch fibers tend to be less economical than your slow-twitch fibers in their use of oxygen. Therefore, your running economy will tend to decrease slightly during the race, meaning that your lactate threshold pace will decrease slightly as well. The result is that your optimal pace will be slightly reduced during the latter stages of the marathon.

For example, if your goal is to run 2:39 for the marathon, then even splits would require you to run 1:19:30 for each half of the race. To run even splits, you would have to increase your oxygen consumption and lactate level as your fatigue level increases during the second half of the race. A more efficient pacing strategy would be to go through halfway in 1:18:00 to 1:19:00 because doing so would allow you to slow by 2 to 3 percent during the second half and still achieve your goal. If you ran negative splits for the marathon (i.e., the second half faster than the first half), chances are that you ran more slowly than optimally during the first half of the race and could have had a faster finishing time.

For world-class marathoners, whose genetics and training put them on a higher plane, the optimal pacing strategy is likely a bit different. These select few are so highly trained that they have a lower tendency to recruit less-economical muscle fibers as the race progresses. In addition, they can pick up the pace over the last several miles and gradually accumulate lactate to the finish. For the best marathoners in the world, therefore, the most effective pacing strategy is to run the second half of the marathon at the same pace as, or even slightly faster than, the first half.

The last two world records have been set with models of good pacing. In setting the world best of 2:05:42 at the 1999 Chicago Marathon, Khalid Khannouchi's negative splits of 1:03:07 for the first half and 1:02:35 for the second half were close to optimal. When Tegla Loroupe ran her world record of 2:20:43 at the 1999 Berlin Marathon, she ran 1:09:47 for the first half and 1:10:56 for the second half. She likely slowed a bit over the second half because in chasing a sub-2:20 finish, she probably went out a little too fast and had to slow in the second half. In contrast, Khannouchi was concentrating on winning the race and said later that he wasn't aware of his splits in the final miles. Interestingly, Ronaldo da Costa's second half was substantially faster than his first half (1:04:42 vs. 1:01:23) when he set the world best of 2:06:05 in the 1998 Berlin Marathon. This suggests either that the splits were inaccurate or that he could have run even faster with more even pacing.

Although in most cases you should stay with your pacing plan, occasionally the weather or the tactics of other runners merit slightly altering your strategy. If you're running into a head wind, there's a substantial advantage to running in a group of runners and letting others block the wind. Though you may need to do your share in leading the group, you'll still save considerable energy compared to running by yourself into the wind. On a windy day, therefore, you may need to run faster or slower than planned to stay with a group.

Even on a calm day, the best strategy may be to deviate slightly from your goal pace rather than running most of the way by yourself. In a big-city marathon like Boston, New York, or Chicago, being stuck by yourself isn't a problem. At almost any pace, you'll be among a number of runners, and you can work with them to reach your goal time. In a smaller marathon, however, you have a reasonably high chance of running by yourself for many miles. In that situation, you must make a judgment call as to whether to go a few seconds per mile faster or slower than planned to stay with a group.

Although drafting behind other runners will give you a small energy advantage, most of the benefit of staying with a group is psychological. You don't have to set the pace, and you can relax and go along with the group.

Most runners find it quite difficult mentally to run by themselves for long stretches of the marathon. So what's the trade-off between having company and having to compromise your strategy? A rule of thumb is to deviate from your goal pace by no more than 8 to 10 seconds per mile if you would otherwise be running by yourself during the first 20 miles of the race. (Of course,

Brian J. Myers © Photo Run 1999

Khalid Khannouchi used excellent pacing in setting a world best 2:05:42 at the 1999 Chicago Marathon.

you won't know until afterward whether you would have had to run by yourself.) Running 8 to 10 seconds per mile faster than planned may not sound like much, but this difference in effort can put you over the edge after a couple of miles. The best way to judge whether to pick it up to latch on to a group is by how you feel at the time. If you feel as though you can handle it, then go for it. If your breathing is uncomfortable and you can sense that you're working at a higher intensity than you can maintain until the finish, then relax and let the others go. You may find that the group will soon break up and that you'll once again have others to run with.

During the final 6 miles and 385 yards, you can afford to be more independent. If no one else is running at the correct pace for you after you've passed the 20-mile mark, you need to muster the courage to go it alone. Chances are that forging out will work well psychologically because if you have prepared well and run a fairly even pace, you'll be passing other runners throughout the final miles. Nothing lifts the spirits quite like passing another runner late in the marathon.

If you're racing a marathon in which your specific finishing place is an important consideration (e.g., the Olympic trials), then your pacing strategy will be somewhat determined by the actions of others in the race. If a group of 10 runners breaks away, then you had better go after them, even if it means running faster than planned. In general, though, it's best to stick close to your race plan and your goal marathon pace.

What Shoes Should You Wear?

Marathoners vary widely in the types of shoes they prefer to race in. On the theory that even an extra ounce adds up over the course of 26.2 miles, some like to wear as light a shoe as possible. On the other hand, some runners figure that during such a long run, they'll need as much cushioning and support as they can get.

Most competitive marathoners should choose their race-day shoes toward the light end of the spectrum. Most shoe companies make a lightweight trainer that works well in the marathon—these are minimalist enough so that you can feel light on your feet but are built up enough in the heel and midsole to provide some protection, especially as you fatigue late in the race.

Most elites, of course, race the marathon in flats. Bear in mind that these runners are usually whippet thin and have excellent biomechanics. Flats have less support and less heel lift than training shoes. The lack of support increases the risk of injury and can make muscles fatigue that have to work harder because of the decreased support. In addition, the lower heel lift puts more strain on Achilles tendons and calf muscles. Following are some rough guidelines about the most likely candidates to wear flats in the marathon.

Top candidates for wearing flats in the marathon

Male	Female
Faster than 2:40	Faster than 2:55
Weighs less than 160	Weighs less than 140
History of being relatively injury-free	History of being relatively injury-free
Good biomechanics	Good biomechanics

Regardless of which shoes you choose for race day, be sure to test them on tempo runs and at least one of your marathon-pace training runs.

The First Half

You're finally at the starting line, warmed up, and ready for the task ahead. It's all too easy to get carried away and run the first mile too fast. A better approach is to run the first mile at, or a bit slower than, your goal pace. Because you won't have done much of a warm-up before the start, your body won't be prepared to go faster than race pace. Also, if you run too fast at the beginning of the race, your body will burn off extra glycogen and accumulate lactate that could negatively affect the rest of your race.

Once the first mile is out of the way, the best strategy during the next few miles is to settle into a good rhythm. Try to run fast but relaxed. Establishing a relaxed running style early in the race will go a long way toward helping you avoid tightening up so that you can maintain your goal pace to the finish. Think about the elements of relaxed running that were discussed in chapter 6. Go through a mental checklist periodically to make sure your shoulders are relaxed, your body is upright, and so on, to help you maintain good running style throughout the race.

Take a carbohydrate drink at the first aid station. It's important to drink right from the start rather than waiting until you feel that you need carbohydrate or fluid. Your thirst mechanism isn't particularly closely matched to your hydration level, so waiting to drink until you feel thirsty is a mistake. Similarly, if you wait until you feel tired and light-headed to take in carbohydrate, it will be too little too late. The longer you can postpone dehydration and carbohydrate depletion, the longer you will be able to maintain your goal pace. Taking in carbs and fluid early will help postpone or prevent serious dehydration or carbohydrate depletion later. As we discussed in chapter 3, a few seconds lost at each aid station can translate into several minutes gained toward the end of the marathon.

Mentally, the first half of the marathon is the time to cruise. Try to save your mental and emotional energy for the second half of the race. All other factors being equal, if there is a group of runners in the lead pack at halfway, the winner will be the one who has cruised along at the back of the pack saving his or her energy for the demands of the second half of the race. Regardless of your ultimate finishing place in the marathon, you should realize that the second half is much harder than the first half; just try to get the first half out of the way at the correct pace without using any more mental energy than necessary.

//// When Not to Finish

Most of the time, you should finish the marathon even if you're not running as well as you had hoped. The marathon is a test of endurance. If you casually drop out of a marathon once, it will be all too easy to drop out again. Of course, in certain situations, struggling to finish a marathon may compromise your health or your future marathon success. Here are some legitimate reasons to drop out of a marathon:

- If you're limping, then your running mechanics are thrown off. You'll merely aggravate your injury by continuing.
- If you have a specific pain, and that pain is increasing progressively during the race, then you're doing yourself harm and should stop.
- If you're light-headed and unable to concentrate, you should stop.
- If you're overcome by muscle cramps, a torn muscle, heat exhaustion, or the like, then stop.

On to 20 Miles

From the halfway mark to 20 miles is the no-man's-land of the marathon. You're already fairly tired and still have a long way to go. This is where the mental discipline of training will help you to maintain a strong effort and a positive attitude. It's easy to let your pace slip 5 seconds per mile, and then 10 seconds per mile or more, during this stretch. By using all of the available feedback on your pace—whether in the form of kilometer or mile splits— you'll know exactly how you're progressing, and you should be able to concentrate and maintain your goal pace during these miles.

Slowing during this portion of the marathon is often more a matter of not concentrating than of not being able to physically maintain the pace. Focusing on your splits gives you an immediate goal to concentrate on. The ability to do a bit of adding in your head while running is a helpful skill. If you're supposed to be running 5:40 per mile, and there are markers every mile during the marathon, then just add 6:00 to your previous mile split and subtract 20 seconds to calculate what your next split should be. If you're 5 seconds too slow, don't try to make up the lost 5 seconds during the next mile; add 5:40 again as your target to get yourself back on track. By focusing on these incremental goals along the way, you'll prevent a large drift in your pace and should be able to stay very close to your goal.

Focus on your splits.

It's not unusual to have a few miles when you just don't feel good. These bad patches are a test of mental resolve. Often these stretches will last a while and then mysteriously go away. For example, you might feel tight and uncomfortable from miles 15 to 17 but then get back in the groove again and feel good to the finish. The key is to have the confidence that you'll eventually overcome this bad patch.

Pete learned this lesson during the 1983 San Francisco Marathon. After working quite hard from 13 to 16 miles, he had a stretch of about 3 miles when his breathing felt out of sync, and he struggled to stay with the other two leaders. Pete kept telling himself to relax and that the other guys might be hurting, too. Fortunately, he settled back into a comfortable rhythm by 18 miles, felt strong enough to drop the other two runners by the 20-mile mark, and cruised home to victory. If Pete had let himself think negatively during the bad patch and let the other two runners get away, he wouldn't have won that race.

Taking in carbohydrate as often as possible during the second half of the race can help you maintain your mental focus. The only fuel for your brain is glucose (carbohydrate), and when you become carbohydrate depleted, the amount of glucose reaching the brain starts to decrease. If you've carbohydrate loaded, this shouldn't start to affect you until well past the 20-mile mark. Taking in carbohydrate between miles 13 and 20, however, will help ensure that you stay alert and think clearly throughout the race.

///// **Dropping Out**

In my marathon career, I started 18 marathons and finished 16, including 8 victories. Of the two dropouts, one was because of injury, and the other was because of stupidity. Both occurred in 1986.

The dropout because of stupidity was the Boston Marathon. This was the first professional Boston Marathon, with lots of media excitement and financial incentives. I ignored my usual race plan of running even splits and got carried away early. During the first 10 miles, Greg Meyer and I exchanged the lead several times. Whenever Greg would take the lead, I would try to take it back.

This was overly aggressive racing for so early in the marathon. Meanwhile, Rob DeCastella, who won that day, sat in behind us, probably laughing to himself at the lack of patience of the two Americans. By 12 miles, my breathing wasn't in its usual rhythm, my legs were already pretty beat up, and my intestines were becoming increasingly uncomfortable. During the next mile, I fell off the lead bunch and started to tighten up. Knowing that I had gone too hard too early, I stopped just past the halfway mark and quietly cursed myself. It was a lesson well learned and a mistake I never made again. It also doesn't fall under the list of legitimate reasons to drop out of a marathon.

The only positive aspect of dropping out so early was that I recovered fully in about a week. A few weeks later, I used my fitness and frustration to set a personal best of 28:41 for 10,000 meters on the track, and that summer, I placed sixth in the event at the national championships. In July, I redeemed myself over 26.2 miles by winning the San Francisco Marathon in 2:13:29.

My other dropout was in the 1986 Twin Cities Marathon, which was also the trial race for the next year's World Championships. I went into the race with a tight hamstring from stretching too hard after a track workout several weeks earlier. It felt okay early in the race but gradually tightened up in the drizzly 40-degree weather. At 20 miles, I was at the back of the lead pack when the hamstring tightened completely. I couldn't run another step. After walking for about a mile, I gratefully accepted a ride to the finish. That dropout was easier mentally because the decision was out of my hands.

Having had a frustrating year in the marathon, I was determined to get a decent one under my belt as quickly as possible. My physical therapist said that the hamstring wasn't too badly damaged and that I should run easily for about 10 days. With regular massage, it loosened up, and I decided to run the New York City Marathon, which was 3 weeks after Twin Cities. I ran conservatively and gradually moved from 30th place at halfway to finish 9th in 2:14:09. It had been a year of lessons learned.

Pete Pfitzinger

The Final 6 Miles and 385 Yards

Having made it to 20 miles, you're at the most rewarding stage of the marathon. This is the part that you have prepared for during your long months of training. This is when your long runs, during which you worked hard over the last stages, will really pay off. Until now, everything required the patience to hold back. Now, you're free to see what you've got. During these final 6 miles and 385 yards, you get to dig deep and use up any energy that you have left. This is what the marathon is all about. It's the stretch that poorly prepared marathoners fear and well-prepared marathoners relish.

The key from 20 miles to the finish is to push as hard as you can without having disaster strike in the form of a cramp or very tight muscles. You will have prepared yourself for this during your long runs, your marathon-pace runs, and, to a lesser extent, your tempo runs. You need to use your body's feedback to determine just how hard you can push. Chances are that, by now, your calf muscles, hamstrings, quads, or some combination of these are on edge and will limit how fast you can go. You need to test the waters a bit and push to what you perceive to be the limit that your muscles will tolerate. This is a progressive meting-out process, in which you can take progressively greater risks as the finish line nears.

If you've been taking in fluid and carbohydrate throughout the race, your muscles should be in pretty good condition. Keep drinking until 25 miles. Keeping up your blood sugar level will keep you alert so that you can

As you approach the finish line, give a little more effort and finish strong.

concentrate well to the end. When you see the finish line approaching, give a little more effort so that you run strongly over the line. Show yourself that you have mastered the marathon and are able to kick it in a bit to the finish. Then enjoy the fruits of your labor.

In these first several chapters, we've looked at preparing for and running the marathon from all the necessary angles. Now it is time to put theory into practice. The rest of this book contains training schedules that implement the physiological principles of marathoning. The knowledge gained from this first section of the book, combined with the marathon-specific fitness that following the schedules will bring you, should leave you well prepared for marathon success.

PART
II

Training
Programs

One Marathon on up to 55 Miles per Week

This chapter is for mid-mileage marathoners who typically train less than 40 miles per week but who are willing to up their mileage to 55 miles per week during marathon preparation. It includes three schedules: a 24-week schedule that starts at 30 miles per week, an 18-week schedule that starts at 33 miles per week, and a 12-week schedule that starts at 35 miles per week. Each of these schedules increases weekly mileage progressively to a peak of 55 miles.

As discussed in chapter 2, it's useful to divide your overall training schedule into phases, called mesocycles. The training schedules consist of four mesocycles, which focus on endurance, lactate threshold and endurance, race preparation, and tapering, respectively. A final schedule, which contains a 5-week postmarathon recovery program, can follow any of the other schedules.

Of the three training schedules presented in this chapter, we recommend the 18-week schedule for most situations. Eighteen weeks are plenty of time to stimulate the necessary adaptations to improve your marathon performance. At the same time, 18 weeks are short enough that you can focus your efforts without becoming bored with the process.

> *The 18-week schedule is recommended for most situations.*

At times, however, you simply don't have 18 weeks to prepare for your marathon. The 12-week schedule includes the same mesocycles as the 18- and 24-week schedules, but because of the short time for preparation, each of these mesocycles is abbreviated. If you go into a marathon in a rush, you must realize that your preparation won't be as thorough as if you had longer to prepare. The 12-week schedule takes into account that sometimes circumstances don't allow you the optimal length of time for preparation and strives to provide a compact yet effective training program.

Although the 24-week training schedule provides even more preparation time than the 18-week schedule, it's ideal only in special situations—usually, when you're preparing for a marathon that's so important to you that you have little doubt that you'll be able to stay focused for such a long time. Trying to qualify for the Boston Marathon for the first time would be a situation that might call for the 24-week schedule. Of course, it's not our place to tell you which marathons should matter most in your life; any number of situations may be especially important for you, and that's when the 24-week schedule is optimal.

Before Starting the Schedules

These schedules are challenging right from the start and get harder as your marathon approaches. So that you can progress as the training increases in quantity and quality, and to minimize your chances of injury, you should be able to complete the first week of the schedule without too much effort.

Be realistic in assessing whether you're ready for the first week of the schedule. For example, if you've been running 20 miles per week and your longest run in the last several weeks is 6 miles, now isn't the time to suddenly

1996 Boston Marathon. The 24-week schedule is ideal if you are preparing for a race of personal importance, such as Boston.

jump to a 33-mile week containing a 12-mile run, as the first week of the 18-week schedule calls for. The idea behind the schedules isn't to make you as tired as possible as soon as possible but to apply repeated training stresses that you absorb and benefit from.

As a rule, you should be running at least 25 miles a week before starting these schedules, and in the last month you should have comfortably completed a run close in length to the long run called for in the first week of the schedule.

Reading the Schedules

The schedules are presented in a day-by-day format. This is in response to requests from readers of our first book, *Road Racing for Serious Runners*, to provide schedules that specify what to do each day of the week.

The main limitation with this approach is that it's impossible to guess the myriad of outside factors that may influence your day-to-day nonrunning life. Work schedules, family life, relationships, school commitments, and Mother Nature all have their parts in determining when you get to do your long runs and other aspects of marathon preparation. You'll no doubt require some flexibility in your training and will need to juggle days around from time to time. That's expected, and as long as you don't try to make up for lost time by doing several hard days in a row, you should be able to avoid injury and overtraining. By following the principles covered in the earlier chapters, you'll be able to safely fine-tune the training schedules to suit your circumstances.

Following the Schedules

Each column of the schedules represents a week's training. For example, in the 12-week schedule, the column for 11 weeks to goal indicates that at the end of that week you have 11 weeks until your marathon. The schedules continue week by week until race week.

We have included the specific workout for each day as well as the category of training for that day. For example, in the 18-week schedule, on the Friday of the 7-weeks-to-goal column, the specific workout is a 12-mile run and the category of training for that day is medium-long run. This aspect of the schedules allows you to quickly see the balance of training during each week and the progression of workouts from week to week. Look again at the 18-week schedule—it's easy to see that with 7 weeks to go until the marathon, there are 4 recovery days, along with a lactate threshold session, a long run, and a medium-long run.

Looking at the row for Sunday, it's easy to see how the long runs progress and then taper in the last few weeks before the marathon.

The workouts are divided into the following eight categories: long runs, medium-long runs, general aerobic, lactate threshold, $\dot{V}O_2max$, speed, recovery, and marathon-specific runs. Each of these categories is explained briefly. The various types of training are explained in depth in chapter 2.

Long Runs

A long run is any run of 17 miles or longer. The intention of long runs is (obviously) to improve your endurance in preparation for the marathon's 26.2 miles. The specific physiological benefits of long runs are discussed in detail in chapter 2. To gain the most from your long runs, do them at the correct intensity. Long runs shouldn't be slow jogs during which you just accumulate time on your feet. The most beneficial intensity range for your long runs is 10 to 20 percent slower than your goal marathon race pace. The reason for this intensity range is explained in chapter 2.

Medium-Long Runs

A medium-long run is any run of 11 to 16 miles. Medium-long runs reinforce the physiological benefits of your long runs. To gain the greatest physiological benefits, the pace for these runs should be similar to the pace for long runs.

General Aerobic Runs

General aerobic runs include any run of 10 miles or less that's done at a steady pace. Faster runs of this length fall into the lactate threshold category, whereas slower runs are specifically for recovery. In other words, these are your standard, moderate-effort, putting-in-the-miles runs. The intention of your general aerobic runs is to enhance your overall aerobic conditioning through boosting your training volume; these runs improve your marathon readiness because many of the beneficial adaptations that improve endurance are related to the total volume of your training.

Lactate Threshold

Lactate threshold runs are tempo runs in which you run for at least 20 minutes at your lactate threshold pace. This coincides closely with your current 15K race pace. Tempo runs provide a strong stimulus to improve your lactate threshold pace, which leads to similar improvements in your marathon race pace. The lactate threshold sessions are done after a 2- to 3-mile warm-up. The tempo runs in this chapter are from 4 to 7 miles long. Slower runners should run closer to their 15K race pace on tempo runs, whereas faster runners should run closer to their half marathon race pace during these workouts.

Naoko Takahashi

**Fastest Marathon: 2:21:47
Marathon Career Highlights: 2000
Olympic marathon champion.
Japanese record holder.**

Victah Sailer © Photo Run 2000

Naoko Takahashi is an exemplar of the Japanese marathoning tradition, both in her devotion to the distance and in her preparation for it.

Born in 1972, Takahashi began running in junior high school. She competed throughout high school and college, and although she was above average with a 9:13 3,000-meter time in college, she was hardly seen to be a future Olympic champion. After college, she joined one of the corporate running teams that are the backbone of Japan's development system. She remained a solid but unspectacular runner until 1996, when her 10,000-meter best improved to 31:48, nearly 3 minutes faster than what her PR had been a year earlier.

Takahashi made her marathon debut in 1997. (That she won the Olympics 3 years later is further proof that Olympic marathon champions are usually relatively new to the distance.) Because of not having gone farther than 30 kilometers in training, she slowed significantly over the final miles and finished in 2:31:32. Although she was eager to run another marathon soon, her coach, Yoshio Koide, wanted her to get more endurance training in while also honing her shorter distance potential. As a result, she ran the 5,000-meter race at the 1997 world championships, placing 13th, and didn't run her second marathon until the spring of 1998.

That race, the Nagoya Ladies Marathon, was held close to her hometown, and Takahashi responded to the presence of supporters on the course and a solid year of training by winning in 2:25:48, then a national record. The race was Takahashi's first display of her ability to run quickly late in the marathon—after passing 30 kilometers at an average of just under 35:30 per 10K, she ran the next 10K in just under 32:30. Later that year, Takahashi won the Asian Games Marathon in 2:21:47, despite the hot, humid conditions of Bangkok. In that race, she started out fast and ran alone to the finish.

Takahashi's capacity for surging late in the marathon or holding on after a searing early pace comes from her training. Like many leading Japanese runners

(continued)

Naoko Takahashi *(continued)*

(and American David Morris, who ran 2:09 after training in Japan), she builds her training around high mileage of 130 miles per week or more, and long, high-quality tempo runs. Takahashi also runs 10K and 20K time trials to assess her fitness before marathons. In 1999, she covered a 14-mile course 5 minutes faster than her compatriot, Hiromi Suzuki, had before winning the 1997 world championships. Takahashi also trains extensively at altitude, sometimes residing in Albuquerque, New Mexico, or Boulder, Colorado. Before winning in Sydney, she did two 40-kilometer runs above 10,000 feet of altitude.

Her coach, Koide, says, "Takahashi's strongest points are that she really loves running, and she is very easy to coach because she follows my direction very well. When I first saw her run, I sensed that her best event would be the marathon."

Another element of her success might be her ability to temporarily drop the routine of hard training after a marathon. While recovering, she is reported to put on as much as 15 pounds, and she sometimes eats 40 pieces of sushi or 4 pounds of steak at all-you-can-eat restaurants. These are admittedly extremes and probably shouldn't be emulated, but Takahashi illustrates how even the best marathoners in the world recognize the need for a physical and mental break after a peak effort.

$\dot{V}O_2$max

$\dot{V}O_2$max runs are intervals of 600 meters to 2,000 meters duration, which are run at 95 to 100 percent of your current $\dot{V}O_2$max pace. This coincides closely with your current 3K to 5K race pace. These sessions provide a strong stimulus to improve your $\dot{V}O_2$max.

Careful readers will notice that none of the $\dot{V}O_2$max sessions calls for repeats longer than 1,600 meters. As we noted in chapter 2, the optimal duration for $\dot{V}O_2$max intervals is 2 minutes to 6 minutes; only elite runners will cover 2,000 meters in a 6-minute interval. The longer your repeats are in these workouts, the more days you'll need after the workout for recovery. Though $\dot{V}O_2$max work is an important part of your marathon preparation, it's not as crucial in the marathon as it is in races such as 5K and 10K. The $\dot{V}O_2$max sessions in these schedules, then, feature repeats that strike a balance between being long enough to provide a powerful training stimulus and short enough to leave you fresh for your other important workouts of the week.

The same reasoning applies for the prescribed pace in these $\dot{V}O_2$max workouts: whereas runners focusing on shorter races need to do some of their intervals closer to 3K race pace, marathoners gain maximum benefit from sticking to 5K race pace.

Speed

Speed runs are repetitions of 50 to 150 meters that improve leg speed and running form. These sessions are done after a thorough warm-up and often toward the end of a general aerobic run or a recovery run. Allow yourself plenty of rest between repetitions so that you can run each one with good technique.

Recovery

Recovery runs are relatively short runs done at a relaxed pace to enhance recovery for your next hard workout. These runs aren't necessarily jogs, but they should be noticeably slower than your other workouts of the week.

Marathon-Pace Runs

Marathon-pace runs are medium-long or long runs during which you run most of the miles at your goal marathon pace. These runs provide the precise physiological benefit of allowing you to practice the pace, form, and so on of race day. They're also a great confidence booster. Start these runs comfortably, as you would other medium-long or long runs, and then run the last portion at marathon race pace. For example, if the schedule calls for 16 miles with 12 miles at marathon race pace, gradually pick up the pace during the first 4 miles, and then run the last 12 miles at marathon goal pace.

A Word About "Hard" Days

Looking at these schedules, you might be wondering, "Where are all the 'speed' workouts?" After all, it's normal to think that anyone preparing for a marathon should be training as hard as possible, and what better way to be sure that you're doing so than by hitting the track at least once a week for lung-searing intervals, right?

In chapter 2, we explained at length the principles underlying these schedules. Briefly put, we designed the schedules to provide the optimal stimuli to the physiological systems that most determine marathoning success—endurance, lactate threshold, and $\dot{V}O_2$max, in that order of importance. In the long run, so to speak, it's your long runs and tempo runs that have the most relevance to your performance on marathon day, not how often you've churned out a sterling set of half mile repeats.

During your long buildup, understanding the components of marathon success can provide confidence that you're training properly. Use the explanation of marathon physiology from chapter 2 not only to explain to your training buddies why you won't be joining them for quarters next week but also to remind yourself why you're doing yet another 12-miler in the middle of the workweek. If your running friends continue to chide you that you're not training hard enough, invite them to follow the schedules along with you for a few weeks, then report back. We suspect they'll have gotten the message by then.

Racing Strategies

In chapter 7, we discussed at length race strategies appropriate for all marathoners. If you follow one of the schedules in this chapter, you're probably a midpack runner. Unlike the situation the runners at the front of the field often face, you'll probably have plenty of people around you to run with from start to finish. This can be good and bad.

On the plus side, obviously, is that you're less likely to face lonely stretches of nobody to run with. Use this probability to your advantage—soon after the start, try to find other runners who look capable of maintaining your goal pace through at least 20 miles and encourage them to work with you. (If they fall apart at 21 miles, that's their problem, right?)

By following one of this chapter's schedules, you'll be better able to hold up past 20 miles than most of the runners at your pace in the first part of the race. Your superior preparation will mean that you'll have the pleasure of continually passing people until the finish. Look forward to this time. Pick a runner a few hundred yards up the road, and set the short-term goal of catching him or her. Then go after your next victim, and keep doing so until the finish.

On the not-so-good side, you're more likely than those at the front of the field to feel crowded in the early miles. Try not to let this upset you. Tell yourself that the crowds are helping you not to go out too fast, and if need be, work up gradually to your goal pace.

Don't try to make up lost time suddenly if a break in the crowd appears. Instead, when you have clear running room, run no more than 10 seconds per mile faster than goal pace until you're back on schedule because you will burn less glycogen and be less likely to accumulate lactate. If the deficit you have to make up isn't too great, 5 seconds per mile faster than goal pace is even better because you'll burn less glycogen and accumulate less lactate. Once you're back on track, ease off to goal pace.

After the Marathon

The final schedule in this chapter is a 5-week recovery schedule for after the marathon. This is the fifth mesocycle; it completes the training program and leaves you ready to prepare for future challenges.

The recovery schedule is purposely conservative. You have little to gain by rushing back into training, and your risk of injury is exceptionally high at this point, owing to the reduced resiliency of your muscles and connective tissue after the marathon.

The schedule starts with 2 days off from running, which is the bare minimum of time away from running you should allow yourself. If you still have acute soreness or tightness so severe that it will alter your form, or if you just don't feel like running, certainly feel free to take more than 2 days off. If ever there was a time to lose your marathoner's mind-set, the week after your goal race is it. Even most of the top runners in the world take days off after a marathon. They know that the nearly negligible benefits of a short run at this time are far outweighed by the risks. Not running now also will increase your chances of being inspired to resume hard training when your body allows it.

To aid your recovery, try some light cross-training, such as swimming or cycling. These activities increase blood flow through your muscles without subjecting them to pounding. Walking will also achieve this in the week after the marathon.

One way to ensure that you don't run too hard too soon after your marathon is to use a heart rate monitor. As discussed in chapter 4, a heart rate monitor can help prevent you from going too fast on recovery days. During the first few weeks after the marathon, keep your heart rate below 75 percent of your maximal heart rate or 70 percent of your heart rate reserve. Running at this intensity will help your body overcome the stress of the marathon as quickly as possible.

During this 5-week recovery schedule, the number of days of running per week increases from 3 to 5. At the end of the 5 weeks, you should be fully recovered from the marathon and, with a little luck, injury-free and mentally fresh.

Mesocycle 1 Endurance

	Weeks to goal				
	23	**22**	**21**	**20**	**Recovery week 19**
Monday	Rest or cross-training	Rest or cross-training	Rest or cross-training	Rest or cross-training	Rest or cross-training
Tuesday	General aerobic + speed 7 mi w/ 10 × 100 m strides	General aerobic + speed 8 mi w/ 10 × 100 m strides	Lactate threshold 8 mi w/ 4 mi @ 15K to half marathon race pace	General aerobic + speed 8 mi w/ 10 × 100 m strides	General aerobic + speed 7 mi w/ 10 × 100 m strides
Wednesday	Rest or cross-training	Rest or cross-training	Recovery 4 mi	Recovery 5 mi	Rest or cross-training
Thursday	General aerobic 8 mi	General aerobic 9 mi	General aerobic 8 mi	General aerobic 9 mi	General aerobic 9 mi
Friday	Rest or cross-training	Rest or cross-training	Rest or cross-training	Rest or cross-training	Rest or cross-training
Saturday	Recovery 4 mi	Recovery 4 mi	Recovery 4 mi	Recovery 4 mi	Recovery 5 mi
Sunday	Medium-long run 11 mi	Medium-long run 12 mi	Medium-long run 13 mi	Medium-long run 14 mi	Medium-long run 11 mi
Weekly mileage	30	33	37	40	32

	Weeks to goal				
	18	**17**	**16**	**15**	**Recovery week 14**
Monday	Rest or cross-training	Rest or cross-training	Rest or cross-training	Rest or cross-training	Rest or cross-training
Tuesday	Lactate threshold 9 mi w/ 4 mi @ 15K to half marathon race pace	General aerobic + speed 9 mi w/ 10 × 100 m strides	General aerobic + speed 9 mi w/ 10 × 100 m strides	Lactate threshold 10 mi w/ 5 mi @ 15K to half marathon race pace	General aerobic + speed 8 mi w/ 10 × 100 m strides
Wednesday	Recovery 5 mi	Recovery 5 mi	Recovery 5 mi	Recovery 5 mi	Recovery 5 mi
Thursday	General aerobic 9 mi	General aerobic 9 mi	General aerobic 10 mi	General aerobic 10 mi	General aerobic 8 mi
Friday	Rest or cross-training	Rest or cross-training	Rest or cross-training	Rest or cross-training	Rest or cross-training
Saturday	Recovery 4 mi	Recovery 5 mi	Recovery 5 mi	Recovery 5 mi	Recovery 5 mi
Sunday	Medium-long run 15 mi	Medium-long run 16 mi	Long run 17 mi	Long run 18 mi	Medium-long run 13 mi
Weekly mileage	42	44	46	48	39

Mesocycle 2 Lactate Threshold + Endurance

	Weeks to goal		
	13	12	11
Monday	Rest or cross-training	Rest or cross-training	Rest or cross-training
Tuesday	Lactate threshold 10 mi w/ 5 mi @ 15K to half marathon race pace	Recovery 6 mi	Recovery + speed 6 mi w/ 6 × 100 m strides
Wednesday	Recovery 5 mi	$\dot{V}O_2$max 9 mi w/ 6 × 800 m @ 5K race pace; jog 2 min between	Lactate threshold 11 mi w/ 6 mi @ 15K to half marathon race pace
Thursday	Medium-long run 11 mi	Medium-long run 12 mi	Rest or cross-training
Friday	Rest or cross-training	Rest or cross-training	Medium-long run 13 mi
Saturday	Recovery 5 mi	Recovery + speed 6 mi w/ 6 × 100 m strides	Recovery 5 mi
Sunday	Long run 17 mi	Long run 18 mi	Long run 20 mi
Weekly mileage	48	51	55

	Weeks to goal		
	10	Recovery week 9	8
Monday	Rest or cross-training	Rest or cross-training	Rest or cross-training
Tuesday	General aerobic + speed 9 mi w/ 10 × 100 m strides	Recovery 5 mi	Recovery + speed 6 mi w/ 6 × 100 m strides
Wednesday	Recovery 6 mi	$\dot{V}O_2$max 8 mi w/ 5 × 600 m @ 5K race pace; jog 90 sec between	Lactate threshold 12 mi w/ 7 mi @ 15K to half marathon race pace
Thursday	Medium-long run 13 mi	Rest or cross-training	Rest or cross-training
Friday	Rest or cross-training	Medium-long run 11 mi	Medium-long run 12 mi
Saturday	Recovery + speed 5 mi w/ 6 × 100 m strides	General aerobic + speed 7 mi w/ 8 × 100 m strides	Recovery 5 mi
Sunday	Marathon specific 16 mi w/ 12 mi @ marathon race pace	Medium-long run 13 mi	Long run 20 mi
Weekly mileage	49	44	55

Mesocycle 3 Race Preparation

	Weeks to goal				
	7	**6**	**5**	**4**	**3**
Monday	Rest or cross-training	Rest or cross-training	Rest or cross-training	Rest or cross-training	Rest or cross-training
Tuesday	$\dot{V}O_2$max 8 mi w/ 5 × 600 m @ 5K race pace; jog 90 sec between	General aerobic 8 mi	$\dot{V}O_2$max 8 mi w/ 5 × 600 m @ 5K race pace;	Recovery + speed 5 mi w/ 6 × 100 m strides jog 90 sec between	$\dot{V}O_2$max 8 mi w/ 5 × 600 m @ 5K race pace; jog 90 sec between
Wednesday	Medium-long run 11 mi	$\dot{V}O_2$max 9 mi w/ 5 × 1000 m @ 5K race pace; jog 2 min between	Medium-long run 11 mi	$\dot{V}O_2$max 10 mi w/ 4 × 1,200 m @ 5K race pace; jog 2 min between	General aerobic 8 mi
Thursday	Rest or cross-training	Rest or cross-training	Rest or cross-training	Rest or cross-training	Rest or cross-training
Friday	Recovery + speed 4 mi w/ 6 × 100 m	Medium-long run 11 mi	Recovery + speed 4 mi w/ 6 × 100 m strides	General aerobic 10 mi	Recovery + speed 4 mi w/ 6 × 100 m strides
Saturday	8-10K tune-up race	Recovery + speed 5 mi w/ 6 × 100 m strides	8-15K tune-up race	Recovery 5 mi	8-15K tune-up race
Sunday	Long run 17 mi	Marathon specific 17 mi w/ 14 mi @ marathon race pace	Medium-long run 15 mi	Long run 21 mi	Long run 17 mi
Weekly mileage	50	50	48	51	47

Mesocycle 4 Taper and Race

	Weeks to goal		
	2	**1**	**Race week**
Monday	Rest or cross-training	Rest or cross-training	Rest
Tuesday	General aerobic + speed 7 mi w/ 8 × 100 m strides	General aerobic + speed 7 mi w/ 8 × 100 m strides	Recovery 6 mi
Wednesday	General aerobic 8 mi	$\dot{V}O_2$max 8 mi w/ 3 × 1,600 m @ 5K race pace; jog 2 min between	Dress rehearsal 7 mi w/ 2 mi @ marathon race pace
Thursday	Rest or cross-training	Rest or cross-training	Rest
Friday	Recovery + speed 4 mi w/ 6 × 100 m strides	Recovery + speed 5 mi w/ 6 × 100 m strides	Recovery + speed 5 mi w/ 6 × 100 m strides
Saturday	Lactate threshold 8 mi w/ 4 mi @ 15K to half marathon race pace	Rest or cross-training	Recovery 4 mi
Sunday	Medium-long run 16 mi	Medium-long run 12 mi	Goal marathon
Weekly mileage	43	32	22 (6 days prerace)

Mesocycle 1 Endurance

	Weeks to goal		
	17	**16**	**15**
Monday	Rest or cross-training	Rest or cross-training	Rest or cross-training
Tuesday	General aerobic + speed 7 mi w/ 10 × 100 m strides	General aerobic + speed 8 mi w/ 10 × 100 m strides	Lactate threshold 8 mi w/ 4 mi @ 15K to half marathon race pace
Wednesday	Rest or cross-training	Rest or cross-training	Recovery 4 mi
Thursday	General aerobic 9 mi	General aerobic 10 mi	General aerobic 10 mi
Friday	Rest or cross-training	Rest or cross-training	Rest or cross-training
Saturday	Recovery 4 mi	Recovery 5 mi	Recovery 4 mi
Sunday	Medium-long run 12 mi	Medium-long run 13 mi	Medium-long run 14 mi
Weekly mileage	32	36	40

	Weeks to goal		
	14	**13**	**Recovery week 12**
Monday	Rest or cross-training	Rest or cross-training	Rest or cross-training
Tuesday	General aerobic + speed 8 mi w/ 10 × 100 m strides	Lactate threshold 9 mi w/ 4 mi @ 15K to half marathon race pace	General aerobic + speed 8 mi w/ 8 × 100 m strides
Wednesday	Recovery 5 mi	Recovery 5 mi	Recovery 5 mi
Thursday	General aerobic 10 mi	General aerobic 10 mi	General aerobic 8 mi
Friday	Rest or cross-training	Rest or cross-training	Rest or cross-training
Saturday	Recovery 4 mi	Recovery 5 mi	Recovery 4 mi
Sunday	Medium-long run 15 mi	Medium-long run 17 mi	Medium-long run 12 mi
Weekly mileage	42	46	37

Mesocycle 2 Lactate Threshold + Endurance

	Weeks to goal				
	11	**10**	**9**	**Recovery week** **8**	**7**
Monday	Rest or cross-training	Rest or cross-training	Rest or cross-training	Rest or cross-training	Rest or cross-training
Tuesday	Lactate threshold 10 mi w/ 5 mi @ 15K to half marathon race pace	Recovery + speed 6 mi w/ 6 × 100 m strides	Recovery 6 mi	General aerobic 8 mi	Recovery + speed 6 mi w/ 6 × 100 m strides
Wednesday	Recovery 4 mi	Medium-long run 12 mi	Medium-long run 14 mi	$\dot{V}O_2$max 8 mi w/ 5 x 600 m @ 5K race pace; jog 90 sec between	Lactate threshold 12 mi w/ 7 mi @ 15K to half marathon race pace
Thursday	Medium-long run 11 mi	Rest or cross-training	Recovery 6 mi	Recovery 5 mi	Rest or cross-training
Friday	Rest or cross-training	Lactate threshold 11 mi w/ 6 mi @ 15K to half marathon race pace	Rest or cross-training	Rest or cross-training	Medium-long run 12 mi
Saturday	General aerobic + speed 7 mi w/ 8 × 100 m strides	Recovery 5 mi	Recovery + speed 6 mi w/ 6 × 100 m strides	General aerobic + speed 8 mi w/ 8 × 100 m strides	Recovery 5 mi
Sunday	Long run 18 mi	Long run 20 mi	Marathon specific 15 mi w/ 12 mi @ marathon race pace	Medium-long run 14 mi	Long run 20 mi
Weekly mileage	50	54	47	43	55

Mesocycle 3 Race Preparation

	Weeks to goal			
	6	**5**	**4**	**3**
Monday	Rest or cross-training	Rest or cross-training	Rest or cross-training	Rest or cross-training
Tuesday	$\dot{V}O_2$max 8 mi w/ 5 × 600 m @ 5K race pace; jog 90 sec between	General aerobic 8 mi	$\dot{V}O_2$max 8 mi w/ 5 × 600 m @ 5K race pace; jog 90 sec between	Recovery + speed 5 mi w/ 6 × 100 m strides
Wednesday	Medium-long run 11 mi	$\dot{V}O_2$max 9 mi w/ 5 × 1,000 m @ 5K race pace; jog 2 min between	Medium-long run 11 mi	$\dot{V}O_2$max 10 mi w/ 4 × 1,200 m @ 5K race pace; jog 2 min between
Thursday	Rest or cross-training	Rest or cross-training	Rest or cross-training	Rest or cross-training
Friday	Recovery + speed 4 mi w/ 6 × 100 m strides	Medium-long run 12 mi	Recovery + speed 4 mi w/ 6 × 100 m strides	General aerobic 10 mi
Saturday	8-15K tune-up race	Recovery 5 mi	8-15K tune-up race	Recovery 4 mi
Sunday	Long run 17 mi	Marathon specific 17 mi w/ 14 mi @ marathon race pace	Long run 17 mi	Long run 20 mi
Weekly mileage	50	51	50	49

Mesocycle 4 Taper and Race

	Weeks to goal		
	2	**1**	**Race week**
Monday	Rest or cross-training	Rest or cross-training	Rest
Tuesday	$\dot{V}O_2max$ 8 mi w/ 5 × 600 m @ 5K race pace; jog 90 sec between	General aerobic + speed 7 mi w/ 8 × 100 m strides	Recovery 6 mi
Wednesday	Recovery 5 mi	$\dot{V}O_2max$ 8 mi w/ 3 × 1,600 m @ 5K race pace; jog 2 min between	Dress rehearsal 7 mi w/ 2 mi @ marathon race pace
Thursday	Rest or cross-training	Rest or cross-training	Rest
Friday	Recovery + speed 4 mi w/ 6 × 100 m strides	Recovery + speed 5 mi w/ 6 × 100 m strides	Recovery + speed 5 mi w/ 6 × 100 m strides
Saturday	8-10K tune-up race	Rest or cross-training	Recovery 4 mi
Sunday	Medium-long run 16 mi	Medium-long run 12 mi	Goal marathon
Weekly mileage	43	32	22 (6 days prerace)

Mesocycle 1 Endurance

	Weeks to goal			
	11	**10**	**9**	**8**
Monday	Rest or cross-training	Rest or cross-training	Rest or cross-training	Rest or cross-training
Tuesday	General aerobic + speed 8 mi w/ 10 × 100 m strides	Lactate threshold 8 mi w/ 4 mi @ 15K to half marathon race pace	General aerobic + speed 8 mi w/ 10 × 100 m strides	Lactate threshold 10 mi w/ 5 mi @ 15K to half marathon race pace
Wednesday	Rest or cross-training	Rest or cross-training	Recovery 4 mi	Recovery 4 mi
Thursday	General aerobic 9 mi	Medium-long run 11 mi	Medium-long run 11 mi	Medium-long run 11 mi
Friday	Rest or cross-training	Rest or cross-training	Rest or cross-training	Rest or cross-training
Saturday	Recovery 5 mi	Recovery 5 mi	Recovery 4 mi	Recovery 5 mi
Sunday	Medium-long run 13 mi	Medium-long run 15 mi	Medium-long run 16 mi	Long run 17 mi
Weekly mileage	35	39	43	47

Mesocycle 2 Lactate Threshold + Endurance

	Weeks to goal		
	7	**6**	**5**
Monday	Rest or cross-training	Rest or cross-training	Rest or cross-training
Tuesday	Recovery 5 mi	Recovery 5 mi	Recovery + speed 6 mi w/ 6 × 100 m strides
Wednesday	Medium-long run 12 mi	$\dot{V}O_2$max 10 mi w/ 5 × 1,000 m @ 5K race pace; jog 2 min between	Lactate threshold 12 mi w/ 7 mi @ 15K to half marathon race pace
Thursday	Rest or cross-training	Medium-long run 12 mi	Rest or cross-training
Friday	Lactate threshold 11 mi w/ 6 mi @ 15K to half marathon race pace	Rest or cross-training	Medium-long run 12 mi
Saturday	Recovery 5 mi	Recovery + speed 6 mi w/ 6 × 100 m strides	Recovery 5 mi
Sunday	Long run 18 mi	Marathon specific 15 mi with 12 mi @ marathon race pace	Long run 20 mi
Weekly mileage	51	48	55

Mesocycle 3 Race Preparation

	Weeks to goal		
	4	**3**	**2**
Monday	Rest or cross-training	Rest or cross-training	Rest or cross-training
Tuesday	$\dot{V}O_2$max 8 mi w/ 5 × 600 m @ 5K race pace; jog 90 sec between	Recovery + speed 5 mi w/ 6 × 100 m strides	$\dot{V}O_2$max 8 mi w/ 5 × 600 m @ 5K race pace; jog 90 sec between
Wednesday	Medium-long run 11 mi	$\dot{V}O_2$max 10 mi w/ 4 × 1,200 m @ 5K race pace; jog 2 min between	Recovery 5 mi
Thursday	Rest or cross-training	Rest or cross-training	Rest or cross-training
Friday	Recovery + speed 4 mi w/ 6 × 100 m strides	General aerobic 10 mi	Recovery + speed 4 mi w/ 6 × 100 m strides
Saturday	8-15K tune-up race	Recovery 4 mi	8-10K tune-up race
Sunday	Long run 17 mi	Long run 20 mi	Medium-long run 16 mi
Weekly mileage	50	49	43

Mesocycle 4 Taper and Race

	Weeks to goal	
	1	**Race week**
Monday	Rest or cross-training	Rest
Tuesday	General aerobic + speed 7 mi w/ 8 × 100 m strides	Recovery 6 mi
Wednesday	$\dot{V}O_2$max 8 mi w/ 3 × 1,600 m @ 5K race pace; jog 2 min between	Dress rehearsal 7 mi w/ 2 mi @ marathon race pace
Thursday	Rest or cross-training	Rest
Friday	Recovery + speed 5 mi w/ 6 × 100 m strides	Recovery + speed 5 mi w/ 6 × 100 m strides
Saturday	Rest or cross-training	Recovery 4 mi
Sunday	Medium-long run 12 mi	Goal marathon
Weekly mileage	32	22 (6 days prerace)

Mesocycle 5 Recovery

	Weeks postmarathon				
	1	**2**	**3**	**4**	**5**
Monday	Rest or cross-training	Rest or cross-training	Rest or cross-training	Rest or cross-training	Rest or cross-training
Tuesday	Rest or cross-training	Recovery 5 mi	Recovery 5 mi	General aerobic 7 mi	General aerobic 7 mi
Wednesday	Recovery 4 mi	Recovery 5 mi	Recovery 5 mi	Recovery 5 mi	Recovery 5 mi
Thursday	Rest or cross-training	Rest or cross-training	Rest or cross-training	Rest or cross-training	Rest or cross-training
Friday	Recovery 4 mi	Recovery 4 mi	General aerobic + speed 7 mi w/ 8 × 100 m strides	General aerobic + speed 8 mi w/ 8 × 100 m strides	General aerobic + speed 8 mi w/ 8 × 100 m strides
Saturday	Rest or cross-training	Rest or cross-training	Rest or cross-training	Rest or cross-training	Recovery 4 mi
Sunday	Recovery 5 mi	Recovery 7 mi	General aerobic 9 mi	General aerobic 10 mi	Medium-long run 11 mi
Weekly mileage	13	21	26	30	35

One Marathon on up to 70 Miles per Week

This chapter is for mid- to high-mileage marathoners who train 50 to 70 miles per week. It includes three schedules: a 24-week schedule that starts at 50 miles per week, an 18-week schedule that starts at 53 miles per week, and a 12-week schedule that starts at 55 miles per week. Each of these schedules increases weekly mileage progressively to a peak of 70 miles.

As discussed in chapter 2, it's useful to divide your overall training schedule into phases, called mesocycles. The training schedules consist of four mesocycles, which focus on endurance, lactate threshold and endurance, race preparation, and tapering, respectively. A final schedule, which contains a 5-week postmarathon recovery program, can follow any of the other schedules.

Of the three training schedules presented in this chapter, we recommend the 18-week schedule for most situations. Eighteen weeks are plenty of time to stimulate the necessary adaptations to improve your marathon performance. At the same time, 18 weeks are short enough that you can focus your efforts without becoming bored with the process.

At times, however, you simply don't have 18 weeks to prepare for your marathon. The 12-week schedule includes the same mesocycles as the 18- and 24-week schedules, but because of the short time for preparation, each of these mesocycles is abbreviated. If you go into a marathon in a rush, you must realize that your preparation won't be as thorough as if you had longer to prepare. The 12-week schedule takes into account that sometimes circumstances don't allow you the optimal length of time for preparation and strives to provide a compact yet effective training program.

The 12-week schedule provides a compact yet effective training program.

Although the 24-week training schedule provides even more preparation time than the 18-week schedule, it's ideal only in special situations—usually, when you're preparing for a marathon that's so important to you that you have little doubt that you'll be able to stay focused for such a long time. Trying to qualify for the Boston Marathon for the first time would be a situation that might call for the 24-week schedule. Of course, it's not our place to tell you which marathons should matter most in your life; any number of situations may be especially important for you, and that's when the 24-week schedule is optimal.

Before Starting the Schedules

These schedules are challenging right from the start and get harder as your marathon approaches. So that you can progress as the training increases in quantity and quality, and to minimize your chances of injury, you should be able to complete the first week of the schedule without too much effort.

Be realistic in assessing whether you're ready for the first week of the schedule. For example, if you've been running 30 miles per week and your longest run in the last several weeks is 8 miles, now isn't the time to suddenly jump to a 53-mile week containing a 15-mile run, as the first week of the 18-week schedule calls for. The idea behind the schedules isn't to make you as tired as possible as soon as possible but to apply repeated training stresses that you absorb and benefit from.

As a rule, you should be running at least 40 miles a week before starting these schedules, and in the last month you should have comfortably completed a run close in length to the long run called for in the first week of the schedule.

Reading the Schedules

The schedules are presented in a day-by-day format. This is in response to requests from readers of our first book, *Road Racing for Serious Runners*, to provide schedules that specify what to do each day of the week.

The main limitation with this approach is that it's impossible to guess the myriad of outside factors that may influence your day-to-day nonrunning life. Work schedules, family life, relationships, school commitments, and Mother Nature all have their parts in determining when you get to do your long runs and other aspects of marathon preparation. You'll no doubt require some flexibility in your training and will need to juggle days around from time to time. That's expected, and as long as you don't try to make up for lost time by doing several hard days in a row, you should be able to avoid injury and overtraining. By following the principles covered in the earlier chapters, you'll be able to safely fine-tune the training schedules to suit your circumstances.

Following the Schedules

Each column of the schedules represents a week's training. For example, in the 12-week schedule, the column for 11 weeks to goal indicates that at the end of that week you have 11 weeks until your marathon. The schedules continue week by week until race week.

We have included the specific workout for each day as well as the category of training for that day. For example, in the 18-week schedule, on the Tuesday of the 7-weeks-to-go column, the specific workouts are a 6-mile run and a 4-mile run and the category of training for that day is recovery. This aspect of the schedules allows you to quickly see the balance of training during each week

Mother Nature may dictate when you can do your hard runs.

and the progression of workouts from week to week. Look again at the 18-week schedule—it's easy to see that with 7 weeks to go until the marathon, there are 4 recovery days that week, along with a lactate threshold session, a long run, and a medium-long run.

Looking at the row for Sunday, it's easy to see how the long runs progress and then taper in the last few weeks before the marathon.

The workouts are divided into the following eight categories: long runs, medium-long runs, general aerobic, lactate threshold, $\dot{V}O_2max$, speed, recovery, and marathon-specific runs. Each of these categories is explained briefly. The various types of training are explained in depth in chapter 2.

Long Runs

A long run is any run of 17 miles or longer. The intention of long runs is (obviously) to improve your endurance in preparation for the marathon's

26.2 miles. The specific physiological benefits of long runs are discussed in detail in chapter 2. To gain the most from your long runs, do them at the correct intensity. Long runs shouldn't be slow jogs during which you just accumulate time on your feet. The most beneficial intensity range for your long runs is 10 to 20 percent slower than your goal marathon race pace. The reason for this intensity range is explained in chapter 2.

Medium-Long Runs

A medium-long run is any run of 11 to 16 miles. Medium-long runs reinforce the physiological benefits of your long runs. To gain the greatest physiological benefits, the pace for these runs should be similar to the pace for long runs.

General Aerobic Runs

General aerobic runs include any run of 10 miles or less that's done at a steady pace. Faster runs of this length fall into the lactate threshold category, whereas slower runs are specifically for recovery. In other words, these are your standard, moderate-effort, putting-in-the-miles runs. The intention of your general aerobic runs is to enhance your overall aerobic conditioning through boosting your training volume; these runs improve your marathon readiness because many of the beneficial adaptations that improve endurance are related to the total volume of your training.

Lactate Threshold

Lactate threshold runs are tempo runs in which you run for at least 20 minutes at your lactate threshold pace. This coincides closely with your current 15K to half marathon race pace. Tempo runs provide a strong stimulus to improve your lactate threshold pace, which leads to similar improvements in your marathon race pace. The lactate threshold sessions are done after a 2- to 3-mile warm-up. The tempo runs in this chapter are from 4 to 7 miles long. Slower runners should run closer to their 15K race pace on tempo runs, whereas faster runners should run closer to their half marathon race pace during these workouts.

$\dot{V}O_2$max

$\dot{V}O_2$max runs are intervals of 600 meters to 2,000 meters duration, which are run at 95 to 100 percent of your current $\dot{V}O_2$max pace. This coincides closely with your current 3K to 5K race pace. These sessions provide a strong stimulus to improve your $\dot{V}O_2$max.

Careful readers will notice that none of the $\dot{V}O_2$max sessions calls for repeats longer than 1,600 meters. As we noted in chapter 2, the optimal duration for $\dot{V}O_2$max intervals is 2 to 6 minutes; only elite runners will cover

2,000 meters in a 6-minute interval. The longer your repeats are in these workouts, the more days you'll need after the workout for recovery. Though $\dot{V}O_2$max work is an important part of your marathon preparation, it's not as crucial in the marathon as it is in races such as 5K and 10K. The $\dot{V}O_2$max sessions in these schedules, then, feature repeats that strike a balance between being long enough to provide a powerful training stimulus and short enough to leave you fresh for your other important workouts of the week.

The same reasoning applies for the prescribed pace in these $\dot{V}O_2$max workouts: whereas runners focusing on shorter races need to do some of their intervals closer to 3K race pace, marathoners gain maximum benefit from sticking to 5K race pace.

Speed

Speed runs are repetitions of 50 to 150 meters that improve leg speed and running form. These sessions are done after a thorough warm-up and often toward the end of a general aerobic run or a recovery run. Allow yourself plenty of rest between repetitions so that you can run each one with good technique.

Recovery

Recovery runs are relatively short runs done at a relaxed pace to enhance recovery for your next hard workout. These runs aren't necessarily jogs, but they should be noticeably slower than your other workouts of the week.

Marathon-Pace Runs

Marathon-pace runs are medium-long or long runs during which you run most of the miles at your goal marathon pace. These runs provide the precise physiological benefit of allowing you to practice the pace, form, and so on of race day. They're also a great confidence booster. Start these runs comfortably, as you would other medium-long or long runs, and then run the last portion at marathon race pace. For example, if the schedule calls for 16 miles with 12 miles at marathon race pace, gradually pick up the pace during the first 4 miles, and then run the last 12 miles at marathon goal pace.

Doing Doubles

As discussed in chapter 5, sometimes marathoners benefit from running twice a day. This is obviously the case for elites cranking out 130-mile weeks, but it isn't necessary on a regular basis if you're running 50 to 70 miles per week. In these schedules, doubles are called for only on the occasional recovery day, with a total of 10 miles for the day. On these days, your recovery will be enhanced by doing a 6-miler and a 4-miler rather than putting in one 10-mile run. Instead of making you more tired, splitting your mileage like this on easy days will speed your recovery because each run will increase blood flow to your muscles yet take so little out of you.

A Word About "Hard" Days

Looking at these schedules, you might be wondering, "Where are all the 'speed' workouts?" After all, it's normal to think that anyone preparing for a marathon should be training as hard as possible, and what better way to be sure that you're doing so than by hitting the track at least once a week for lung-searing intervals, right?

In chapter 2, we explained at length the principles underlying these schedules. Briefly put, we designed the schedules to provide the optimal stimuli to the physiological systems that most determine marathoning success—endurance, lactate threshold and $\dot{V}O_2max$, in that order of importance. In the long run, so to speak, it's your long runs and tempo runs that have the most relevance to your performance on marathon day, not how often you've churned out a sterling set of half mile repeats.

During your long buildup, understanding the components of marathon success can provide confidence that you're training properly. Use the explanation of marathon physiology from chapter 2 not only to explain to your training buddies why you won't be joining them for quarters next week but also to remind yourself why you're doing a 15-miler in the middle of the workweek. If your running friends continue to chide you that you're not training hard enough, invite them to follow the schedules with you for a few weeks, then report back. We suspect they'll have gotten the message by then.

Racing Strategies

We discussed marathon race strategy at length in chapter 7. Part of that discussion centered on running with a group when possible. If you follow one of the schedules in this chapter, you might well be finishing within the top quarter or third of the field in your marathon. That means that you're likely to have runners around you throughout the marathon, especially in a big-city race, but there won't be so many people in front of you at the start that you'll spend the first few miles navigating around crowds. Make use of this probable position within the field; once you feel as if you're running comfortably at your goal pace, look around for other runners who appear that they can sustain the pace until the end. Talk to them, ask what their goals are, and try to find others to run with.

In chapter 7, we also discussed the importance of a conservative early pace. Although you'll be well trained if you follow one of these schedules, you won't have as large a margin of error as those who have regularly put in 85 miles a week or more. If you run intelligently in the early part of the race, then you'll have runners to pick off regularly in the last 10 miles or so because others who are either less prepared or more foolhardy will come back to you.

After the Marathon

The fourth schedule in this chapter is a 5-week recovery schedule for after the marathon. This is the fifth mesocycle; it completes the training program and leaves you ready to prepare for future challenges.

The recovery schedule is purposely conservative. You have little to gain by rushing back into training, and your risk of injury is exceptionally high at this point, owing to the reduced resiliency of your muscles and connective tissue after the marathon.

The schedule starts with 2 days off from running, which is the bare minimum of time away from running you should allow yourself. If you still have acute soreness or tightness so severe that it will alter your form, or if you just don't feel like running, certainly feel free to take more than 2 days off. If ever there was a time to lose your marathoner's mind-set, the week after your goal race is it. Even most of the top runners in the world take days off after a marathon. They know that the nearly negligible benefits of a short run at this time are far outweighed by the risks. Not running now also will increase your chances of being inspired to resume hard training when your body allows it.

Of course, some people don't consider themselves real runners unless they run pretty much every day of their lives. Plod through a few miles if you must, but be aware that you're prolonging your recovery.

What better aids recovery during this time is light cross-training, such as swimming or cycling. These activities increase blood flow through your muscles without subjecting them to pounding. Walking will also achieve this in the week after the marathon.

One way to ensure that you don't run too hard too soon after your marathon is to use a heart rate monitor. As discussed in chapter 4, a heart rate monitor can help prevent you from going too fast on recovery days. During the first few weeks after the marathon, keep your heart rate below 75 percent of your maximal heart rate or 70 percent of your heart rate reserve. Running at this intensity will help your body overcome the stress of the marathon as quickly as possible.

During this 5-week recovery schedule, the number of days of running per week increases from 3 to 5. At the end of the 5 weeks, you should be fully recovered from the marathon and, with a little luck, injury-free and mentally fresh.

Mesocycle 1 Endurance

	Weeks to goal				
	23	**22**	**21**	**20**	**Recovery week 19**
Monday	Rest or cross-training	Rest or cross-training	Rest or cross-training	Rest or cross-training	Rest or cross-training
Tuesday	General aerobic + speed 7 mi w/ 10 × 100 m strides	General aerobic + speed 8 mi w/ 10 × 100 m strides	Lactate threshold 9 mi w/ 4 mi @ 15K to half marathon race pace	General aerobic + speed 8 mi w/ 10 × 100 m strides	General aerobic + speed 7 mi w/ 10 × 100 m strides
Wednesday	General aerobic 10 mi	General aerobic 10 mi	General aerobic 10 mi	Medium-long run 11 mi	Medium-long run 11 mi
Thursday	Recovery 5 mi	Recovery 5 mi	Recovery 5 mi	Recovery 5 mi	Recovery 5 mi
Friday	General aerobic 10 mi	General aerobic 10 mi	Medium-long run 11 mi	Medium-long run 11 mi	General aerobic 10 mi
Saturday	Recovery 5 mi	Recovery 5 mi	Recovery 5 mi	Recovery 5 mi	Recovery 5 mi
Sunday	Medium-long run 13 mi	Medium-long run 14 mi	Medium-long run 16 mi	Long run 17 mi	Medium-long run 13 mi
Weekly mileage	50	52	56	57	51

	Weeks to goal				
	18	**17**	**16**	**15**	**Recovery week 14**
Monday	Rest or cross-training	Rest or cross-training	Rest or cross-training	Rest or cross-training	Rest or cross-training
Tuesday	Lactate threshold 9 mi w/ 4 mi @ 15K to half marathon race pace	General aerobic + speed 10 mi w/ 10 × 100 m strides	General aerobic + speed 10 mi w/ 10 × 100 m strides	Lactate threshold 10 mi w/ 5 mi @ 15K to half marathon race pace	General aerobic + speed 9 mi w/ 10 × 100 m strides
Wednesday	Medium-long run 12 mi	Medium-long run 12 mi	Medium-long run 13 mi	Medium-long run 14 mi	Medium-long run 11 mi
Thursday	Recovery 5 mi	Recovery 5 mi	Recovery 5 mi	Recovery 6 mi	Recovery 5 mi
Friday	Medium-long run 11 mi	Medium-long run 12 mi	Medium-long run 12 mi	Medium-long run 12 mi	Medium-long run 11 mi
Saturday	Recovery 5 mi	Recovery 5 mi	Recovery 5 mi	Recovery 5 mi	Recovery 5 mi
Sunday	Long run 17 mi	Long run 18 mi	Long run 19 mi	Long run 20 mi	Medium-long run 14 mi
Weekly mileage	59	62	64	67	55

Mesocycle 2 Lactate Threshold + Endurance

	Weeks to goal		
	13	**12**	**11**
Monday	Rest or cross-training	Rest or cross-training	Rest or cross-training
Tuesday	Lactate threshold 10 mi w/ 5 mi @ 15K to half marathon race pace	Medium-long run 11 mi	Recovery 6 mi
Wednesday	Medium-long run 13 mi	$\dot{V}O_2$max 10 mi w/ 8 × 800 m @ 5K race pace; jog 2 min between	Medium-long run 15 mi
Thursday	Recovery 5 mi	Recovery 6 mi	Recovery 6 mi
Friday	Medium-long run 12 mi	Medium-long run 14 mi	Lactate threshold 11 mi w/ 6 mi @ 15K to half marathon race pace
Saturday	General aerobic + speed 8 mi w/ 10 × 100 m strides	General aerobic + speed 8 mi w/ 10 × 100 m strides	General aerobic + speed 8 mi w/ 10 × 100 m strides
Sunday	Long run 20 mi	Long run 21 mi	Long run 18 mi
Weekly mileage	68	70	64

		Recovery week	
	10	**9**	**8**
Monday	Rest or cross-training	Rest or cross-training	Rest or cross-training
Tuesday	Recovery 6 mi a.m. 4 mi p.m.	Recovery 6 mi	Recovery 6 mi
Wednesday	Medium-long run 15 mi	$\dot{V}O_2$max 9 mi w/ 6 × 600 m @ 5K race pace; jog 90 sec between	Lactate threshold 12 mi w/ 7 mi @ 15K to half marathon race pace
Thursday	Recovery 6 mi	Recovery 6 mi	Recovery 6 mi
Friday	Medium-long run 13 mi	Medium-long run 11 mi	Medium-long run 15 mi
Saturday	General aerobic + speed 8 mi w/ 10 × 100 m strides	General aerobic + speed 9 mi w/ 10 × 100 m strides	General aerobic + speed 8 mi w/ 10 × 100 m strides
Sunday	Marathon specific 16 mi w/ 12 mi @ marathon race pace	Medium-long run 14 mi	Long run 23 mi
Weekly mileage	68	55	70

Mesocycle 3 Race Preparation

	Weeks to goal				
	7	**6**	**5**	**4**	**3**
Monday	Rest or cross-training	Rest or cross-training	Rest or cross-training	Rest or cross-training	Rest or cross-training
Tuesday	$\dot{V}O_2$max 9 mi w/ 5 3 600 m @ 5K race pace; jog 90 sec between	Medium-long run 11 mi	$\dot{V}O_2$max 9 mi w/ 5 3 600 m @ 5K race pace; jog 90 sec between	Recovery 6 mi a.m. 4 mi p.m.	$\dot{V}O_2$max 9 mi w/ 6 × 600 m @ 5K race pace; jog 90 sec between
Wednesday	Medium-long run 13 mi	$\dot{V}O_2$max 10 mi w/ 5 × 1,000 m @ 5K race pace; jog 2 min between	Medium-long run 14 mi	$\dot{V}O_2$max 11 mi w/ 6 × 1,200 m @ 5K race pace; jog 2 min between	Medium-long run 13 mi
Thursday	Recovery + speed 6 mi w/ 6 × 100 m strides 4 mi p.m.	Recovery 8 mi	Recovery + speed 6 mi w/ 6 × 100 m strides 4 mi p.m.	Medium-long run 15 mi	Recovery + speed 6 mi w/ 6 × 100 m strides
Friday	Recovery 5 mi	Medium-long run 11 mi	Recovery 5 mi	General aerobic + speed 8 mi w/ 10 × 100 m strides	Recovery 5 mi
Saturday	8-10K tune-up race	General aerobic + speed 7 mi w/ 6 × 100 m strides	8-15K tune-up race	Recovery 5 mi	8-15K tune-up race
Sunday	Long run 20 mi	Marathon specific 17 mi w/ 14 mi @ marathon race pace	Long run 18 mi	Long run 21 mi	Long run 20 mi
Weekly mileage	68	64	67	70	64

Mesocycle 4 Taper and Race

	Weeks to goal		
	2	**1**	**Race week**
Monday	Rest or cross-training	Rest	Rest
Tuesday	General aerobic + speed 8 mi w/ 8 × 100 m strides	General aerobic + speed 8 mi w/ 8 × 100 m strides	Recovery 5 mi a.m. 4 mi p.m.
Wednesday	Medium-long run 12 mi	Recovery 5 mi	Dress rehearsal 7 mi w/ 2 mi @ marathon race pace
Thursday	Recovery + speed 7 mi w/ 6 × 100 m strides	$\dot{V}O_2max$ 8 mi w/ 3 × 1,600 m @ 5K race pace; jog 2 min between	Recovery 5 mi
Friday	Recovery 5 mi	Recovery 5 mi	Recovery + speed 5 mi w/ 6 × 100 m strides
Saturday	Lactate threshold 9 mi w/ 5 mi @ 15K to half marathon race pace	General aerobic + speed 7 mi w/ 8 × 100 m strides	Recovery 4 mi
Sunday	Long run 17 mi	Medium-long run 13 mi	Goal marathon
Weekly mileage	58	46	30 (6 days prerace)

Mesocycle 1 Endurance

	Weeks to goal		
	17	**16**	**15**
Monday	Rest or cross-training	Rest or cross-training	Rest or cross-training
Tuesday	General aerobic + speed 8 mi w/ 10 × 100 m strides	General aerobic + speed 8 mi w/ 10 × 100 m strides	Lactate threshold 9 mi w/ 4 mi @ 15K to half marathon race pace
Wednesday	Medium-long run 11 mi	Medium-long run 12 mi	Medium-long run 13 mi
Thursday	Recovery 5 mi	Recovery 5 mi	Recovery 5 mi
Friday	General aerobic 9 mi	General aerobic 9 mi	Medium-long run 11 mi
Saturday	Recovery 5 mi	Recovery 5 mi	Recovery 5 mi
Sunday	Medium-long run 15 mi	Long run 17 mi	Medium-long run 15 mi
Weekly mileage	53	56	58

	Weeks to goal		
	14	**13**	**Recovery week 12**
Monday	Rest or cross-training	Rest or cross-training	Rest or cross-training
Tuesday	General aerobic + speed 9 mi w/ 10 × 100 m strides	Lactate threshold 9 mi w/ 4 mi @ 15K to half marathon race pace	General aerobic + speed 8 mi w/ 10 × 100 m strides
Wednesday	Medium-long run 14 mi	Medium-long run 14 mi	Medium-long run 12 mi
Thursday	Recovery 5 mi	Recovery 5 mi	Recovery 5 mi
Friday	Medium-long run 11 mi	Medium-long run 12 mi	Medium-long run 11 mi
Saturday	Recovery 5 mi	Recovery 5 mi	Recovery 5 mi
Sunday	Long run 18 mi	Long run 20 mi	Medium-long run 14 mi
Weekly mileage	62	65	55

Mesocycle 2 Lactate Threshold + Endurance

	Weeks to goal				
	11	**10**	**9**	**Recovery week** **8**	**7**
Monday	Rest or cross-training	Rest or cross-training	Rest or cross-training	Rest or cross-training	Rest or cross-training
Tuesday	Lactate threshold 10 mi w/ 5 mi @ 15K to half marathon race pace	Recovery 6 mi a.m. 4 mi p.m.	Recovery 6 mi a.m. 4 mi p.m.	General aerobic 10 mi	Recovery 6 mi a.m. 4 mi p.m.
Wednesday	Medium-long run 14 mi	Medium-long run 14 mi	Medium-long run 15 mi	V̇O$_2$max 9 mi w/ 6 × 600 m @ 5K race pace; jog 90 sec between	Medium-long run 15 mi
Thursday	Recovery 5 mi	Recovery 5 mi	Recovery 6 mi	Recovery 6 mi	Recovery 6 mi
Friday	Medium-long run 11 mi	Lactate threshold 11 mi w/ 6 mi @ 15K to half marathon race pace	Medium-long run 13 mi	Medium-long run 11 mi	Lactate threshold 12 mi w/ 7 mi @ 15K to half marathon race pace
Saturday	General aerobic + speed 8 mi w/ 10 × 100 m strides	Recovery 6 mi	Recovery + speed 7 mi w/ 6 × 100 m strides	General aerobic + speed 8 mi w/ 10 × 100 m strides	Recovery 5 mi
Sunday	Long run 21 mi	Long run 20 mi	Marathon specific 15 mi w/ 12 mi @ marathon race pace	Medium-long run 15 mi	Long run 22 mi
Weekly mileage	69	66	66	59	70

Mesocycle 3 Race Preparation

	Weeks to goal			
	6	**5**	**4**	**3**
Monday	Rest or cross-training	Rest or cross-training	Rest or cross-training	Rest or cross-training
Tuesday	$\dot{V}O_2$max 9 mi w/ 5 × 600 m @ 5K race pace; jog 90 sec between	$\dot{V}O_2$max 11 mi w/ 6 × 1,000 m @ 5K race pace; jog 90 sec between	$\dot{V}O_2$max 9 mi w/ 5 × 600 m @ 5K race pace; jog 2 min between	Recovery 6 mi a.m. 4 mi p.m.
Wednesday	Medium-long run 14 mi	Medium-long run 15 mi	Medium-long run 13 mi	$\dot{V}O_2$max 11 mi w/ 6 × 1,200 m @ 5K race pace; jog 2 min between
Thursday	Recovery + speed 6 mi w/ 6 × 100 m strides 4 mi p.m.	Recovery 6 mi a.m. 4 mi p.m.	Recovery + speed 6 mi w/ 6 × 100 m strides	Medium-long run 14 mi
Friday	Recovery 5 mi	Medium-long run 12 mi	Recovery 5 mi	General aerobic + speed 8 mi w/ 8 × 100 m strides
Saturday	8-15K tune-up race	Recovery 5 mi	8-15K tune-up race	Recovery 5 mi
Sunday	Long run 18 mi	Marathon specific 17 mi w/ 14 mi @ marathon race pace	Long run 18 mi	Long run 20 mi
Weekly mileage	68	70	63	68

Mesocycle 4 Taper and Race

		Weeks to goal	
	2	**1**	**Race week**
Monday	Rest or cross-training	Rest	Rest
Tuesday	General aerobic + speed 7 mi w/ 8 × 100 m strides	General aerobic + speed 8 mi w/ 8 × 100 m strides	Recovery 5 mi a.m. 4 mi p.m.
Wednesday	Medium-long run 12 mi	Recovery 5 mi	Dress rehearsal 7 mi with 2 mi @ marathon race pace
Thursday	Recovery + speed 6 mi w/ 6 × 100 m strides	$\dot{V}O_2$max 8 mi w/ 3 × 1,600 m @ 5K race pace; jog 2 min between	Recovery 5 mi
Friday	Recovery 5 mi	Recovery 5 mi	Recovery + speed 5 mi w/ 6 × 100 m strides
Saturday	8-10K tune-up race	General aerobic + speed 7 mi w/ 8 × 100 m strides	Recovery 4 mi
Sunday	Long run 17 mi	Medium-long run 13 mi	Goal marathon
Weekly mileage	56	46	30 (6 days prerace)

Mesocycle 1 Endurance

	Weeks to goal			
	11	**10**	**9**	**8**
Monday	Rest or cross-training	Rest or cross-training	Rest or cross-training	Rest or cross-training
Tuesday	General aerobic + speed 8 mi w/ 10 × 100 m strides	Lactate threshold 9 mi w/ 4 mi @ 15K to half marathon race pace	General aerobic + speed 9 mi w/ 10 × 100 m strides	Lactate threshold 10 mi w/ 5 mi @ 15K to half marathon race pace
Wednesday	Medium-long run 11 mi	Medium-long run 11 mi	Medium-long run 14 mi	Medium-long run 15 mi
Thursday	Recovery 5 mi	Recovery 5 mi	Recovery 5 mi	Recovery 5 mi
Friday	Medium-long run 11 mi	Medium-long run 12 mi	Medium-long run 12 mi	Medium-long run 13 mi
Saturday	Recovery 5 mi	Recovery 5 mi	Recovery 5 mi	Recovery 5 mi
Sunday	Medium-long run 15 mi	Long run 17 mi	Long run 18 mi	Long run 17 mi
Weekly mileage	55	59	63	65

Mesocycle 2 Lactate Threshold + Endurance			
	Weeks to goal		
	7	**6**	**5**
Monday	Rest or cross-training	Rest or cross-training	Rest or cross-training
Tuesday	General aerobic + speed 8 mi w/ 10 × 100 m strides	Recovery 6 mi a.m. 4 mi p.m.	General aerobic + speed 8 mi w/ 10 × 100 m strides
Wednesday	Medium-long run 15 mi	$\dot{V}O_2$max 11 mi w/ 5 × 1,200 m @ 5K race pace; jog 2½ min between	Medium-long run 14 mi
Thursday	Recovery 5 mi	Medium-long run 15 mi	Recovery 5 mi
Friday	Lactate threshold 11 mi w/ 6 mi @ 15K to half marathon pace Recovery 4 mi p.m.	General aerobic 10 mi	Lactate threshold 12 mi w/ 7 mi @ 15K to half marathon race pace Recovery 4 mi p.m.
Saturday	General aerobic + speed 7 mi w/ 6 × 100 m strides	Recovery 6 mi	Recovery 6 mi
Sunday	Long run 20 mi	Marathon specific 16 mi with 12 mi @ marathon race pace	Long run 21 mi
Weekly mileage	70	68	70

Mesocycle 3 Race Preparation

	Weeks to goal		
	4	**3**	**2**
Monday	Rest or cross-training	Rest or cross-training	Rest or cross-training
Tuesday	$\dot{V}O_2$max 9 mi w/ 5 × 600 m @ 5K race pace; jog 90 sec between	Recovery 6 mi a.m. 4 mi p.m.	$\dot{V}O_2$max 9 mi w/ 5 × 600 m @ 5K race pace; jog 90 sec between
Wednesday	Medium-long run 15 mi	$\dot{V}O_2$max 11 mi w/ 6 × 1,000 m @ 5K race pace; jog 2 min between	Medium-long run 11 mi
Thursday	Recovery + speed 7 mi w/ 6 × 100 m strides	Medium-long run 15 mi	Recovery + speed 6 mi w/ 6 × 100 m strides
Friday	Recovery 6 mi	General aerobic 8 mi	Recovery 5 mi
Saturday	8-15K tune-up race	Recovery 6 mi	8-10K tune-up race
Sunday	Long run 18 mi	Long run 20 mi	Long run 17 mi
Weekly mileage	68	70	59

Mesocycle 4 Taper and Race

	Weeks to goal	
	1	**Race week**
Monday	Rest or cross-training	Rest
Tuesday	General aerobic + speed 8 mi w/ 8 × 100 m strides	Recovery 5 mi a.m. 4 mi p.m.
Wednesday	Recovery 5 mi	Dress rehearsal 7 mi with 2 mi @ marathon race pace
Thursday	$\dot{V}O_2max$ 8 mi w/ 3 × 1,600 m @ 5K race pace; jog 2 min between	Recovery 5 mi
Friday	Recovery 5 mi	Recovery + speed 5 mi w/ 6 × 100 m strides
Saturday	General aerobic + speed 7 mi w/ 10 × 100 m strides	Recovery 4 mi
Sunday	Medium-long run 13 mi	Goal marathon
Weekly mileage	46	30 (6 days prerace)

Mesocycle 5 Recovery

	Weeks postmarathon				
	1	**2**	**3**	**4**	**5**
Monday	Rest or cross-training	Rest or cross-training	Rest or cross-training	Rest or cross-training	Rest or cross-training
Tuesday	Rest or cross-training	Recovery 5 mi	Recovery 5 mi	Recovery 5 mi	Recovery 6 mi
Wednesday	Recovery 4 mi	Recovery 5 mi	Recovery 5 mi	General aerobic 7 mi	General aerobic 8 mi
Thursday	Rest or cross-training	Rest or cross-training	Rest or cross-training	Rest or cross-training	Rest or cross-training
Friday	Recovery 5 mi	Recovery 5 mi	General aerobic + speed 7 mi w/ 8 × 100 m strides	General aerobic + speed 8 mi w/ 8 × 100 m strides	General aerobic + speed 9 mi w/ 8 × 100 m strides
Saturday	Rest or cross-training	Rest or cross-training	Recovery 5 mi	Recovery 5 mi	Recovery 6 mi
Sunday	Recovery 6 mi	Recovery 8 mi	General aerobic 9 mi	Medium-long rtun 11 mi	Medium-long run 12 mi
Weekly mileage	15	23	31	36	41

One Marathon on More Than 70 Miles per Week

This chapter is for high-mileage marathoners. It includes three schedules: a 24-week schedule that starts at 60 miles per week, an 18-week schedule that starts at 64 miles per week, and a 12-week schedule that starts at 66 miles per week. Each of these schedules increases weekly mileage progressively, with the 18- and 24-week schedules building to a peak of 93 miles and the 12-week schedule topping out at 90 miles.

As discussed in chapter 2, it's useful to divide your overall training schedule into phases, called mesocycles. The training schedules consist of four mesocycles, which focus on endurance, lactate threshold and endurance, race preparation, and tapering, respectively. A final schedule, which contains a 5-week postmarathon recovery program, can follow any of the other schedules.

Of the three training schedules presented in this chapter, we recommend the 18-week schedule for most situations. Eighteen weeks are plenty of time to stimulate the necessary adaptations to improve your marathon performance. At the same time, 18 weeks are short enough that you can focus your efforts without becoming bored with the process.

Victah Sailer © Photo Run 2000

Rod DeHaven

**Fastest Marathon: 2:13:01
Marathon Career Highlights: First place, 2000 Olympic marathon trials. Top American at the 1999 World Championships Marathon.**

As does Joe LeMay, Rod DeHaven shows that high-level achievement in the marathon—and high mileage—are possible around the constraints of a "normal" life. DeHaven is a father of two who works as a computer programmer. Although he reduced his hours in the months before winning the 2000 Olympic marathon trials, he was still putting in 30 hours each week at the office. Moreover, he logged 120-mile weeks, ran his personal best in 1998, and represented the United States at the 1999 World Championships while working full-time.

Given his nonrunning responsibilities, DeHaven says that a key to his marathon training is doing his main run of the day before work. "Do your longer run of the day prior to work when you're not likely to have conflicts," he advises. "My experience is that if something comes up at work or home, I might scale back or forgo running altogether if I haven't run. Consistency is very important."

For a typical workday during marathon training, here's how DeHaven describes his schedule: "I rise at 5:30 A.M., get out the door by 5:45, and run for 60 to 75 minutes. I occasionally stretch for a few minutes and then get ready for work. Fortunately, it takes only 10 minutes to get from home to my desk. I run again for half an hour during my lunch hour. I usually work until 5:00 to 5:30 P.M. Typically, on Wednesdays I'll do an interval workout, so I'll cut my morning run to 30 minutes and skip the run at lunch. When I get home, my life is much like anyone else's. Usually, our kids go to bed around 9:30, and then I try to get to sleep by 10:00 to 10:30 P.M. Between the kids' bedtime and mine, I'll try to do some stretching." At work, he drinks a lot of water and gets up to walk around at least once every 90 minutes.

DeHaven sticks to his early schedule on weekends, again to minimize conflicts with the rest of his life. "On Saturdays, I'll usually do my hard workout around 8:00 A.M.," he says. "That will usually be a tempo run. After that, my wife and I will try to have something scheduled to do with the kids. In the afternoon, I'll try to take a nap with my boys. I'll typically sleep for an hour and then squeeze in a 30- to 45-minute run. On Sunday, I usually get out the door between 7:00 and 8:00 A.M. and run for 1:45 to 2:30. I'll nap again in the afternoon. The one thing that makes all the running possible is that my wife handles a lot of the errand running. She's very efficient and has been very understanding of my hobby."

When asked how his running has suffered over the years because of his work schedule, DeHaven says, "Before working part-time prior to the trials, I used to think that I didn't make any compromises as long as I got out of bed. But working part-time, I discovered some things that helped my marathon fitness, such as hill running, doing strides after a run, and consistent stretching." Because you probably won't be spending as much time running as DeHaven, it's possible to regularly incorporate some of these aspects of training on a full-time work schedule.

DeHaven says that his pretrials buildup taught him another valuable lesson. "Typically, my focus for a marathon has been limited to 8 weeks when I have been working full-time," he says. "For the trials, the buildup was along the lines of 14 weeks. The longer buildup allowed me to use some discretion when some minor injuries cropped up." In part for similar reasons, we recommend that most readers follow the 18-week schedules presented in this book.

At times, however, you simply don't have 18 weeks to prepare for your marathon. The 12-week schedule includes the same mesocycles as the 18- and 24-week schedules, but because of the short time for preparation, each of these mesocycles is abbreviated. If you go into a marathon in a rush, you must realize that your preparation won't be as thorough as if you had longer to prepare. The 12-week schedule takes into account that sometimes circumstances don't allow you the optimal length of time for preparation and strives to provide a compact yet effective training program.

Although the 24-week training schedule provides even more preparation time than the 18-week schedule, it's ideal only in special situations—usually, when you're preparing for a marathon that's so important to you that you have little doubt that you'll be able to stay focused for such a long time. The Olympic trials would be such a special situation for elite marathoners, while trying to qualify for the Boston Marathon for the first time might fit the bill for locally competitive runners. Of course, it's not our place to tell you which marathons should matter most in your life; any number of situations may be especially important for you, and that's when the 24-week schedule is optimal.

Use the 24-week schedule to prepare for personally important marathons.

Before Starting the Schedules

These schedules are challenging right from the start and get harder as your marathon approaches. So that you can progress as the training increases in quantity and quality and to minimize your chances of injury, you should be able to complete the first week of the schedule without too much effort.

Be realistic in assessing whether you're ready for the first week of the schedule. For example, if you've been running 40 miles per week and your longest run in the last several weeks is 12 miles, now isn't the time to suddenly jump to a 64-mile week containing a 17-mile run, as the first week of the 18-week schedule calls for. The idea behind the schedules isn't to make you as tired as possible as soon as possible but to apply repeated training stresses that you absorb and benefit from.

As a rule, you should be running at least 50 to 55 miles a week before starting these schedules, and in the last month, you should have comfortably completed a run close in length to the long run called for in the first week of the schedule.

Reading the Schedules

The schedules are presented in a day-by-day format. This is in response to requests from readers of our first book, *Road Racing for Serious Runners*, to provide schedules that specify what to do each day of the week.

The main limitation with this approach is that it's impossible to guess the myriad of outside factors that may influence your day-to-day nonrunning life (assuming you still have one at this level of mileage). Work schedules, family life, relationships, school commitments, and Mother Nature all have their parts in determining when you get to do your long runs and other aspects of marathon preparation. You'll no doubt require some flexibility in your training and will need to juggle days around from time to time. That's expected, and as long as you don't try to make up for lost time by doing several hard days in a row, you should be able to avoid injury and overtraining. By following the principles covered in the earlier chapters, you will be able to safely fine-tune the training schedules to suit your circumstances.

Following the Schedules

Each column of the schedules represents a week's training. For example, in the 12-week schedule, the column for 11 weeks to goal indicates that at the end of that week you have 11 weeks until your marathon. The schedules continue week by week until race week.

We have included the specific workout for each day as well as the category of training for that day. For example, in the 18-week schedule, on the Monday of the 7-weeks-to-go column, the specific workouts are a 6-mile run and a 4-mile run and the category of training for that day is recovery. This aspect of the schedules allows you to quickly see the balance of training during each week and the progression of workouts from week to week. Look again at the 18-week schedule—it's easy to see that with 7 weeks to go until the marathon, there are 4 recovery days that week with a lactate threshold session, a long run, and a medium-long run.

Looking at the row for Sunday, it's easy to see how the long runs progress and then taper in the last few weeks before the marathon.

The workouts are divided into the following eight categories: long runs, medium-long runs, general aerobic, lactate threshold, $\dot{V}O_2$max, speed, recovery, and marathon-specific runs. Each of these categories is explained briefly. The various types of training are explained in depth in chapter 2.

Long Runs

A long run is any run of 17 miles or longer. The intention of these runs is (obviously) to improve your endurance in preparation for the marathon's 26.2 miles. The specific physiological benefits of long runs are discussed in detail in chapter 2. To gain the most from your long runs, do them at the correct intensity. Long runs shouldn't be slow jogs during which you just accumulate time on your feet. The most beneficial intensity range for your long runs is 10 to 20 percent slower than your goal marathon race pace. The reason for this intensity range is explained in chapter 2.

Medium-Long Runs

A medium-long run is any run of 11 to 16 miles. Medium-long runs reinforce the physiological benefits of your long runs. To gain the most specific physiological benefits for the marathon, the pace for these runs should be similar to the pace for long runs.

General Aerobic Runs

General aerobic runs include any run of 10 miles or less that's done at a steady pace. Faster runs of this length fall into the lactate threshold category, whereas slower runs are specifically for recovery.

© Tony Demin/International Stock

Your pace for long and medium-long runs should be 10 to 20 percent slower than goal marathon race pace.

In other words, these are your standard, moderate-effort, putting-in-the-miles runs. The intention of your general aerobic runs is to enhance your overall aerobic conditioning through boosting your training volume; these runs improve your marathon readiness because many of the beneficial adaptations that improve endurance are related to the total volume of your training.

Lactate Threshold

Lactate threshold runs are tempo runs in which you run for at least 20 minutes at your lactate threshold pace. This coincides closely with your current 15K to half marathon race pace. Tempo runs provide a strong stimulus to improve your lactate threshold pace, which leads to similar improvements in your marathon race pace. The lactate threshold sessions are done after a 2- to 3-mile warm-up. The tempo runs in this chapter are from 4 to 7 miles long. Slower runners should run closer to their 15K race pace on tempo runs, whereas faster runners should run closer to their half marathon race pace during these workouts.

$\dot{V}O_2max$

$\dot{V}O_2max$ runs are intervals of 600 meters to 2,000 meters duration, which are run at 95 to 100 percent of your current $\dot{V}O_2max$ pace. This coincides closely with your current 3K to 5K race pace. These sessions provide a strong stimulus to improve your $\dot{V}O_2max$.

Careful readers will notice that none of the $\dot{V}O_2max$ sessions call for repeats longer than 1,600 meters. As we noted in chapter 2, the optimal duration for $\dot{V}O_2max$ intervals is 2 to 6 minutes; only elite runners will cover 2,000 meters in a 6-minute interval. The longer your repeats are in these workouts, the more days you'll need after the workout for recovery. Though $\dot{V}O_2max$ work is an important part of your marathon preparation, it's not as crucial in the marathon as it is in races such as 5K and 10K. The $\dot{V}O_2max$ sessions in these schedules, then, feature repeats that strike a balance between being long enough to provide a powerful training stimulus and short enough to leave you fresh for your other important workouts of the week.

The same reasoning applies for the prescribed pace in these $\dot{V}O_2max$ workouts—whereas runners focusing on shorter races need to do some of their intervals closer to 3K race pace, marathoners gain maximum benefit from sticking to 5K race pace.

Speed

Speed runs are repetitions of 50 to 150 meters that improve leg speed and running form. These sessions are done after a thorough warm-up and often toward the end of a general aerobic run or a recovery run. Allow yourself plenty of rest between repetitions so that you can run each one with good technique.

Recovery

Recovery runs are relatively short runs done at a relaxed pace to enhance recovery for your next hard workout. These runs aren't necessarily jogs, but they should be noticeably slower than your other workouts of the week.

Marathon-Pace Runs

Marathon-pace runs are medium-long or long runs during which you run most of the miles at your goal marathon pace. These runs provide the precise physiological benefit of allowing you to practice the pace, form, and so on of race day. Think of marathon-pace runs as integrating all of the other aspects of your training. They also are a great confidence booster. Start these runs comfortably, as you would other medium-long or long runs, and then run the last portion at marathon race pace. For example, if the schedule calls for 17 miles with 12 miles at marathon race pace, gradually pick up the pace during the first 5 miles, and then run the last 12 miles at marathon goal pace.

Doing Doubles

As discussed in chapter 5, sometimes marathoners benefit from running twice a day. This is obviously the case for elites cranking out 130-mile weeks, but it can also be so for anyone running more than 70 miles a week. In these schedules, for example, recovery days of 10 miles are often broken into two short runs. Rather than making you more tired, splitting your mileage like this on easy days will speed your recovery because each run will increase blood flow to your muscles yet take so little out of you.

As we mentioned at the beginning of this chapter, we know that not everyone will be able to follow these schedules exactly as they appear. That applies on the days here that call for a lactate threshold workout in the morning and an easy recovery run in the evening. If your schedule makes it more likely that you'll do a high-quality tempo run in the evening rather than the morning, then simply flip the workouts prescribed for these days. Just be sure to make the short morning run a true recovery run.

When a second run is called for on the day of a medium-long run, however, try to stick to the schedule as written. As explained in chapter 5, a short evening run on these days provides an additional endurance boost, whereas doing a short morning run and a medium-long run in the evening will likely detract from the quality of the medium-long run. Again, though, use your best judgment. If your schedule means that you'll have to do a midweek medium-long run at 4:30 A.M., you're probably better off making time for it in the evening.

When 93 Miles per Week Just Isn't Enough

The hardy few among you might want to do more mileage than what's prescribed in the schedules. (Generally speaking, these are people whose days are 27 hours long; how else do they find the time?) If you're in this group, be sure to follow the spirit of the schedules when adding miles—that is, your mileage should build gradually during mesocycle 1, peak at the end of mesocycle 2, come down slightly during mesocycle 3, and fall dramatically during mesocycle 4.

Where should you add miles to the schedules? Try adding a bit of mileage to the general aerobic runs and medium-long runs if you sense that doing so doesn't detract from your week's most important sessions. (Remember, mileage is a means to a goal, not a primary goal in itself.) You could also add miles to your warm-ups and cool-downs on $\dot{V}O_2max$ and lactate threshold workout days. If you're going to do more doubles than the schedules stipulate, refer to the section on two-a-day runs in chapter 5.

A Word About "Hard" Days

Looking at these schedules, you might be wondering, "Where are all the 'speed' workouts?" After all, it's normal to think that anyone preparing for a marathon should be training as hard as possible, and what better way to be sure that you're doing so than by hitting the track at least once a week for lung-searing intervals, right?

In chapter 2, we explained at length the principles underlying these schedules. Briefly put, we designed the schedules to provide the optimal stimuli to the physiological systems that most determine marathoning success—endurance, lactate threshold, and $\dot{V}O_2max$, in that order of importance. In the long run, so to speak, it's your long runs and tempo runs that have the most relevance to your performance on marathon day, not how often you've churned out a sterling set of half mile repeats.

During your long buildup, understanding the components of marathon success can provide confidence that you're training properly. Use the explanation of marathon physiology from chapter 2 not only to explain to your training buddies why you won't be joining them for quarters next week but also to remind yourself why you're doing yet another 15-miler in the middle of the workweek. If your running friends continue to chide you that you're not training hard enough, invite them to follow the schedules with you for a few weeks, then report back. We suspect they'll have gotten the message by then.

Racing Strategies

We discussed marathon race strategy at length in chapter 7. Here, we'll merely add that if you follow the schedules in this chapter, you will be more thoroughly prepared for your marathon than most of the other runners in the race. Few others in the field will have done the combination of mileage and targeted quality that you have.

Despite your commitment and eagerness, though, you'll need to not get carried away in the early miles, even if your goal pace in the first half feels quite easy. The temptation to try to capitalize on that good feeling will be strong. Perhaps more than any other readers of this book, you will have to be disciplined in the early miles to stick to your goal pace, so that you can use your fitness in the second half of the race and run even splits. Although your outstanding preparation makes you less likely than most to blow up late in the race from a too-hasty start, there's still no point in squandering months of hard work with an overly ambitious early pace.

At the same time, it's likely that among readers of this book you'll be attempting to race the marathon at the greatest differential from your normal training pace. For that reason, in the days before your marathon, your goal pace might seem especially daunting. Draw confidence from your long runs, tempo runs, and marathon-pace runs that you can sustain your ambitious goal pace for 26.2 miles. Also, focus on your goal-pace splits to increase your chances of running the first half of the race intelligently and thereby vastly increasing your chances of being able to hold goal pace past 20 miles.

After the Marathon

The final schedule in this chapter is a 5-week recovery schedule for after the marathon. This is the fifth mesocycle; it completes the training program and leaves you ready to prepare for future challenges.

The recovery schedule is purposely conservative. You have little to gain by rushing back into training, and your risk of injury is exceptionally high at this point, owing to the reduced resiliency of your muscles and connective tissue after the marathon.

The schedule starts with 2 days off from running, which is the bare minimum of time away from running you should allow yourself. If you still have acute soreness or tightness so severe that it will alter your form, or if you just don't feel like running, certainly feel free to take more than 2 days off. If ever there was a time to lose your marathoner's mind-set, the week after your goal race is it. Even most of the top runners in the world take days off after a marathon. They know that the nearly negligible benefits of a short run at this time are far outweighed by the risks. Not running now also will increase your chances of being inspired to resume hard training when your body allows it.

Of course, some people don't consider themselves real runners unless they run pretty much every day of their lives. Plod through a few miles if you must, but be aware that you're prolonging your recovery.

What better aids recovery during this time is light cross-training, such as swimming or cycling. These activities increase blood flow through your muscles without subjecting them to pounding. Walking will also achieve this in the week after the marathon.

One way to ensure that you don't run too hard too soon after your marathon is to use a heart rate monitor. As discussed in chapter 4, a heart rate monitor can help prevent you from going too fast on recovery days. During the first few weeks after the marathon, keep your heart rate below 75 percent of your maximal heart rate or 70 percent of your heart rate reserve. Running at this intensity will help your body to overcome the stress of the marathon as quickly as possible.

During this 5-week recovery schedule, the number of days of running per week increases from 3 to 6. At the end of the 5 weeks, you should be fully recovered from the marathon and, with a little luck, injury-free and mentally fresh.

Mesocycle 1 Endurance

		Weeks to goal			
	23	**22**	**21**	**20**	**Recovery week 19**
Monday	Recovery 6 mi	Recovery 6 mi	Recovery 6 mi	Recovery 5 mi a.m. 4 mi p.m.	Recovery 6 mi
Tuesday	General aerobic + speed 7 mi w/ 10 × 100 m strides	General aerobic + speed 8 mi w/ 10 × 100 m strides	Lactate threshold 9 mi w/ 4 mi @ 15K to half marathon race pace	General aerobic + speed 8 mi w/ 10 × 100 m strides	General aerobic + speed 7 mi w/ 10 × 100 m strides
Wednesday	Medium-long run 11 mi	Medium-long run 11 mi	Medium-long run 12 mi	Medium-long run 12 mi	Medium-long run 12 mi
Thursday	Recovery 5 mi	Recovery 6 mi	Recovery 6 mi	Recovery 6 mi	Recovery 6 mi
Friday	General aerobic 10 mi	General aerobic 10 mi	Medium-long run 11 mi	Medium-long run 11 mi	General aerobic 10 mi
Saturday	Recovery 6 mi	Recovery 6 mi	Recovery 6 mi	Recovery 6 mi	Recovery 6 mi
Sunday	Medium-long run 15 mi	Medium-long run 16 mi	Long run 17 mi	Long run 18 mi	Medium-long run 15 mi
Weekly mileage	60	63	67	70	62

		Weeks to goal			
	18	**17**	**16**	**15**	**Recovery week 14**
Monday	Recovery 6 mi a.m. 4 mi p.m.	Recovery 6 mi a.m. 4 mi p.m.	Recovery 6 mi a.m. 4 mi p.m.	Recovery 6 mi a.m. 4 mi p.m.	Recovery 6 mi a.m. 4 mi p.m.
Tuesday	Lactate threshold 10 mi w/ 4 mi @ 15K to half marathon race pace	General aerobic + speed 10 mi w/ 10 × 100 m strides	General aerobic + speed 10 mi w/ 10 × 100 m strides	Lactate threshold 10 mi w/ 5 mi @ 15K to half marathon race pace	General aerobic + speed 9 mi w/ 10 × 100 m strides
Wednesday	Medium-long run 13 mi	Medium-long run 13 mi	Medium-long run 14 mi	Medium-long run 14 mi	Medium-long run 12 mi
Thursday	Recovery 6 mi	Recovery 6 mi	Recovery 7 mi	Recovery 6 mi a.m. 4 mi p.m.	Recovery 6 mi
Friday	Medium-long run 11 mi	Medium-long run 12 mi	Medium-long run 12 mi	Medium-long run 13 mi	Medium-long run 11 mi
Saturday	Recovery 6 mi	Recovery 7 mi	Recovery 7 mi	Recovery 7 mi	Recovery 7 mi
Sunday	Long run 18 mi	Long run 19 mi	Long run 20 mi	Long run 21 mi	Medium-long run 15 mi
Weekly mileage	74	77	80	85	70

Mesocycle 2 Lactate Threshold + Endurance

	Weeks to goal		
	13	**12**	**11**
Monday	Recovery 6 mi a.m., 4 mi p.m.	Recovery 6 mi a.m., 4 mi p.m.	Recovery 6 mi a.m., 4 mi p.m.
Tuesday	Lactate threshold 10 mi w/ 5 mi @ 15K to half marathon race pace	$\dot{V}O_2$max 10 mi w/ 8 × 800 m @ 5K race pace; jog 2 min between	Recovery 6 mi a.m. 4 mi p.m.
Wednesday	Medium-long run 14 mi	Medium-long run 15 mi	Medium-long run 15 mi
Thursday	Recovery 6 mi a.m., 4 mi p.m.	Recovery 6 mi a.m., 4 mi p.m.	Recovery 6 mi a.m., 4 mi p.m.
Friday	Medium-long run 13 mi	Medium-long run 13 mi Recovery 4 mi p.m.	Lactate threshold 12 mi w/ 6 mi @ 15K to half marathon race pace Recovery 4 mi p.m.
Saturday	General aerobic + speed 8 mi w/ 10 × 100 m strides	General aerobic + speed 9 mi w/ 10 × 100 m strides	General aerobic + speed 8 mi w/ 10 × 100 m strides
Sunday	Long run 20 mi	Long run 22 mi	Long run 18 mi
Weekly mileage	85	93	87

	Weeks to goal		
	10	**Recovery week 9**	**8**
Monday	Recovery 6 mi a.m., 4 mi p.m.	Recovery 6 mi a.m., 4 mi p.m.	Recovery 6 mi a.m., 4 mi p.m.
Tuesday	Recovery 6 mi a.m., 4 mi p.m.	Recovery 6 mi a.m., 4 mi p.m.	Recovery 6 mi a.m., 4 mi p.m.
Wednesday	Medium-long run 15 mi	$\dot{V}O_2$max 9 mi w/ 6 × 600 m @ 5K race pace; jog 90 sec between	Lactate threshold 12 mi w/ 7 mi @ 15K to half marathon race pace Recovery 4 mi p.m.
Thursday	Recovery 6 mi a.m., 4 mi p.m.	Recovery 6 mi a.m., 4 mi p.m.	Recovery 6 mi a.m., 4 mi p.m.
Friday	Medium-long run 13 mi Recovery 4 mi p.m.	Medium-long run 11 mi	Medium-long run 15 mi
Saturday	General aerobic + speed 8 mi w/ 10 × 100 m strides	General aerobic + speed 9 mi w/ 10 × 100 m strides	General aerobic + speed 8 mi w/ 10 × 100 m strides
Sunday	Marathon specific 17 mi w/ 12 mi @ marathon race pace	Medium-long run 16 mi	Long run 24 mi
Weekly mileage	87	75	93

Mesocycle 3 Race Preparation

	Weeks to goal				
	7	**6**	**5**	**4**	**3**
Monday	Recovery 6 mi a.m. 4 mi p.m.	Recovery 6 mi a.m. 4 mi p.m.	Recovery 6 mi a.m. 4 mi p.m.	Recovery 6 mi a.m. 4 mi p.m.	Recovery 6 mi a.m. 4 mi p.m.
Tuesday	$\dot{V}O_2$max 9 mi w/ 5 × 600 m @ 5K race pace; jog 90 sec between	$\dot{V}O_2$max 11 mi w/ 5 × 1,000 m @ 5K race pace; jog 2 min between	$\dot{V}O_2$max 9 mi w/ 5 × 600 m @ 5K race pace; jog 90 sec between	Recovery 6 mi a.m. 4 mi p.m.	$\dot{V}O_2$max 9 mi w/ 5 × 600 m @ 5K race pace; jog 90 sec between
Wednesday	Medium-long run 15 mi Recovery 5 mi p.m.	Medium-long run 15 mi	Medium-long run 14 mi Recovery 4 mi p.m.	$\dot{V}O_2$max 12 mi w/ 6 × 1,200 m @ 5K race pace; jog 2 min between	Medium-long run 14 mi
Thursday	Recovery + speed 6 mi w/ 6 × 100 m strides 4 mi p.m.	Recovery 6 mi a.m. 4 mi p.m.	Recovery + speed 6 mi w/ 6 × 100 m strides a.m. 4 mi p.m.	Medium-long run 15 mi Recovery 4 mi p.m.	Recovery + speed 6 mi w/ 6 × 100 m strides 4 mi p.m.
Friday	Recovery 6 mi a.m. 4 mi p.m.	Medium-long run 12 mi Recovery 4 mi p.m.	Recovery 6 mi	General aerobic + speed 8 mi w/ 10 × 100 m strides	Recovery 6 mi
Saturday	8-10K tune-up race	General aerobic + speed 8 mi w/ 6 × 100 m strides	8-15K tune-up race	Recovery 6 mi a.m. 4 mi p.m.	8-15K tune-up race
Sunday	Long run 20 mi	Marathon specific 18 mi w/ 15 mi @ marathon race pace	Long run 18 mi	Long run 22 mi	Long run 20 mi
Weekly mileage	90	88	82	91	80

Mesocycle 4 Taper and Race

	Weeks to goal		
	2	**1**	**Race week**
Monday	Recovery 6 mi a.m. 4 mi p.m.	Recovery 6 mi	Recovery 6 mi
Tuesday	General aerobic + speed 10 mi w/ 8 × 100 m strides	General aerobic + speed 9 mi w/ 8 × 100 m strides	Recovery 5 mi a.m. 4 mi p.m.
Wednesday	Medium-long run 14 mi	Recovery 6 mi	Dress rehearsal 8 mi w/ 2 mi @ marathon race pace
Thursday	Recovery + speed 7 mi w/ 6 × 100 m strides	$\dot{V}O_2$max 9 mi w/ 3 × 1,600 m @ 5K race pace; jog 2 min between	Recovery 6 mi
Friday	Recovery 6 mi	Recovery 6 mi	Recovery + speed 5 mi w/ 6 × 100 m strides
Saturday	Lactate threshold 10 mi w/ 5 mi @ 15K to half marathon race pace	General aerobic + speed 8 mi w/ 8 × 100 m strides	Recovery 4 mi
Sunday	Long run 17 mi	Medium-long run 13 mi	Goal marathon
Weekly mileage	74	57	38 (6 days prerace)

Mesocycle 1 Endurance

	Weeks to goal		
	17	**16**	**15**
Monday	Recovery 5 mi	Recovery 6 mi	Recovery 6 mi
Tuesday	General aerobic + speed 8 mi w/ 10 × 100 m strides	General aerobic + speed 8 mi w/ 10 × 100 m strides	Lactate threshold 10 mi w/ 4 mi @ 15K to half marathon race pace
Wednesday	Medium-long run 12 mi	Medium-long run 13 mi	Medium-long run 14 mi
Thursday	Recovery 6 mi	Recovery 6 mi	Recovery 6 mi
Friday	General aerobic 10 mi	Medium-long run 11 mi	Medium-long run 12 mi
Saturday	Recovery 6 mi	Recovery 6 mi	Recovery 6 mi
Sunday	Long run 17 mi	Long run 18 mi	Medium-long run 16 mi
Weekly mileage	64	68	70

	Weeks to goal		
	14	**13**	**Recovery week** **12**
Monday	Recovery 6 mi a.m. 4 mi p.m.	Recovery 6 mi a.m. 4 mi p.m.	Recovery 6 mi a.m. 4 mi p.m.
Tuesday	General aerobic + speed 10 mi w/ 10 × 100 m strides	Lactate threshold 10 mi w/ 4 mi @ 15K to half marathon race pace	General aerobic + speed 10 mi w/ 10 × 100 m strides
Wednesday	Medium-long run 14 mi	Medium-long run 15 mi	Medium-long run 13 mi
Thursday	Recovery 6 mi	Recovery 6 mi	Recovery 6 mi
Friday	Medium-long run 12 mi	Medium-long run 13 mi	Medium-long run 11 mi
Saturday	Recovery 6 mi	Recovery 6 mi	Recovery 6 mi
Sunday	Long run 19 mi	Long run 20 mi	Medium-long run 16 mi
Weekly mileage	77	80	72

Mesocycle 2 Lactate Threshold + Endurance

	Weeks to goal				
				Recovery week	
	11	**10**	**9**	**8**	**7**
Monday	Recovery 6 mi a.m. 4 mi p.m.	Recovery 6 mi a.m. 4 mi p.m.	Recovery 6 mi a.m. 4 mi p.m.	Recovery 6 mi a.m. 4 mi p.m.	Recovery 6 mi a.m. 4 mi p.m.
Tuesday	Lactate threshold 11 mi w/ 5 mi @ 15K to half marathon race pace	Recovery 6 mi a.m. 4 mi p.m.	Recovery 6 mi a.m. 4 mi p.m.	General aerobic 9 mi	Recovery 6 mi a.m. 4 mi p.m.
Wednesday	Medium-long run 15 mi	Medium-long run 15 mi	Medium-long run 15 mi Recovery 4 mi p.m.	$\dot{V}O_2$max 9 mi w/ 6 × 600 m @ 5K race pace; jog 90 sec between	Medium-long run 15 mi
Thursday	Recovery 6 mi a.m. 4 mi p.m.	Recovery 6 mi a.m. 4 mi p.m.	Recovery 6 mi a.m. 4 mi p.m.	Recovery 6 mi a.m. 4 mi p.m.	Recovery 6 mi a.m. 4 mi p.m.
Friday	Medium-long run 12 mi	Lactate threshold 12 mi w/ 6 mi @ 15K to half marathon race pace	Medium-long run 13 mi	Medium-long run 11 mi Recovery 4 mi p.m.	Lactate threshold 12 mi w/ 7 mi @ 15K to half marathon race pace Recovery 4 mi p.m.
Saturday	General aerobic + speed 8 mi w/ 10 × 100 m strides	Recovery 8 mi	Recovery + speed 7 mi w/ 6 × 100 m strides	General aerobic + speed 8 mi w/ 10 × 100 m strides	Recovery 8 mi
Sunday	Long run 20 mi	Long run 22 mi	Marathon specific 16 mi w/ 12 mi @ marathon race pace	Medium-long run 16 mi	Long run 24 mi
Weekly mileage	86	87	85	77	93

Mesocycle 3 Race Preparation

	Weeks to goal			
	6	**5**	**4**	**3**
Monday	Recovery 6 mi a.m. 4 mi p.m.	Recovery 6 mi a.m. 4 mi p.m.	Recovery 6 mi a.m. 4 mi p.m.	Recovery 6 mi a.m. 4 mi p.m.
Tuesday	$\dot{V}O_2max$ 9 mi w/ 5 × 600 m @ 5K race pace; jog 90 sec between	$\dot{V}O_2max$ 12 mi w/ 6 × 1,000 m @ 5K race pace; jog 2 min between	$\dot{V}O_2max$ 9 mi w/ 5 × 600 m @ 5K race pace; jog 90 sec between	Recovery 6 mi a.m. 4 mi p.m.
Wednesday	Medium-long run 15 mi Recovery 4 mi p.m.	Medium-long run 15 mi	Medium-long run 14 mi	$\dot{V}O_2max$ 12 mi w/ 6 × 1,200 m @ 5K race pace; jog 2 min between
Thursday	Recovery + speed 7 mi w/ 6 × 100 m strides	Recovery 6 mi a.m. 4 mi p.m.	Recovery + speed 7 mi w/ 6 × 100 m strides	Medium-long run 15 mi Recovery 4 mi
Friday	Recovery 6 mi	Medium-long run 12 mi Recovery 4 mi p.m.	Recovery 6 mi	General aerobic + speed 8 mi w/ 8 × 100 m strides
Saturday	8-15K tune-up race	Recovery 7 mi	8-15K tune-up race	Recovery 6 mi a.m. 4 mi p.m.
Sunday	Long run 18 mi	Marathon specific 18 mi w/ 15 mi @ marathon race pace	Long run 20 mi	Long run 22 mi
Weekly mileage	82	88	79	91

Mesocycle 4 Taper and Race

	Weeks to goal		
	2	**1**	**Race week**
Monday	Recovery 6 mi a.m. 4 mi p.m.	Recovery 6 mi	Recovery 6 mi
Tuesday	General aerobic + speed 10 mi w/ 8 × 100 m strides	General aerobic + speed 9 mi w/ 8 × 100 m strides	Recovery 5 mi a.m. 4 mi p.m.
Wednesday	Medium-long run 14 mi	Recovery 6 mi	Dress rehearsal 8 mi with 2 mi @ marathon race pace
Thursday	Recovery + speed 7 mi w/ 6 × 100 m strides	$\dot{V}O_2$max 9 mi w/ 3 × 1,600 m @ 5K race pace; jog 2 min between	Recovery 6 mi
Friday	Recovery 6 mi	Recovery 6 mi	Recovery + speed 5 mi w/ 6 × 100 m strides
Saturday	Lactate threshold 10 mi w/ 5 mi @ 15K to half marathon race pace	General aerobic + speed 8 mi w/ 8 × 100 m strides	Recovery 4 mi
Sunday	Long run 17 mi	Medium-long run 13 mi	Goal marathon
Weekly mileage	74	57	38 (6 days prerace)

Mesocycle 1 Endurance

	Weeks to goal			
	11	**10**	**9**	**8**
Monday	Recovery 6 mi	Recovery 6 mi a.m. 4 mi p.m.	Recovery 6 mi a.m. 4 mi p.m.	Recovery 6 mi a.m. 4 mi p.m.
Tuesday	General aerobic + speed 8 mi w/ 10 × 100 m strides	Lactate threshold 10 mi w/ 4 mi @ 15K to half marathon race pace	General aerobic + speed 8 mi w/ 10 × 100 m strides	Lactate threshold 10 mi w/ 5 mi @ 15K to half marathon race pace
Wednesday	Medium-long run 12 mi	Medium-long run 11 mi	Medium-long run 13 mi	Medium-long run 15 mi
Thursday	Recovery 6 mi	Recovery 6 mi	Recovery 6 mi	Recovery 6 mi
Friday	Medium-long run 11 mi	Medium-long run 12 mi	Medium-long run 13 mi	Medium-long run 13 mi Recovery 4 mi p.m.
Saturday	Recovery 6 mi	Recovery 6 mi	Recovery 6 mi	Recovery 6 mi
Sunday	Long run 17 mi	Long run 18 mi	Long run 19 mi	Long run 17 mi
Weekly mileage	66	73	75	81

Mesocycle 2 Lactate Threshold + Endurance			
	Weeks to goal		
	7	**6**	**5**
Monday	Recovery 6 mi a.m. 4 mi p.m.	Recovery 6 mi a.m. 4 mi p.m.	Recovery 6 mi a.m. 4 mi p.m.
Tuesday	General aerobic + speed 8 mi w/ 10 × 100 m strides	Recovery 6 mi a.m. 4 mi p.m.	General aerobic + speed 9 mi w/ 10 × 100 m strides
Wednesday	Medium-long run 15 mi Recovery 4 mi p.m.	$\dot{V}O_2$max 12 mi w/ 5 × 1,200 m @ 5K race pace; jog 2½ min between	Medium-long run 15 mi
Thursday	Recovery 6 mi	Medium-long run 15 mi Recovery 4 mi p.m.	Recovery 6 mi a.m. 4 mi p.m.
Friday	Lactate threshold 12 mi w/ 6 mi @ 15K to half marathon race pace Recovery 4 mi p.m.	General aerobic 9 mi Recovery 5 mi p.m.	Lactate threshold 12 mi w/ 7 mi @ 15K to half marathon race pace Recovery 4 mi p.m.
Saturday	General aerobic + speed 7 mi w/ 6 × 100 m strides	Recovery + speed 7 mi w/ 6 × 100 m strides	General aerobic + speed 8 mi w/ 6 × 100 m strides
Sunday	Long run 20 mi	Marathon specific 17 mi with 12 mi @ marathon race pace	Long run 22 mi
Weekly mileage	86	89	90

Mesocycle 3 Race Preparation

	Weeks to goal		
	4	**3**	**2**
Monday	Recovery 6 mi a.m. 4 mi p.m.	Recovery 6 mi a.m. 4 mi p.m.	Recovery 6 mi a.m. 4 mi p.m.
Tuesday	$\dot{V}O_2$max 9 mi w/ 5 × 600 m @ 5K race pace; jog 90 sec between	Recovery 6 mi a.m. 4 mi p.m.	$\dot{V}O_2$max 9 mi w/ 5 × 600 m @ 5K race pace; jog 90 sec between
Wednesday	Medium-long run 15 mi Recovery 4 mi p.m.	$\dot{V}O_2$max 11 mi w/ 6 × 1,000 m @ 5K race pace; jog 2 min between	Medium-long run 12 mi
Thursday	Recovery + speed 7 mi w/ 6 × 100 m strides	Medium-long run 15 mi	Recovery + speed 6 mi w/ 6 × 100 m strides a.m. 4 mi p.m.
Friday	Recovery 6 mi a.m.	General aerobic 9 mi a.m. Recovery 4 mi p.m.	Recovery 6 mi
Saturday	8-15K tune-up race	General aerobic + speed 8 mi w/ 6 × 100 m strides	8-15K tune-up race
Sunday	Long run 18 mi	Long run 20 mi	Long run 17 mi
Weekly mileage	82	87	75

Mesocycle 4 Taper and Race

	Weeks to goal	
	1	**Race week**
Monday	Recovery 6 mi	Recovery 6 mi
Tuesday	General aerobic + speed 9 mi w/ 8 × 100 m strides	Recovery 5 mi a.m. 4 mi p.m.
Wednesday	Recovery 6 mi	Dress rehearsal 8 mi with 2 mi @ marathon race pace
Thursday	$\dot{V}O_2$max 9 mi w/ 3 × 1,600 m @ 5K race pace; jog 2 min between	Recovery 6 mi
Friday	Recovery 6 mi	Recovery + speed 5 mi w/ 6 × 100 m strides
Saturday	General aerobic + speed 8 mi w/ 10 × 100 m strides	Recovery 4 mi
Sunday	Medium-long run 13 mi	Goal marathon
Weekly mileage	57	38 (6 days prerace)

Mesocycle 5 Recovery

	Weeks postmarathon				
	1	**2**	**3**	**4**	**5**
Monday	Rest or cross-training	Rest or cross-training	Rest or cross-training	Rest or cross-training	Rest or cross-training
Tuesday	Rest or cross-training	Recovery 5 mi	Recovery 6 mi	Recovery 6 mi	Recovery 6 mi
Wednesday	Recovery 4 mi	Recovery 5 mi	Recovery 6 mi	General aerobic 9 mi	General aerobic 9 mi
Thursday	Rest or cross-training	Rest or cross-training	Rest or cross-training	Rest or cross-training	Recovery 6 mi
Friday	Recovery 5 mi	Recovery 5 mi	General aerobic + speed 8 mi w/ 8 × 100 m strides	General aerobic + speed 9 mi w/ 8 × 100 m strides	General aerobic + speed 10 mi w/ 8 × 100 m strides
Saturday	Rest or cross-training	Recovery 5 mi	Recovery 6 mi	Recovery 6 mi	Recovery 6 mi
Sunday	Recovery 7 mi	General aerobic 10 mi	General aerobic 10 mi	Medium-long run 12 mi	Medium-long run 13 mi
Weekly mileage	16	30	36	42	50

11

Multiple Marathoning

This chapter is for those occasions when, for whatever perverse reason, you've decided to do two marathons with 12 weeks or less between. Though doing two (or more) marathons in rapid succession generally isn't the best way to go after a personal best time, this chapter focuses on structuring your training to maximize your likelihood of success. It includes five schedules, covering 12, 10, 8, 6, and 4 weeks between marathons.

These schedules are substantially different from the schedules in chapters 8 to 10, in that these schedules must start with helping you to recover from marathon number 1 and then help you train and taper for marathon number 2. The number of weeks between marathons dictates how much time you devote to recovery, training, and tapering. For example, the 12-week schedule allows a relatively luxurious 4 weeks for recovery, whereas the 6-week schedule can allocate only 2 weeks to recovery.

The schedules in this chapter were written for marathoners who typically build to 60 to 70 miles per week during marathon preparation. The 10- and 12-week schedules build to a peak weekly mileage of 67, whereas the 8-, 6-, and 4-week schedules peak at 65, 59, and 48 miles, respectively. If your mileage during marathon preparation is typically more than 70 miles per week, then scale up the volume in these schedules moderately. Similarly, if your mileage typically peaks at less than 60 miles per week, then scale the training back proportionately.

The schedules assume that you want to do your best in your second marathon. Though this might not mean running a personal best or even running as fast as in the first one in your double (or triple, or whatever), it does mean toeing the line with the intention of running as fast as you can that day. If your multiple-marathoning goal is to cruise comfortably through a second or third marathon soon after a peak effort, then ignore these schedules. Simply focus on recovering from your first one while interspersing enough long runs to maintain your endurance until your next one.

///// Why Multiple Marathoning?

Frank Shorter said that you can't run another marathon until you've forgotten your last one. If that's so, then a lot of runners out there have short memories.

Although statistics in this area are hard to come by, anecdotal evidence suggests that many runners choose to circumvent the conventional wisdom—which is to do, at most, a spring and a fall marathon—and are running three, four, or more marathons a year. Some run a marathon a month. And we're not just talking about middle-of-the-packers here. Some leading runners, such as 1998 New York City Marathon winner Franca Fiacconi, who has produced world-class times only a week apart, and Doug Kurtis, who has run a world-record 75 sub-2:20 marathons, have shown that it's possible to run successive high-quality 26.2-milers in a startlingly short time.

Someone like Fiacconi, of course, has significant financial incentive for attempting repeat marathons. Should you try to do so? We can't answer that question for you other than to describe why some people are drawn to multiple marathoning.

UNMET GOALS

It's rare to finish a marathon and—after the obligatory utterance of "Never again"—not think that you could have run at least a little faster, if only X, Y, and/or Z hadn't occurred. If you've run a less-than-satisfying marathon, but it didn't seem to take too much out of you, and if another likely site for a good race looms several weeks ahead, then you might want to consider your horse-remounting skills.

BUILDING BLOCKS

A marathon run at a controlled but honest pace a few months before a peak effort can provide a significant training boost and a good measure of your fitness. If you run one too hard or too close to your real goal race, of course, this is akin to pulling up roots to see how your carrots are growing. Certainly these are excellent opportunities to test your marathon drink, shoes, and the like in battle conditions.

TRAVEL

As the growing popularity of destination marathons shows, a special knowledge of an area comes from covering it at length on foot. Many runners plan vacations around a scenic marathon for a chance to view the scenery in a way that you can't experience from a tour bus. When you combine such trips with a standard marathon schedule, you're likely to run into instances of short turnaround times.

VARIETY

Some runners simply like to run marathons and to experience them in all their permutations, from intimate affairs like Washington, D.C.'s Last Plain to Boston (fewer than 100 runners doing 8.5 laps around Hains Point), to medium-size marathons like Napa Valley (1,800 runners traversing California wine country) and Twin Cities (8,000 runners along the Mississippi River at peak fall foliage), on up to the mega events like Chicago and Berlin. Even though marathons are held throughout the year, the traditional spring and fall clustering can mean that sampling the marathon world requires becoming a multiple marathoner.

A FOOLISH CONSISTENCY

How can we put this gently? Some runners are drawn to challenges for no better reason than because they sound good. This would include such undertakings as running a marathon a month for a year, running a marathon in all 50 U.S. states plus the District of Columbia, running one in every province and territory in Canada, and completing a marathon on every continent. The marathon-a-month goal obviously requires scant time between efforts but so can the geographically based ones, given that you'll be at the mercy of marathon planners.

WHY NOT?

"Normal" marathoners should check the amount of glass in their houses before throwing stones at multiple marathoners. After all, the bulk of this book has been devoted to detailing how to maximize your chances of success at an activity that the human body isn't really suited for. So if some runners want to give the standard reason for undertaking such a challenge—"Because it's there"—several times a year, well, it's not as if they're clubbing seals.

Reading the Schedules

The schedules are presented in a day-by-day format. This is in response to requests from readers of our first book, *Road Racing for Serious Runners*, to provide schedules that specify what to do each day of the week.

The main limitation with this approach is that it's impossible to guess the myriad of outside factors that may influence your day-to-day nonrunning life. Work schedules, family life, relationships, school commitments, and Mother Nature all have their parts in determining when you get to do your long runs and other aspects of marathon preparation. You'll no doubt require some flexibility in your training and will need to juggle days around from time to time. That's expected, and as long as you don't try to make up for lost time by doing several hard days in a row, you should be able to avoid injury and overtraining.

Because of the large variation between runners in the time required for marathon recovery, you should approach these schedules with a high degree of flexibility. Also, if, in your first marathon, the weather was hot, you became severely dehydrated, or you became unusually hobbled, then your recovery is likely to take longer than usual. When a conflict arises between what the schedule says to do and what your body indicates it's willing to do, listen to your body. With these tight time frames between marathons, your best strategy is first to focus on recovery and then to worry about the other aspects of training. If you're not able to follow the schedules closely for one reason or another, then follow the priorities discussed later in this chapter in choosing which workouts to do and which to miss.

> **Listen to your body.**

For all the schedules in this chapter, remember that in the first few weeks after marathon number 1, recovery is your primary objective and that during the last 3 weeks, tapering to consolidate your energy reserves is paramount. If you're worn out or injured going into marathon number 2, then any extra workouts you squeezed in won't have been worth the effort.

One way to ensure that you don't run too hard during the first few weeks after your previous marathon is to use a heart rate monitor. As discussed in chapter 4, a heart rate monitor can help prevent you from going too fast on your easy days. During the first few weeks after the marathon, keep your heart rate below 75 percent of your maximal heart rate or 70 percent of your heart rate reserve to help speed your recovery.

/// Pete's 1983 Trifecta

In 1983, I ran three high-quality marathons in 17 weeks. Nine weeks after winning the San Francisco Marathon in 2:14:44, I finished second in the Montreal Marathon in 2:12:33. Eight weeks after that, I won the Auckland Marathon in 2:12:19. At the time, the last two races were personal bests.

I did a few things wrong between San Francisco and Montreal but was able to hold my body together through a combination of luck, enthusiasm, and youth (I was 26). After San Francisco, I was remarkably stiff for several days. I'm not sure whether that was from standing around in the cold for a couple of hours after the race or because it was my first marathon in almost 2 years. I hobbled a 2-miler 2 days after the race and racked up 46 miles for the week. Regular massage helped to bring my legs around.

Fortunately, my body bounced back really well after that first week, and I was up to 100 miles for the third week after, including a session of eight 800-meter repeats on the track. My mileage climbed to 116 and 122 for the fourth and fifth weeks, which was about as high as I used to get back then. (I hadn't made an Olympic team yet, so I was working full-time.) There was just enough time to fit in two tune-up races, a 5-miler in 23:35 and a third-place finish in the New Haven 20K, and then it was time to taper again. Eight days before Montreal, I went to the track and did two repeats of 1,600 meters in 4:24 and 4:23, which was really fast for me and a good omen. The last 2 weeks before the race I tried to get caught up on sleep, and I felt really ready going into Montreal.

The night after Montreal, I stayed out until 5 A.M., took an 8 A.M. flight back to Boston, and caught a cab directly to work. This didn't help my recovery. After that, though, I settled down, and in the first 3 weeks after Montreal covered 48, 72, and 97 miles. Lots of sleep and weekly massage kept me injury-free, and, except for the occasional "felt like hell" notation in my diary, training went pretty well.

Three weeks before the Auckland Marathon, I started my leave of absence from work at New Balance to prepare for the Olympic trials and flew to New Zealand with my training partner, Tom Ratcliffe, who was also running Auckland. We got a bit carried away with the excitement and probably overtrained the first week there. The second week in New Zealand, I ran a 10K tune-up race in 29:12, which I was very pleased with. During the last week before the marathon, however, I could tell that my body was on a fine edge, and I decided to back right off. Three days before the race, I was still feeling pretty tired. Fortunately, on race day, I felt strong and broke away after 17 miles. It had been a very positive experience in multiple marathoning that was excellent practice for the following year's Olympic trials and marathon.

Following the Schedules

Each column of the schedules represents a week's training. For example, in the 10-week schedule, the column for 9 weeks to goal indicates that at the end of that week you have 9 weeks until your second marathon. The schedules continue week by week until race week.

We have included the specific workout for each day as well as the category of training for that day. For example, in the 10-week schedule on the Friday of the 5-weeks-to-go column, the specific workout is a 9-mile run, and the category of training for that day is general aerobic conditioning. This aspect of the schedules allows you to quickly see the balance of training during each week and the progression of workouts from week to week. Look again at the 10-week schedule—it's easy to see that with 5 weeks to go until the marathon, there are 3 recovery days that week with a $\dot{V}O_2max$ session, a long run, a medium-long run, and a general aerobic conditioning run.

Looking at the row for Sunday, it's easy to see how the long runs progress and then taper in the last few weeks before the marathon.

The workouts are divided into the following eight categories: long runs, medium-long runs, general aerobic, lactate threshold, $\dot{V}O_2max$, speed, recovery, and (for the 12-week schedule only) marathon-specific runs. Each of these categories is explained briefly below. The various types of training are explained in depth in chapter 2.

Long Runs

A long run is any run of 17 miles or longer. The intention of long runs is (obviously) to improve your endurance in preparation for the marathon's 26.2 miles. The specific physiological benefits of these runs are discussed in detail in chapter 2. To gain the most from your long runs, do them at the correct intensity. Long runs shouldn't be slow jogs during which you just accumulate time on your feet. The most beneficial intensity range for your long runs is 10 to 20 percent slower than your goal marathon race pace. The reason for this intensity range is explained in chapter 2.

Medium-Long Runs

A medium-long run is any run of 11 to 16 miles. Medium-long runs reinforce the physiological benefits of your long runs. To gain the greatest physiological benefits, the pace for these runs should be similar to the pace for long runs.

General Aerobic Runs

General aerobic runs include any run of 10 miles or less that's done at a steady pace. Faster runs of this length fall into the lactate threshold category, whereas slower runs are specifically for recovery. In other words, these are your standard, moderate-effort, putting-in-the-miles runs. The intention of your general aerobic runs is to enhance your overall aerobic conditioning through boosting your training volume; these runs improve your marathon readiness because many of the beneficial adaptations that improve endurance are related to the total volume of your training.

Lactate Threshold

Lactate threshold runs are tempo runs in which you run for at least 20 minutes at your lactate threshold pace. This coincides closely with your current 15K to half marathon race pace. Tempo runs provide a strong stimulus to improve your lactate threshold

General aerobic runs enhance aerobic conditioning by increasing training volume.

pace, which leads to similar improvements in your marathon race pace. The lactate threshold sessions are done after a 2- to 3-mile warm-up. The tempo runs in this chapter are 4 or 5 miles long, whereas in chapters 8 to 10 the tempo runs extend up to 7 miles. The reason for the difference is that with the short time frames of the schedules in this chapter and the fact that you've just run a marathon, lactate threshold training isn't as high a priority.

$\dot{V}O_2$max

$\dot{V}O_2$max runs consist of intervals of 600 meters to 1,600 meters duration, which are run at 95 to 100 percent of your current $\dot{V}O_2$max pace. This coincides closely with your current 3K to 5K race pace. These sessions provide a strong stimulus to improve your $\dot{V}O_2$max.

Speed

Speed runs are repetitions of 50 meters to 150 meters that improve leg speed and running form. These sessions are done after a thorough warm-up and often toward the end of a general aerobic run or a recovery run. Allow yourself plenty of rest between repetitions so that you can run each one with good technique.

Recovery

Recovery runs are relatively short runs done at a relaxed pace to enhance recovery from your previous marathon and for your next hard workout. These runs aren't necessarily jogs, but they should be noticeably slower than your other workouts of the week.

Marathon-Pace Runs

Only one marathon-pace run is called for in this chapter, and it occurs in the 12-week schedule, with 6 weeks until marathon number 2. These sessions are so hard and require so much recovery that they don't have a role in the schedules of 10 weeks or less. Start the marathon-pace run in the 12-week schedule comfortably, as you would other medium-long runs, and then run the last 12 miles at marathon race pace.

Doing Doubles

As discussed in chapter 5, sometimes marathoners benefit from running twice a day. This isn't the case when you have a short time frame between marathons. These schedules don't include doubles because the weekly mileage doesn't warrant it and because the maximum distance on recovery days is 7 miles.

//// Pete's 1984 Dynamic Double

On May 26, 1984, I ran 2:11:43 to win the Olympic marathon trials, and then on August 12, I placed 11th in 2:13:53 in the Olympics. Here's how I approached the 11 weeks in between.

I was on a bit of a high after winning the trials, to say the least. I took the next day off and went for a relaxed swim and a pathetic 3-mile shuffle 2 days after the race. The next day, I had my weekly massage, and my muscles weren't too bad. Building toward the Olympics, massage each week helped to keep me injury-free despite the short recovery. I ran 45 miles the week after the trials. Using the philosophy that I needed to get the training in as quickly as possible to be able to taper again and be in top form for the Olympics, I initially ran as I felt and got in 112 miles the second week and 151 miles the third week. During the second week after the trials, I started doing a few strideouts every couple of days to try to get my legs turning over. This seemed to help quite a bit.

In retrospect, I should have run 80 to 90 miles the second week and 110 to 120 the third week. Doing the amount I did showed a lack of confidence because I wouldn't have lost fitness by doing fewer miles. In fact, if I had run a bit less mileage right after the trials, I probably would have performed better at the Olympics. But I didn't understand that at the time.

The problem I faced was that in 11 weeks I couldn't very well do a 4-week recovery and a 3-week taper because that would have left only 4 weeks to train to compete against the best runners in the world. I got around that by cutting back the recovery and getting back into fairly high-quality long intervals by the fourth or fifth week posttrials. The beauty of the short recovery after the trials was that I was fit enough to do my long intervals at a good clip right away, so I didn't need as long to build into them. For example, in the fifth week posttrials, I did a 3-mile time trial on the track in 14:02.

I did continue, however, to train according to how I felt, with flexibility both ways. For example, one day I headed out for a 15-miler, felt good, and wound up going 26. On other days, I would postpone a track workout for a day or 2 until my legs felt like they could give a good effort without getting injured.

I tapered more for the Olympics than for the trials. This was somewhat necessitated by tightness that I developed in my back during the last 3 weeks before the race. It was also out of a realization that I had trained a bit too hard in the weeks after the trials and that my energy level needed time to come up a notch. This is a very subjective matter, but I could tell during my training runs that a bit of zip was missing and that it was better to cut back and regain my strength. I did this by making my easy days— in terms of speed and distance—easier. I also trimmed the volume of my long runs and my speed workouts. This taper became the model that I followed for the rest of my racing career.

Multiple Marathoning Priorities

The following sections explain the priorities for the training schedules in this chapter. But what if you don't have 12, 10, 8, 6, or 4 weeks between marathons?

If you have less than 4 weeks between marathons, you're on your own. Your main concern should be recovery, recovery, and more recovery not only from your first marathon but also from the lobotomy that led you to come up with this plan.

For other amounts of time between marathons, follow these guidelines:

- Eleven weeks between. Do the 12-week schedule but skip the week "6 weeks to goal."
- Nine weeks between. Do the 10-week schedule, but skip the week "5 weeks to goal," and with 35 days to go, increase the distance of the run to 18 miles.
- Seven weeks between. Do the 8-week schedule, but skip the week "3 weeks to goal," and with 21 days to go, increase the distance of the run to 18 miles.
- Five weeks between. Do the 6-week schedule but skip the week "2 weeks to goal," and with 14 days to go, increase the medium-long run to 16 miles.

12-Week Schedule

Twelve weeks between marathons aren't too bad. There's a real risk, however, of either taking it too easy and gradually losing marathon-specific fitness or overdoing it and finding yourself at the starting line of marathon number 2 feeling tired and wondering why you're there. You need to find the perfect balance for your individual situation. The best strategy is to really take it easy for the first 3 to 4 weeks after your previous marathon to ensure that your body is fully recovered. That leaves 8 or 9 weeks until the next marathon, including 5 or 6 weeks of solid training and a 3-week taper.

The key training time is the 6-week period lasting from 7 weeks to go through 2 weeks until the second marathon. The most important workouts during those weeks are the tune-up races with 15 and 29 days to go; the marathon-specific run with 42 days to go; the long runs with 21, 28, 35, and 49 days to go; the $V.O_2max$ sessions with 25, 33, and 39 days to go; and the medium-long runs with 24, 32, 38, 44, and 52 days until marathon number 2.

Victah Sailer © Agence Shot 1990

Bill Rodgers

Fastest Marathon: 2:09:27
Marathon Career Highlights: Won Boston and New York City marathons four times each. Member of 1976 Olympic team. Twice set American record. Ran 28 sub-2:15s.

Bill Rodgers deservedly secured his spot in running history by winning the two most competitive American marathons of his era, Boston and New York City, four times each. What's less remembered about Rodgers's running of that era was the frequency with which he won other marathons while preparing for and recovering from his two key races each year.

Consider 1977. Rodgers started the year with a marathon win in Kyoto, Japan. Hot weather quashed his hope of winning Boston for a second time that April, and he dropped out at the top of Heartbreak Hill. To capitalize on his fitness and to soothe his psyche, Rodgers ran the Amsterdam Marathon a month later, and he won in 2:12:46. In late October, he ran 2:11:28 to defend his title at New York. In early December, he returned to Japan for the Fukuoka Marathon, which at the time was the closest thing to an unofficial annual world championship. Rodgers won in 2:10:55 and was ranked the top marathoner in the world for the year by *Track and Field News*.

"Some people focus on just one marathon a year and don't mind putting all their eggs in one basket," says Rodgers. "Frank Shorter was great at this. For me, my racing schedule was an offshoot of my personality—I need to be active. I thrive on the competitive and social aspects of our sport. I just want to get out there and run and enjoy it!"

Rodgers usually used lesser marathons as stepping-stones to his main goals. "A good marathon a few months before Boston set me up psychologically," Rodgers says. "My mileage wouldn't drop too much before the first one, and after laying low for a week or so afterward, I'd be right back into regular training."

In fact, Rodgers followed this approach even between two important marathons. The day after winning New York in 1977, he ran 3 miles. The next day, he had a 14-mile day on two 7-milers, and on the next day, he ran 9 miles in the morning and 10 in the evening. The following week, he ran 168 miles because, he says, "I wanted to be ready for Fukuoka in another month or so."

Lest we all ignore the need for proper tapering and recovery, Rodgers notes that his nearly unmatched mileage base—at his peak, he averaged 130 miles per week for several years, even after taking tapering and recovery periods into account—allowed him to skirt around the need for downtime that most runners have. In addition, he says, "I didn't do a lot of brutal, intense speed work, and a lot of my mileage was run at a relatively easy pace. I was putting in a lot of miles, but I wasn't killing myself every day."

Moreover, Rodgers adds, his relative nonchalance toward rest occasionally backfired on him. "I had some wipeouts," he says, "and some times when I didn't race as well as I should have. If the weather was good, I could usually get away with it, but if it was hot, I would get zapped."

"We didn't know how to train for the damn marathon," Rodgers laughs. "We were all experimenting. Today, we know so much more about how to approach each workout, how to taper, and so on. I'm still a big believer in high mileage, and I'd still race a lot, but in retrospect, if I were doing it today, I'd give myself more of a break before and after marathons."

10-Week Schedule

Allowing 10 weeks between marathons is almost reasonable, and the schedule reflects this by providing 3 weeks of solid recovery, 4 weeks of solid training, and a 3-week taper.

The key training weeks are those that end with 6, 5, 4, 3, and 2 weeks until your second marathon. The most important workouts during those weeks are the tune-up races with 15 and 29 days to go; the long runs with 14, 21, 28, and 35 days to go; the lactate threshold session with 44 days to go; the $\dot{V}O_2$max sessions with 25 and 39 days to go; and the medium-long runs with 24, 32, and 38 days until marathon number 2. The only word of caution concerning a 10-week time frame between marathons is to allow yourself to recover fully from your previous marathon before training too intensely for the next one.

8-Week Schedule

The 8-week schedule allows you to recover thoroughly from your previous marathon, train well for about 3 weeks, and then taper for marathon number 2. Eight weeks between marathons are far less risky than 4 or 6 weeks. Even if your first marathon was hot, or if you came out of it with a minor injury, with a bit of luck you should still be okay for marathon number 2.

The key training weeks are those that end with 4, 3, and 2 weeks until the second marathon. The most important workouts during those weeks are the tune-up race with 15 days to go; the long runs with 14, 21, and 28 days to go; the lactate threshold session with 30 days to go; and the medium-long runs with 18 and 24 days until the marathon. Try to avoid doing more than the schedules call for because 8 weeks between marathons are still brief enough that you don't have much room for error.

6-Week Schedule

The 6-week schedule was difficult to put together because 6 weeks is just enough time to start to lose fitness if you don't train enough, but it is also just barely enough time to recover from marathon number 1 before your need to taper for marathon number 2. The most important training weeks are those that end 3 weeks and 2 weeks before marathon number 2. Those weeks provide a small window during which you can train fairly hard without wearing yourself out for the second marathon.

The key workouts during those weeks are the tune-up race with 15 days to go, the long run with 14 days to go, the $\dot{V}O_2max$ sessions with 19 and 23 days to go, and the medium-long runs with 18 and 21 days until the marathon. This brief training stimulus will keep you in peak marathon fitness so that after tapering, you should be close to your best.

4-Week Schedule

The 4-week schedule is about as compact as you can get. This program consists of 2 weeks of recovery merging into 2 weeks of taper. The objective is to get you to the starting line injury-free, fully recovered from your previous marathon, and still in top shape. The mileage for this program starts at 25 miles and builds to 48 miles during the third week. Unfortunately, that's also the penultimate week before the marathon, so mileage and intensity-building abruptly halt and merge into a taper.

The most important workouts in this schedule are the medium-long runs with 10 and 14 days until marathon number 2, and the $\dot{V}O_2max$ session with 12 days to go. If you need to do two marathons 4 weeks apart (and "need" is a relative term), then this schedule should maximize your chances of success.

Racing Strategies

Don't do it!

Just kidding. You should definitely set a clear goal for the second (or third, fourth, etc.) marathon you're running within a brief time frame. Otherwise, you might very well find yourself a few miles into it already wondering, "What am I doing here?" Being able to state what you want to accomplish in your multiple marathoning will provide en route direction and motivation. The longer that you've allowed between marathons, the more precisely you should be able to state your goals for marathon number 2 (beyond "to get through it").

Once you've picked your goal, map out the splits you'll need to hit. Throughout this book, we've stressed the merits of showing restraint early in the marathon to maximize your chances of being able to run a strong second half. That advice is especially pertinent if you've already finished one marathon in the last 12 weeks or sooner. Your multiple-marathoning experience will almost certainly become a self-fulfilling death march if you run too fast early in the race in the hope of building a cushion against an inevitably slower second half.

Wait until the week before your second marathon to decide on a time goal. Be realistic, taking into account how your recovery from your first one went; the quality of your long runs, tempo runs, and interval sessions in the interim; and whether you've felt your energy level rise during your taper for marathon number 2.

Also consider the circumstances of your previous marathon. For example, if you ran a huge PR off of negative splits, then there's probably room for improvement this time around. Or say you wilted over the last 10K the last time around and realize in retrospect that this was because of a too-aggressive first 10 miles; you should be able to make another attempt at your goal time for the first marathon. If, however, you prepared with monklike devotion for 24 weeks for your previous marathon, and shaved 3 seconds off your lifetime best in your 28th marathon, and your second marathon is 4 weeks later, well, sorry, but this probably isn't the time to try for a 10-minute PR.

If you've never consciously tried to run a marathon with negative splits, this might be the occasion to do so. Give yourself the first several miles to get an accurate feel for how your body is responding to the challenge you've set for it, and pick up the pace only when you're fairly confident that you can sustain it to the end.

After the Marathon

If you've just run two or more marathons within a brief time span, your best strategy for future success is to take a well-deserved break. (You might also want to check what they've been putting in your coffee at work.) A few weeks of no running or easy training will help your body to recover and your mind to develop new challenges. You have little to gain by rushing back into training, and your risk of injury is exceptionally high at this point, owing to the reduced resiliency of your muscles and connective tissue after running multiple marathons. If you choose to keep training, then the 5-week recovery schedule (mesocycle 5) in chapter 9 will help you recover and rebuild your training safely.

	Weeks to goal			
	11	**10**	**9**	**8**
Monday	Rest or cross-training	Rest or cross-training	Rest or cross-training	Rest or cross-training
Tuesday	Rest or cross-training	Recovery 5 mi	Recovery 6 mi	General aerobic + speed 8 mi w/ 10 × 100 m strides
Wednesday	Recovery 5 mi	Recovery 5 mi	General aerobic 9 mi	Medium-long run 12 mi
Thursday	Rest or cross-training	Rest or cross-training	Rest or cross-training	Recovery 4 mi
Friday	Recovery 5 mi	General aerobic + speed 7 mi w/ 8 × 100 m strides	General aerobic + speed 9 mi w/ 8 × 100 m strides	Lactate threshold 9 mi w/ 4 mi @ 15K to half marathon race pace
Saturday	Recovery 5 mi	Recovery 5 mi	Recovery 5 mi	Recovery + speed 5 mi w/ 6 × 100 m m strides
Sunday	Recovery 7 mi	General aerobic 10 mi	Medium-long run 13 mi	Medium-long run 16 mi
Weekly mileage	22	32	42	54

	Weeks to goal			
	7	**6**	**5**	**4**
Monday	Rest or cross-training	Rest or cross-training	Rest or cross-training	Rest or cross-training
Tuesday	$\dot{V}O_2$max 9 mi w/ 6 × 800 m @ 5K race pace; jog 2 min between	General aerobic + speed 8 mi w/ 10 × 100 m strides	Recovery 6 mi	$\dot{V}O_2$max 9 mi w/ 6 × 600 m @ 5K race pace; jog 90 sec between
Wednesday	Recovery 6 mi	Medium-long run 15 mi	$\dot{V}O_2$max 10 mi w/ 4 × 1,200 m @ 5K race pace; jog 2½ min between	Medium-long run 11 mi
Thursday	Medium-long run 13 mi	Recovery 6 mi	Medium-long run 15 mi	Recovery + speed 6 mi w/ 6 × 100 m strides
Friday	General aerobic + speed 8 mi w/ 10 × 100 m strides	Medium-long run 13 mi	General aerobic 9 mi	Recovery 5 mi
Saturday	Recovery 6 mi	Recovery + speed 7 mi w/ 6 × 100 m strides	Recovery 6 mi	8-15K tune-up race
Sunday	Long run 18 mi	Marathon specific 15 mi w/ 12 mi @ marathon race pace	Long run 20 mi	Long run 17 mi
Weekly mileage	60	64	66	59

	Weeks to goal			
	3	**2**	**1**	**Race week**
Monday	Rest or cross-training	Rest or cross-training	Rest or cross-training	Rest
Tuesday	Recovery 6 mi	$\dot{V}O_2$max 9 mi w/ 6 × 600 m @ 5K race pace; jog 90 sec between	General aerobic + speed 8 mi w/ 8 × 100 m strides	Recovery 6 mi
Wednesday	$\dot{V}O_2$max 11 mi w/ 6 × 1,000 m @ 5K race pace; jog 2 min between	Medium-long run 11 mi	Recovery 5 mi	Dress rehearsal 7 mi with 2 mi @ marathon race pace
Thursday	Medium-long run 15 mi	Recovery + speed 6 mi w/ 6 × 100 m strides	$\dot{V}O_2$max 9 mi w/ 3 × 1,600 m @ 5K race pace; jog 2 min between	Recovery 6 mi
Friday	General aerobic 9 mi	Recovery 5 mi	Recovery 5 mi	Recovery + speed 5 mi w/ 6 × 100 m strides
Saturday	Recovery 6 mi	8-10K tune-up race	General aerobic + speed 7 mi w/ 10 × 100 m strides	Recovery 4 mi
Sunday	Long run 20 mi	Long run 17 mi	Medium-long run 13 mi	Second marathon
Weekly mileage	67	59	47	28 (6 days prerace)

	Weeks to goal				
	9	**8**	**7**	**6**	**5**
Monday	Rest or cross-training	Rest or cross-training	Rest or cross-training	Rest or cross-training	Rest or cross-training
Tuesday	Rest or cross-training	Recovery 5 mi	Recovery 6 mi	General aerobic + speed 8 mi w/ 10 × 100 m strides	Recovery 6 mi
Wednesday	Recovery 5 mi	Recovery 5 mi	General aerobic 9 mi	Medium-long run 12 mi	$\dot{V}O_2$max 10 mi w/ 4 × 1,200 m @ 5K race pace; jog 2$\frac{1}{2}$ min between
Thursday	Rest or cross-training	Rest or cross-training	Rest or cross-training	Recovery 4 mi	Medium-long run 15 mi
Friday	Recovery 5 mi	General aerobic + speed 7 mi w/ 8 × 100 m strides	General aerobic + speed 9 mi w/ 8 × 100 m strides	Lactate threshold 9 mi w/ 5 mi @ 15K to half marathon race pace	General aerobic 9 mi
Saturday	Recovery 5 mi	Recovery 5 mi	Recovery 5 mi	Recovery + speed 5 mi w/ 6 × 100 m strides	Recovery 6 mi
Sunday	Recovery 7 mi	General aerobic 10 mi	Medium-long run 13 mi	Long run 17 mi	Long run 19 mi
Weekly mileage	22	32	42	55	65

	Weeks to goal				
	4	**3**	**2**	**1**	**Race week**
Monday	Rest or cross-training	Rest or cross-training	Rest or cross-training	Rest or cross-training	Rest
Tuesday	$\dot{V}O_2max$ 9 mi w/ 6 × 600 m @ 5K race pace; jog 90 sec between	Recovery 6 mi	$\dot{V}O_2max$ 9 mi w/ 6 × 600 m @ 5K race pace; jog 90 sec between	General aerobic + speed 8 mi w/ 8 × 100 m strides	Recovery 6 mi
Wednesday	Medium-long run 11 mi	$\dot{V}O_2max$ 11 mi w/ 6 × 1,000 m @ 5K race pace; jog 2 min between	Medium-long run 11 mi	Recovery 5 mi	Dress rehearsal 7 mi with 2 mi @ marathon race pace
Thursday	Recovery + speed 6 mi w/ 6 × 100 m strides	Medium-long run 15 mi	Recovery + speed 6 mi w/ 6 × 100 m strides	$\dot{V}O_2max$ 9 mi w/ 3 × 1,600 m @ 5K race pace; jog 2 min between	Recovery 6 mi
Friday	Recovery 5 mi	General aerobic 9 mi	Recovery 5 mi	Recovery 5 mi	Recovery + speed 5 mi w/ 6 × 100 m strides
Saturday	8-15K tune-up race	Recovery 6 mi	8-10K tune-up race	General aerobic + speed 7 mi w/ 10 × 100 m strides	Recovery 4 mi
Sunday	Long run 17 mi	Long run 20 mi	Long run 17 mi	Medium-long run 13 mi	Second marathon
Weekly mileage	59	67	59	47	28 (6 days prerace)

	Weeks to goal			
	7	**6**	**5**	**4**
Monday	Rest or cross-training	Rest or cross-training	Rest or cross-training	Rest or cross-training
Tuesday	Rest or cross-training	Recovery 5 mi	Recovery 6 mi	General aerobic + speed 8 mi w/ 10 × 100 m strides
Wednesday	Recovery 5 mi	Recovery 5 mi	General aerobic 9 mi	Medium-long run 12 mi
Thursday	Rest or cross-training	Rest or cross-training	Rest or cross-training	Recovery 4 mi
Friday	Recovery 5 mi	General aerobic + speed 7 mi w/ 8 × 100 m strides	General aerobic + speed 9 mi w/ 8 × 100 m strides	Lactate threshold 9 mi w/ 5 mi @ 15K to half marathon race pace
Saturday	Recovery 5 mi	Recovery 5 mi	Recovery 5 mi	Recovery + speed 5 mi w/ 6 × 100 m strides
Sunday	Recovery 7 mi	General aerobic 10 mi	Medium-long run 13 mi	Long run 17 mi
Weekly mileage	22	32	42	55

	Weeks to goal			
	3	**2**	**1**	**Race week**
Monday	Rest or cross-training	Rest or cross-training	Rest or cross-training	Rest
Tuesday	Recovery 6 mi	$\dot{V}O_2$max 9 mi w/ 6 × 600 m @ 5K race pace; jog 90 sec between	General aerobic + speed 8 mi w/ 8 × 100 m strides	Recovery 6 mi
Wednesday	$\dot{V}O_2$max 10 mi w/ 5 × 1,000 m @ 5K race pace; jog 2 min between	Medium-long run 11 mi	Recovery 5 mi	Dress rehearsal 7 mi with 2 mi @ marathon race pace
Thursday	Medium-long run 15 mi	Recovery + speed 6 mi w/ 6 × 100 m strides	$\dot{V}O_2$max 9 mi w/ 3 × 1,600 m @ 5K race pace; jog 2 min between	Recovery 6 mi
Friday	General aerobic 9 mi	Recovery 5 mi	Recovery 5 mi	Recovery + speed 5 mi w/ 6 × 100 m strides
Saturday	Recovery 5 mi	8-10K tune-up race	Recovery + speed 6 mi w/ 8 × 100 m strides	Recovery 4 mi
Sunday	Long run 20 mi	Long run 17 mi	Medium-long run 13 mi	Second marathon
Weekly mileage	65	59	46	28 (6 days prerace)

	Weeks to goal		
	5	**4**	**3**
Monday	Rest or cross-training	Rest or cross-training	Rest or cross-training
Tuesday	Rest or cross-training	Recovery 6 mi	General aerobic + speed 7 mi w/ 8 × 100 m strides
Wednesday	Recovery 5 mi	General aerobic 8 mi	Medium-long run 12 mi
Thursday	Rest or cross-training	Rest or cross-training	Recovery 4 mi
Friday	Recovery 6 mi	General aerobic + speed 8 mi w/ 8 × 100 m strides	$\dot{V}O_2max$ 9 mi w/ 7 × 800 m @ 5K race pace; jog 2 min between
Saturday	Recovery 6 mi	Recovery 5 mi	Recovery + speed 5 mi w/ 6 × 100 m strides
Sunday	General aerobic 8 mi	Medium-long run 11 mi	Medium-long run 15 mi
Weekly mileage	25	38	52

	Weeks to goal		
	2	**1**	**Race week**
Monday	Rest or cross-training	Rest or cross-training	Rest
Tuesday	$\dot{V}O_2$max 9 mi w/ 6 × 600 m @ 5K race pace; jog 90 sec between	General aerobic + speed 8 mi w/ 8 × 100 m strides	Recovery 6 mi
Wednesday	Medium-long run 11 mi	Recovery 5 mi	Dress rehearsal 7 mi with 2 mi @ marathon race pace
Thursday	Recovery + speed 6 mi w/ 6 × 100 m strides	$\dot{V}O_2$max 9 mi w/ 3 × 1,600 m @ 5K race pace; jog 2 min between	Recovery 6 mi
Friday	Recovery 5 mi	Recovery 5 mi	Recovery + speed 5 mi w/ 6 × 100 m strides
Saturday	8-10K tune-up race	Recovery + speed 6 mi w/ 8 × 100 m strides	Recovery 4 mi
Sunday	Long run 18 mi	Medium-long run 13 mi	Second marathon
Weekly mileage	59	46	28 (6 days prerace)

	Weeks to goal			
	3	**2**	**1**	**Race week**
Monday	Rest or cross-training	Rest or cross-training	Rest or cross-training	Rest
Tuesday	Rest or cross-training	Recovery 6 mi	$\dot{V}O_2$max 8 mi w/ 5 × 800 m @ 5K race pace; jog 2 min between	Recovery 6 mi
Wednesday	Recovery 5 mi	General aerobic 8 mi	Recovery 5 mi	Dress rehearsal 7 mi with 2 mi @ marathon race pace
Thursday	Rest or cross-training	Rest or cross-training	Medium-long run 15 mi	Recovery 6 mi
Friday	Recovery 6 mi	General aerobic + speed 8 mi w/ 8 × 100 m strides	Recovery 4 mi	Recovery + speed 5 mi w/ 6 × 100 m strides
Saturday	Recovery 6 mi	Recovery 5 mi	Recovery + speed 5 mi w/ 8 × 100 m strides	Recovery 4 mi
Sunday	General aerobic 8 mi	Medium-long run 12 mi	Medium-long run 11 mi	Second marathon
Weekly mileage	25	39	48	28 (6 days prerace)

appendix
A

Marathon Pace Chart

Goal	Pace per mile	5 mi	10K	10 mi	20K	½ way
2:10	4:57.5	24:47	30:48	49:35	1:01:36	1:05:00
2:15	5:09	25:45	32:00	51:30	1:04:00	1:07:30
2:20	5:20.4	26:42	33:11	53:24	1:06:22	1:10:00
2:25	5:31.8	27:39	34:22	55:18	1:08:44	1:12:30
2:30	5:43.2	28:36	35:33	57:12	1:11:06	1:15:00
2:35	5:54.7	29:33	36:44	59:07	1:13:28	1:17:30
2:40	6:06.1	30:30	37:55	1:01:01	1:15:50	1:20:00
2:45	6:17.6	31:28	39:06	1:02:56	1:18:12	1:22:30
2:50	6:29	32:25	40:17	1:04:50	1:20:34	1:25:00
2:55	6:40.5	33:22	41:28	1:06:45	1:22:56	1:27:30
3:00	6:51.9	34:19	42:39	1:08:39	1:25:18	1:30:00
3:05	7:03.3	35:16	43:50	1:10:33	1:27:40	1:32:30
3:10	7:14.8	36:14	45:02	1:12:28	1:30:04	1:35:00
3:15	7:26.2	37:11	46:13	1:14:22	1:32:26	1:37:30
3:20	7:37.7	38:08	47:24	1:16:17	1:34:48	1:40:00
3:25	7:49.1	39:05	48:35	1:18:11	1:37:10	1:42:30
3:30	8:00.5	40:02	49:46	1:20:05	1:39:32	1:45:00
3:35	8:12	41:00	50:57	1:22:00	1:41:54	1:47:30
3:40	8:23.4	41:57	52:08	1:23:54	1:44:16	1:50:00
3:45	8:34.9	42:54	53:19	1:25:49	1:46:38	1:52:30
3:50	8:46.3	43:51	54:30	1:27:43	1:49:00	1:55:00
3:55	8:57.8	44:49	55:41	1:29:38	1:51:22	1:57:30
4:00	9:09.2	45:46	56:53	1:31:32	1:53:46	2:00:00

15 mi	30K	20 mi	40K	25 mi	Finish
1:14:22	1:32:24	1:39:10	2:03:12	2:03:57	2:10
1:17:15	1:36:00	1:43:00	2:08:00	2:08:45	2:15
1:20:06	1:39:33	1:46:48	2:12:44	2:13:30	2:20
1:22:57	1:43:06	1:50:36	2:17:28	2:18:15	2:25
1:25:48	1:46:39	1:54:24	2:22:12	2:23:00	2:30
1:28:40	1:50:12	1:58:14	2:26:56	2:27:47	2:35
1:31:31	1:53:45	2:02:02	2:31:40	2:32:32	2:40
1:34:24	1:57:18	2:05:52	2:36:24	2:37:20	2:45
1:37:15	2:00:51	2:09:40	2:41:08	2:42:05	2:50
1:40:07	2:04:24	2:13:30	2:45:52	2:46:52	2:55
1:42:58	2:07:57	2:17:18	2:50:36	2:51:37	3:00
1:45:49	2:11:30	2:21:06	2:55:20	2:56:22	3:05
1:48:42	2:15:06	2:24:56	3:00:08	3:01:10	3:10
1:51:33	2:18:39	2:28:44	3:04:52	3:05:55	3:15
1:54:25	2:22:12	2:32:34	3:09:36	3:10:42	3:20
1:57:16	2:25:45	2:36:22	3:14:20	3:15:27	3:25
2:00:07	2:29:18	2:40:10	3:19:04	3:20:12	3:30
2:03:00	2:32:51	2:44:00	3:23:48	3:25:00	3:35
2:05:51	2:36:24	2:47:48	3:28:32	3:29:45	3:40
2:08:43	2:39:57	2:51:38	3:33:16	3:34:32	3:45
2:11:34	2:43:30	2:55:26	3:38:00	3:39:17	3:50
2:14:27	2:47:03	2:59:16	3:42:44	3:44:05	3:55
2:17:18	2:50:39	3:03:04	3:47:32	3:48:50	4:00

B

Lactate Threshold Workout Charts

The training schedules in this book call for doing lactate threshold workouts between your current 15K and half marathon race pace, in tempo runs of 4 to 7 miles. The charts that follow give per-mile and split times for tempo runs based on these parameters. The charts include roughly equivalent race times—for example, a 58:00 15K is roughly equivalent to a 1:24 half marathon—so you should be able to find the narrow range of paces to run to provide the greatest stimulus to improve your lactate threshold.

Slower runners should run closer to their 15K race pace on tempo runs. Faster runners should run closer to their half marathon race pace during these workouts.

Remember, though, that it's important to run your tempo runs at an even pace. Doing so provides a greater stimulus to boosting your lactate threshold than doing a 5-miler in which you finish with the same time but during which you start fast, lag in the middle, and finish fast.

If you'll be doing your tempo runs on a track, bear in mind that on a 400-meter track, four laps at a given pace will be short a few seconds per mile. For example, 20 laps at 85 seconds per lap take 28:20. During this time, you'll have covered 8K, which is almost 50 meters short of 5 miles, so you haven't quite averaged 5:40 per mile on this tempo run.

Current 15K race time	Fast end of lactate threshold pace/mile	Split of 2 mi on tempo run at this pace	Split of 3 mi on tempo run at this pace	Split of 4 mi on tempo run at this pace	Split of 5 mi on tempo run at this pace	Split of 6 mi on tempo run at this pace	Split of 7 mi on tempo run at this pace
44:00	4:43	9:26	14:10	18:53	23:36	28:19	33:02
45:00	4:49	9:39	14:29	19:19	24:08	28:58	33:48
46:00	4:56	9:52	14:48	19:44	24:40	29:37	34:33
47:00	5:02	10:05	15:08	20:10	25:13	30:16	35:18
48:00	5:09	10:18	15:27	20:36	25:45	30:54	36:03
49:00	5:15	10:31	15:46	21:02	26:17	31:32	36:48
50:00	5:21	10:44	16:06	21:28	26:49	32:11	37:33
51:00	5:28	10:57	16:25	21:53	27:21	32:50	38:18
52:00	5:34	11:09	16:44	22:19	27:53	33:28	39:03
53:00	5:41	11:22	17:04	22:45	28:26	34:07	39:48
54:00	5:47	11:35	17:23	23:10	28:58	34:46	40:33
55:00	5:54	11:48	17:42	23:36	29:30	35:25	41:19
56:00	6:00	12:01	18:01	24:02	30:02	36:03	42:03
57:00	6:06	12:14	18:21	24:28	30:34	36:41	42:48
58:00	6:13	12:27	18:40	24:54	31:07	37:20	43:34
59:00	6:19	12:40	18:59	25:19	31:39	37:59	44:19
1:00:00	6:26	12:52	19:19	25:45	32:11	38:37	45:03
1:01:00	6:32	13:05	19:38	26:11	32:43	39:16	45:49
1:02:00	6:39	13:18	19:57	26:36	33:15	39:55	46:14
1:03:00	6:45	13:31	20:17	27:02	33:48	40:34	47:19
1:04:00	6:52	13:44	20:36	27:28	34:20	41:12	48:04
1:05:00	6:58	13:57	20:55	27:54	34:52	41:50	48:49
1:06:00	7:04	14:10	21:15	28:20	35:24	42:29	49:34
1:07:00	7:11	14:23	21:34	28:45	35:56	43:08	50:19
1:08:00	7:17	14:35	21:53	29:11	36:28	43:46	51:04
1:09:00	7:24	14:48	22:13	29:37	37:01	44:25	51:49
1:10:00	7:30	15:01	22:32	30:02	37:33	45:04	52:34
1:11:00	7:37	15:14	22:51	30:28	38:05	45:43	53:20
1:12:00	7:43	15:27	23:10	30:54	38:37	46:21	54:04
1:13:00	7:49	15:40	23:30	31:20	39:09	46:59	54:49
1:14:00	7:56	15:53	23:49	31:46	39:42	47:38	55:35
1:15:00	8:02	16:06	24:08	32:11	40:14	48:17	56:20
1:16:00	8:09	16:18	24:28	32:37	40:46	48:55	57:04
1:17:00	8:15	16:31	24:47	33:03	41:18	49:34	57:50
1:18:00	8:22	16:44	25:06	33:28	41:50	50:13	58:35

Current half marathon race time	Slow end of lactate threshold pace/mile	Split of 2 mi on tempo run at this pace	Split of 3 mi on tempo run at this pace	Split of 4 mi on tempo run at this pace	Split of 5 mi on tempo run at this pace	Split of 6 mi on tempo run at this pace	Split of 7 mi on tempo run at this pace
1:04:00	4:52	9:46	14:39	19:32	24:24	29:17	34:10
1:06:00	5:02	10:04	15:06	20:08	25:10	30:13	35:15
1:08:00	5:11	10:22	15:34	20:45	25:56	31:07	36:18
1:10:00	5:20	10:41	16:01	21:22	26:42	32:02	37:23
1:12:00	5:29	10:59	16:28	21:58	27:27	32:57	38:26
1:14:00	5:38	11:17	16:56	22:35	28:13	33:52	39:31
1:16:00	5:47	11:36	17:23	23:11	28:59	34:47	40:35
1:18:00	5:57	11:54	17:51	23:48	29:45	35:42	41:39
1:20:00	6:06	12:12	18:18	24:24	30:30	36:37	42:43
1:22:00	6:15	12:31	18:46	25:01	31:16	37:32	43:47
1:24:00	6:24	12:49	19:13	25:38	32:02	38:26	44:51
1:26:00	6:33	13:07	19:41	26:14	32:48	39:22	45:55
1:28:00	6:42	13:25	20:08	26:51	33:33	40:16	46:59
1:30:00	6:51	13:44	20:36	27:28	34:19	41:11	48:03
1:32:00	7:01	14:02	21:03	28:04	35:05	42:07	49:08
1:34:00	7:10	14:20	21:31	28:41	35:51	43:01	50:11
1:36:00	7:19	14:39	21:58	29:18	36:37	43:56	51:16
1:38:00	7:28	14:57	22:25	29:54	37:22	44:51	52:19
1:40:00	7:37	15:15	22:53	30:31	38:08	45:46	52:24
1:42:00	7:46	15:34	23:20	31:07	38:54	46:41	54:28
1:44:00	7:56	15:52	23:48	31:44	39:40	47:36	55:32
1:46:00	8:05	16:10	24:15	32:20	40:25	48:31	56:36
1:48:00	8:14	16:29	24:43	32:57	41:11	49:26	57:40
1:50:00	8:23	16:47	25:10	33:34	41:57	50:20	58:44
1:52:00	8:32	17:05	25:38	34:10	42:43	51:16	59:48
1:54:00	8:41	17:23	26:05	34:47	43:28	52:10	1:00:52
1:56:00	8:50	17:42	26:33	35:24	44:14	53:05	1:01:56
1:58:00	9:00	18:00	27:00	36:00	45:00	54:00	1:03:00
2:00:00	9:09	18:18	27:28	36:37	45:46	54:55	1:04:04

$\dot{V}O_2$max Workout Chart

The training schedules in this book call for doing $\dot{V}O_2$max workouts at your current 5K race pace, in repeat segments of 600 meters to 1,600 meters. By current 5K race pace, we mean a race run on a reasonable course in good conditions—not, say, a hilly 5K on a cold, windy day.

The chart that follows gives lap and split times on a standard 400-meter track for workouts based on 5K race times of 14:00 to 24:30. (One mile is almost 10 meters longer than four laps of a 400-meter track, so the 1,600-meter splits are slightly faster than the per-mile pace for a given 5K time.)

Current 5K race time	Per-mile pace for VO$_2$max workouts	Split of 400 m at this pace	Split of 600 m at this pace	Split of 800 m at this pace	Split of 1,000 m at this pace	Split of 1,200 m at this pace	Split of 1,600 m at this pace
14:00	4:30.4	1:07.2	1:40.8	2:14.4	2:48	3:21.6	4:28.8
14:30	4:40	1:09.6	1:44.4	2:19.2	2:54	3:28.8	4:38.4
15:00	4:49.7	1:12	1:48	2:24	3:00	3:36	4:48
15:30	4:59.3	1:14.4	1:51.6	2:28.8	3:06	3:43.2	4:57.6
16:00	5:09	1:16.8	1:55.2	2:33.6	3:12	3:50.4	5:07.2
16:30	5:18.6	1:19.2	1:58.8	2:38.4	3:18	3:57.6	5:16.8
17:00	5:28.3	1:21.6	2:02.4	2:43.2	3:24	4:04.8	5:26.4
17:30	5:38	1:24	2:06	2:48	3:30	4:12	5:36
18:00	5:47.6	1:26.4	2:09.6	2:52.8	3:36	4:19.2	5:45.6
18:30	5:57.3	1:28.8	2:13.2	2:57.6	3:42	4:26.4	5:55.2
19:00	6:06.9	1:31.2	2:16.8	3:02.4	3:48	4:33.6	6:04.8
19:30	6:16.6	1:33.6	2:20.4	3:07.2	3:54	4:40.8	6:14.4
20:00	6:26.2	1:36	2:24	3:12	4:00	4:48	6:24
20:30	6:35.9	1:38.4	2:27.6	3:16.8	4:06	4:55.2	6:33.6
21:00	6:45.6	1:40.8	2:31.2	3:21.6	4:12	5:02.4	6:43.2
21:30	6:55.2	1:43.2	2:34.8	3:26.4	4:18	5:09.6	6:52.8
22:00	7:04.9	1:45.6	2:38.4	3:31.2	4:24	5:16.8	7:02.4
22:30	7:14.5	1:48	2:42	3:36	4:30	5:24	7:12
23:00	7:24.2	1:50.4	2:45.6	3:40.8	4:36	5:31.2	7:21.6
23:30	7:33.8	1:52.8	2:49.2	3:45.6	4:42	5:38.4	7:31.2
24:00	7:43.5	1:55.2	2:52.8	3:50.4	4:48	5:45.6	7:40.8
24:30	7:53.1	1:57.6	2:56.4	3:55.2	4:54	5:52.8	7:50.4

D

A Brief Glossary

This glossary is purposefully short. It contains only the main physiological terms used in this book that are highly pertinent to marathon training and racing. It's provided here for easy reference if you're reading the book other than from cover to cover. (Shocking, we know, but some people do so.)

biomechanics—How the various parts of your body work together to create your running form. Although some features of your biomechanics, such as the structure of your bones, are primarily genetically determined, stretching and strengthening exercises may improve your running biomechanics and therefore improve your marathon performance.

capillaries—The smallest blood vessels; several typically border each muscle fiber. With the correct types of training, you'll increase the number of capillaries per muscle fiber. By providing oxygen directly to the individual muscle fibers, increased capillary density allows your rate of aerobic energy production to increase. Capillaries also deliver fuel to the muscle fibers and remove waste products such as carbon dioxide.

fast-twitch muscle fibers—Muscle fibers that contract and fatigue rapidly to power intense, short-term exercise such as sprinting. They're classified into two categories, A and B; fast-twitch A fibers have more of the characteristics of slow-twitch fibers than fast-twitch B. Although your fast-twitch muscle fibers can't be converted to slow-twitch fibers, with general endurance training your fast-twitch A fibers gain more of the characteristics of slow-twitch fibers. These adaptations are beneficial because your fast-twitch fibers then become better at producing energy aerobically.

glycogen—The storage form of carbohydrate in your muscles and the main source of energy during running. Endurance training reduces your body's need to burn glycogen at a given pace and teaches your body to store more glycogen.

hemoglobin—A red blood cell protein that carries oxygen in the blood. The higher your hemoglobin content, the more oxygen that can be carried (per unit of blood) to your muscles to produce energy aerobically.

lactate threshold—The exercise intensity above which your rate of lactate production is substantially greater than your rate of lactate clearance. At effort levels above your lactate threshold, the lactate concentration rises in your muscles and blood. The hydrogen ions associated with lactate production inactivate the enzymes for energy production and may interfere with the uptake of calcium, thereby reducing the muscles' ability to contract. You can't, therefore, maintain a pace faster than your lactate threshold pace for more than a few miles. For well-trained runners, lactate threshold usually occurs at 15K to half marathon race pace.

maximal heart rate—The highest heart rate you can attain during all-out running. Your maximal heart rate is determined genetically. In other words, it doesn't increase with training. Successful marathoners don't have particularly high maximal heart rates, so it isn't a factor in determining success.

maximal oxygen uptake—Commonly referred to as $\dot{V}O_2max$; the maximal amount of oxygen that your heart can pump to your muscles and that your muscles can then use to produce energy. The combination of your training and your genetics determines how high a $\dot{V}O_2max$ you have.

mitochondria—The only part of your muscle fibers in which energy can be produced aerobically. Think of them as the aerobic energy factories in your muscle fibers. The right types of training increase the size of your mitochondria (i.e., make bigger factories) and the number of mitochondria (i.e., make more factories) in your muscle fibers.

running economy—How fast you can run using a given amount of oxygen. If you can run faster than another athlete while using the same amount of oxygen, then you have better running economy. Running economy can also be looked at as how much oxygen is required to run at a given speed. If you use less oxygen while running at the same speed as another runner, then you're more economical.

slow-twitch muscle fibers—Muscle fibers contract and tire slowly and power sustained, submaximal exercise such as endurance running. Slow-twitch muscle fibers naturally resist fatigue, and they have a high aerobic capacity, high capillary density, and other characteristics that make them ideal for marathon running. The proportion of slow-twitch fibers in your muscles is determined genetically and is believed not to change with training.

$\dot{V}O_2max$—See *maximal oxygen uptake.*

References and Recommended Readings

Alter, M. 1998. *Sport stretch* (2nd ed.). Champaign, IL: Human Kinetics.

Bompa, T.O. 1999. *Periodization: Theory and Methodology of Training* (4th ed.). Champaign, IL: Human Kinetics.

Brittenham, G., and D. Brittenham. 1997. *Stronger abs and back.* Champaign, IL: Human Kinetics.

Cavanagh, P.R., and K.R. Williams. 1982. Effect of stride length variation on oxygen uptake during distance running. *Medicine and Science in Sports and Exercise* 14(1):30-35.

Daniels, J. 1998. *Daniels' running formula.* Champaign, IL: Human Kinetics.

Eberle, S.G. 2000. *Endurance sports nutrition.* Champaign, IL.: Human Kinetics.

Eyestone, E.D., G. Fellingham, J. George, and A.G. Fisher. 1993. Effect of water running and cycling on maximum oxygen consumption and 2-mile run performance. *American Journal of Sports Medicine* 21(1):41-44.

Farrell, P.A., J.H., Wilmore, E.F., Coyle, J.E., Billing, and D.L., Costill, 1979. Plasma lactate accumulation and distance running performance. *Medicine and Science in Sports and Exercise* 11:338-344.

Flynn, M.G., K.K. Carroll, H.L. Hall, B.A. Bushman, P.G. Brolinson, and C.A. Weideman. 1998. Cross training: Indices of training stress and performance. *Medicine and Science in Sports and Exercise* 30(2):294-300.

Foster, C. 1998. Monitoring training in athletes with reference to overtraining syndrome. *Medicine and Science in Sports and Exercise* 30(7):1164-68.

Foster, C., L.L. Hector, R. Welsh, M. Schrager, M.A. Green, A.C. Snyder. 1995. Effects of specific versus cross-training on running performance. *European Journal of Applied Physiology and Occupational Physiology* 70(4):367-72.

Hickson, R.C., B.A. Dvorak, E.M. Gorostiaga, T.T. Kurowski, and C. Foster. 1988. Potential for strength and endurance training to amplify endurance performance. *Journal of Applied Physiology* 65(5):2285-2290.

Johnston, R.E., T.J. Quinn, R. Kertzer, and N.B. Vroman. 1997. Strength training female distance runners: Impact on running economy. *Journal of Strength and Conditioning Research* 11:224-229.

Lambert, M. 1998. Is a heart rate monitor worth it? *Marathon and Beyond* 2(6):10-18.

Mujika, I. 1998. The influence of training characteristics and tapering on the adaptation in individuals: A review. *International Journal of Sports Medicine* 19(7): 439-46.

Mutton, D.L., S.F. Loy, D.M. Rogers, G.J. Holland, W.J. Vincent, and M. Heng. 1993. Effect of run vs. combined cycle/run training on $\dot{V}O_2$max and running performance. *Medicine and Science in Sports and Exercise* 25(12):1393-97.

Pfitzinger, P., and S. Douglas. 1999. *Road racing for serious runners*. Champaign, IL.: Human Kinetics.

Svedenhag, J., and J. Seger. 1992. Running on land and in water: Comparative exercise physiology. *Medicine and Science in Sports and Exercise* 24(10):1155-1160.

Tanaka, H. 1994. Effects of cross-training. Transfer of training effects on $\dot{V}O_2$max between cycling, running and swimming. *Sports Medicine* 18(5):330-39.

Wilber, R.L., R.J. Moffatt, B.E. Scott, D.T. Lee, and N.A. Cucuzzo. 1996. Influence of water run training on the maintenance of aerobic performance. *Medicine and Science in Sports and Exercise* 28(8):1056-1062.

Williams, M. 1998. *The ergogenics edge*. Champaign, IL.: Human Kinetics.

Index

Boldface page references indicate where terms are defined; *italic* page references indicate information contained in charts and illustrations.

About the Authors

Pete Pfitzinger, the top American finisher at the 1984 and 1988 Olympic Marathons, is a distance running coach and exercise physiologist. He established himself as one of the best marathoners in U.S. history by outkicking Alberto Salazar to win the 1984 U.S. Olympic Marathon Trials. That same year he received the DeCelle award for America's best distance runner and was named Runner of the Year by the Road Runners' Club of America. He is also a two-time winner of the San Francisco Marathon and he finished third in the 1987 New York City Marathon. As a coach, Pfitzinger has more than 20 years' experience, including working with distance runners at the University of Massachusetts, University of New Hampshire, and Mount Holyoke College.

In his current position as an exercise physiologist, Pfitzinger specializes in working with endurance athletes. He is a contributing editor for *Running Times*, which features his monthly column, "The Pfitzinger Lab Report." His writing has also appeared in *American Health, Runner's World*, and *New England Runner*. A graduate of Cornell University and the University of Massachusetts with a master's in exercise science, Pfitzinger lives in Auckland, New Zealand. He is the general manager of the New Zealand Academy of Sport, where he provides sport science and sports medicine services to Olympic and national class athletes.

Stacey Cramp

Scott Douglas is a former editor-in-chief of *Running Times*. He has published articles in *Runner's World, The Washington Post,* and *Women Outside* and has been a columnist for *Running Times* and *Marathon and Beyond*. He was also an editor of *Running & FitNews,* a publication of the American Running Association. Douglas has coauthored two books with Bill Rodgers: *Bill Rodgers' Lifetime Running Plan* and *The Complete Idiot's Guide to Jogging and Running.*

Douglas has been a competitive runner since 1979, setting personal bests of 30:48 in the 10K, 51:01 in the 10-mile, and 1:08:40 in the half-marathon. Running competitively for almost 20 years, he has kept in tune with runners who have to fit training and racing around the demands of a career. Douglas resides in Bethesda, Maryland.

[handwritten notes:] Pg 24 / Heart Rate / Long Run - 73-83% MHR / (135) / Start 9 min Pace End 8:15 Pace